Dislocations/Relocations

Narratives of Displacement

Edited by

Mike Baynham

University of Leeds, UK

and

Anna De Fina

Georgetown University, USA

ST JEROME
PUBLISHING

St. Jerome Publishing
Manchester, UK & Northampton MA

First published 2005 by
St. Jerome Publishing
2 Maple Road West, Brooklands
Manchester, M23 9HH, United Kingdom
Telephone +44 (0)161 973 9856
Fax +44 (0)161 905 3498
stjerome@compuserve.com
http://www.stjerome.co.uk

ISBN 1-900650-79-7 (pbk)
ISSN 1471-0277 (*Encounters*)

© Mike Baynham and Anna De Fina 2005

Printed and bound in Great Britain by
Alden Group Ltd, Osney Mead, Oxford, UK

Typeset by
Delta Typesetters, Cairo, Egypt
Email: hilali1945@yahoo.co.uk

British Library Cataloguing in Publication Data
A catalogue record of this book is available from the British Library

Library of Congress Cataloguing in Publication Data
Dislocations/relocations : narratives of displacement / edited by Mike Baynham and Anna De Fina.
    p. cm. -- (Encounters)
 Includes bibliographical references and index.
  ISBN 1-900650-79-7 (pbk. : alk. paper)
1. Discourse analysis, Narrative--Social aspects.
2. Refugees--Language.
3. Sociolinguistics. I. Baynham, Mike, 1950- II. De Fina, Anna III. Series.
 P302.84.D579 2005
 401'.41--dc22

                    2005008585

Encounters

A new series on language and diversity
Edited by Jan Blommaert, Marco Jacquemet and Ben Rampton

Diversity has come to be recognized as one of the central concerns in our thinking about society, culture and politics. At the same time, it has proved one of the most difficult issues to deal with on the basis of established theories and methods, particularly in the social sciences. Studying diversity not only challenges widespread views of who we are and what we do in social life; it also challenges the theories, models and methods by means of which we proceed in studying diversity. Diversity exposes the boundaries and limitations of our theoretical models, in the same way it exposes our social and political organizations.

Encounters sets out to explore diversity *in* language, diversity *through* language and diversity *about* language. Diversity *in* language covers topics such as intercultural, gender, class or age-based variations in language and linguistic behaviour. Diversity *through* language refers to the way in which language and linguistic behaviour can contribute to the construction or negotiation of such sociocultural and political differences. And diversity *about* language has to do with the various ways in which language and diversity are being perceived, conceptualized and treated, in professional as well as in lay knowledge - thus including the reflexive and critical study of scientific approaches alongside the study of language politics and language ideologies. In all this, mixedness, creolization, crossover phenomena and heterogeneity are privileged areas of study. The series title, *Encounters*, is intended to encourage a relatively neutral but interested stance towards diversity, moving away from the all too obvious 'cultures-collide' perspective that is dominant within the social sciences. The target public of *Encounters* includes scholars and advanced students of linguistics, communication studies, anthropology, cultural studies, sociology, as well as students and scholars in neighbouring disciplines such as translation studies, gender studies, gay and lesbian studies, postcolonial studies.

Jan Blommaert is former Research Director of the IPRA Research Centre of the University of Antwerp and currently Professor of Languages in Education, Institute of Education, University of London. He is author of *Discourse* (Cambridge University Press, 2005), co-author of *Debating Diversity: Analysing the Discourse of Tolerance* (Routledge, 1998), editor of *Language Ideological Debates* (Mouton de Gruyter 1999), and co-editor of the *Handbook of Pragmatics* (John Benjamins 1995-2003) and *The Pragmatics of Inter-cultural and International Communication* (John Benjamins 1991).

Marco Jacquemet is Assistant Professor of Communication Studies at the University of San Francisco. His work focuses on the complex inter-action of different languages and communicative practices in a globalized world. His current research seeks to assess the communicative mutations resulting from the intersection in the Mediterranean area between mobile people (migrants, local and international aid workers, missionaries, busi-nessmen, etc.) and electronic texts (content distributed by satellites, local television stations, Internet connectivity, cellular telephony). As part of this research, in the early 1990s he studied the communicative practices of criminal networks in Southern Italy and the emerging Italian cyberculture. In 1994 he conducted fieldwork in Morocco and Italy on migratory patterns between the two countries. Since 1998, he has been involved in multi-site ethnographic fieldwork in Albania and Italy, inves-tigating the linguistic and socio-cultural consequences of Albania's entry into the global system of late-modern capitalism. Marco Jacquemet is au-thor of *Credibility in Court: Communicative Practices in the Camorra Trials* (Cambridge University Press 1996).

Ben Rampton is Professor of Applied and Sociolinguistics at King's College London. His work involves ethnographic and interactional dis-course analysis, frequently also drawing on anthropology, sociology and cultural studies. His publications cover urban multilingualism; language, youth, ethnicities and class; language education; second language learn-ing; and research methodology. Ben Rampton is author of *Crossing: Language and Ethnicity among Adolescents* (1995/2005), *Language and Late Modernity: Interaction in an Urban School* (Cambridge University Press, forthcoming), co-author of *Researching Language: Issues of Power & Method* (Routledge 1992), and co-editor of *The Language, Ethnicity & Race Reader* (Routledge 2003).

Contents

Introduction

Dislocations/Relocations
Narratives of Displacement

ANNA DE FINA, *Georgetown University*
MIKE BAYNHAM, *University of Leeds*

Recent years have seen a proliferation of works on narrative in fields as diverse as literary theory, sociolinguistics, discourse analysis, anthropology, sociology, psychology, history and folklore. Following this 'narrative turn' (Riessman, 2002) in sociocultural studies, researchers from a variety of disciplines within the social sciences have started using narratives as data, and narrative analysis as methodology for investigating a whole range of socio-cultural phenomena that in the past were the almost exclusive realm of statistical and quantitative enquiry. Thus, the centrality of narrative analysis in the investigation of social processes and practices has become an established fact in the social sciences.

However, narrative analysts, particularly in linguistics and anthropology, have only recently started to interrogate themselves on the role that different contexts play in the structuring of texts belonging to the genre (Ochs and Capps, 2001) and conversely, on the social functions that narratives can accomplish in different social domains. This task is especially important when we look at social contexts characterized by uncertainty, conflict and inequalities such as the societies typical of the post-modern world in which we live. There is now a widespread rejection of conceptions of the relationships between language and social groups and processes as a mere pairing of linguistic structures with social categories and actions (Hill, 1999) and of linguistic genres as relatively well bound, homogeneous texts. This has brought with it a new emphasis on aspects of language and of texts that had been neglected or relegated to the periphery within accepted sociolinguistic and anthropological traditions.

In narrative, this is the case with the conceptualization of time and space. While the received tradition in narrative analysis underlined the centrality of the orderly sequence of events in narrative structure (see Labov and Waletzky, 1967/97; Chafe, 1994) and paid little attention to other dimensions of narrative construction such as spatial organization (Herman, 2002), recent work on narrative has reconsidered such priorities and attempted to problematize the relationship between time and space through a recontextualization of such categories in historical terms (Fabian, 2001;

Mishler, forthcoming). This has involved exploring how social contexts interplay with the use of narrative categories (Briggs, 1997; Baynham, 2003; De Fina, 2003a) and more generally re-evaluating the role of the 'canonical story' told in a monologic mode as a model to approach other kinds of texts within the genre (Georgakopoulou, 2003).

De Certeau (1988:115) reversed the primacy of time in narrative, arguing that: "Every story is a travel story – a spatial practice". Orientation/disoriention/reorientation, far from being a simple contextual backdrop, often *is* the story, especially in non-canonical narratives and in narratives produced by people who have been both physically and psychologically displaced. De Certeau's emphasis on narrative as spatial practice points to a need to re-theorize space and spatiality in this genre. At the same time, a conception of narrative as discursive practice (Fairclough, 1989) invokes the need to relate particular constructions of time and space to specific interactional and social contexts involving relationships of power and dominance. Following these insights, we have taken narratives of displacement as a starting point not only to discuss narrative theory, but also to consider the role of narrative within social phenomena and movements that are central to modernity.

In this sense, while the focus of this book is theoretical, its topic is necessarily political. In our era public discourses, particularly in the media, increasingly present such displacements through the lenses of nationalist and racist rhetoric (Wodak and Riesigl, 1999), creating atmospheres of social panic in which migrants and refugees are seen as threatening the stable borders of national identities. Thus, there is an urgent need for accounts of such processes 'from the inside', and of discourse-based analyses capable of offering an 'emic' perspective (Harris, 1999) on them and of illustrating the subjective construction of these movements of human beings, rather than their objectivist 'othering' in nationalist or racist mainstream discourses.

The focus on displacement allows a consideration of a variety of social contexts and actors. Here we want to encompass not only the movement across borders of migrants and refugees, but also processes of forced displacement and re-settlement within borders, and of marginalization of minorities and underprivileged groups within social spaces. This book is centred on the stories that are ignored/silenced/othered by the public discourse on displacement, migration and settlement. These 'silenced' stories are revealing of the processes through which marginalized social actors construct narratives about themselves and, therefore, of the linguistic resources through which they build resistance (Gal, 2001) to dominating social practices and 'relocate' themselves not only in physical, but also in social space.

Narratives of displacement are also necessarily revealing about the nature of the public discourses within which migrants and minorities are positioned. In fact, as Wertsch (1994) and Bhabha (1990) have shown, narrative strategies are at work not only in personal and literary contexts, but also in public discourses, in the constitutive stories that nations tell themselves. Thus, the distribution and use of narrative resources inevitably leads to issues of power and inequality. While public discourses construct narratives about nationals and foreigners, insiders and outsiders, friends and foes, institutional practices echo, reinforce, and restate the social representations that the former circulate, creating rules of entextualization (Bauman and Briggs, 1990) that limit the acceptability of personal accounts and their forms of circulation in communicative economies. Investigating, for example, the role of narratives in institutional processes such as asylum seeking-procedures or claims for social aid, thus entails an incursion into the power struggles over what constitutes an acceptable text, over whose voices have the right to be heard and therefore an investigation of narrative and symbolic inequality (Hymes, 1996; Briggs, 1996; Blommaert, 2001).

In this respect, narratives of displacement also allow a reconsideration of an old problem in narrative theory: the question of the relationship between 'facts' and emplotment, truth and representation, reliability and credibility. Narrative theorists have struggled over the iconicity of told events with respect to lived events, often arriving at opposite conclusions. While in the Labovian tradition, stories are always a 'recapitulation' of past experience (Labov, 1972), and analysts are interested in the truth of the facts represented, in interactional accounts of narrative, stories are seen as *creating* experience (Mattingly, 1988) and veracity is not an issue since all represented events are seen as constructed. However, narratives told or used in institutional contexts lead us to revisit questions of truth in that narrators are often not free to represent experience creatively, but are pushed by the institutional context to present acceptable accounts of narrated events and of themselves as actors in them. On the other hand, narratives about conflictive events pose a host of moral questions related to historical truth and responsibility. Thus, such narratives establish a nexus between individual instances of discourse, actors and institutions that reveals the limitations of an approach to discourse that stays at the level of situated interaction, without looking for the nexus between local discursive phenomena and global processes of power and domination.

From what has been said above, it is clear that narrative as a genre

exhibiting complex relations with its contexts of production is a pecu-
liarly rich area for the reflexive investigation of how representations are
constructed, how identities are made and re-made in discourse, and how
narrators orient themselves and others in social worlds. Again, the focus
on narratives that are 'loaded' with social meanings in this collection is
thus timely in a meta-methodological sense. Recent years have seen an
unprecedented production in the area of the relationships between narrative and identity (see Bamberg, 2000; Wortham, 2001; Brockmeier and
Carbaugh, 2001; De Fina, 2003b). At the same time, in reaction to the
relative context insensitivity of the Labovian model and following the
social constructionist emphasis on identity as 'discursive work' (Hall,
2000), researchers in the Conversation Analysis and Ethnomethodology
tradition have proposed a methodological restraint that encourages analysts to "hold off from using all sorts of identities which one might want
to use in, say, a political or cultural frame of analysis" (Antaki and
Widdicombe, 1998:5) and stick to concepts and categories signalled by
participants in talk in interaction. However, the definition of what counts
as an explanatory context for the meanings that get constructed and negotiated in local interaction is far from clear. Thus, discourse analysis,
sociolinguistics and anthropology have witnessed a growing debate on
the need to revisit the opposition between local and global processes of
indexicality, and to rework theoretical instruments and concepts that allow investigators to capture how meanings emerging in specific instances
of interaction are related to ideologies, institutional discursive and social
practices, and material life processes (Blommaert *et al.*, 2003). Such debate has revealed a growing uneasiness with interactionally oriented
methodologies that narrowly focus on the particularities of everyday contexts without looking for their embeddedness into larger social and political
processes. Albeit firmly maintaining the centrality of the focus on the use
of language in concrete communicative practices and the ethnographic
observation of specific instances of discourse, recent reflections on the
micro-macro opposition suggest that "we might need to look beyond the
prevailing vocabularies of interactional discourse analysis to more en-
compassing notions of subjectivity" (Rampton 2003:54). The kinds of
narratives discussed in this volume are well suited to carry out this project
because of their evident embeddedness in social processes.

Volume Overview

Authors in this volume analyze a variety of narrative dimensions and related questions. One of these is the relationship between narratives and

representation. Contributors examine how migrants, refugees, marginalized minorities and their displacement, migration and settlement are portrayed both in the narratives told by individual protagonists and in official discourse. Another dimension on which authors focus their attention is orientation in social worlds and in different chapters contributors deal with ways in which the construction of narrative in time and space indexes the shifts in social identities and processes characteristic of displacement. A third important dimension is the relationship between narratives and institutional practices. Different authors interrogate themselves on ways in which narratives in institutional practices relate to displacement, and on the conflicts that are played out in these kinds of institutional narratives. Following these threads, we have divided the volume into three sections that present thematically linked chapters:

I)   Orientation in social worlds
II) Displacement and spatialization practices
III) Institutional placement/displacement

The chapters in section I focus on the narrative construction by individuals or groups of positions, and hence identities, with respect to social categories, and therefore with respect to their placement in social space. In the opening chapter, Baynham looks at migration narratives told by men and women belonging to the Moroccan community in West London. He first describes and characterizes 'hegemonic' narratives, i.e. generic accounts of the migration process in which the protagonists are young males opening the way for their families in the new country through hard work and sacrifice. The author then looks at narratives told by women who migrated to the UK in search of a better life and argues that these provide alternative, non-hegemonic accounts in form, function and content. Although women's role is usually ignored in official stories, Moroccan women narrators display in their stories a high level of agency and enterprise and thus indirectly challenge the hegemonic tale of the heroic male migrant/provider.

In chapter two, Relaño Pastor and De Fina focus on narratives of language difficulties or conflicts told by a group of Mexican first generation immigrant women in the San Diego California area. The questions these authors ask are: how do these women talk about language difficulties and lack of access to language resources and what kinds of agency do they project for themselves as characters in represented story-worlds and as participants in interactional worlds? In order to answer these questions, the authors examine both action structure and performance devices in the narratives. They argue that the strategies and narrative resources used by women to present themselves as protagonists in the story world point to a type of self construction in which the stress is on resistance to dominant exclu-sionary practices and on the configuration of a moral order that challenges the one established in the host society and experienced by them. The authors also focus on the encoding of emotion in narrative as both a symptom of the centrality of the language problem in the lives of these immigrants and as a narrative resource for constructing a moral self.

In chapter three, Liebscher and Dailey-O'Cain examine narratives emerging in conversations with Germans who lived in West Germany before 1989 and moved to Saxony (in former East Germany) at various times between 1990 and 1998. The authors analyze ways in which 'migration' becomes a constraint and a resource in the stories told by these recent migrants, their construction of the relationship between places and (political) spaces and their positioning with respect to social identities that are ideologically tied to such spaces. Migrants confront themselves in interaction with unspoken, shared categorizations and their positionings with respect to them are achieved through negotiation with interlocutors. The authors look at the mechanisms through which specific identities are locally constructed and/or contested within the interactions at hand, and at the coexistence of different affiliations even within the same narrative. They also discuss how narrative structural points offer specific resources for the construction of such identities.

Papers in section II are centred on the connections between narrative and space, both in the sense that for displaced communities narrative activities are intricately connected with lived spaces and construct space in specific ways, and in the sense that the disruption of old space delimitations brought about by globalization and transnational movements has pushed individuals to redefine their own positionings. In doing so, linguistic and discursive resources are stretched and reconfigured to entextualize these disruptions.

In chapter four, Haviland traces the discursive tracks of migration and displacement, analyzing narratives which document the 'treks North' of Zinacantec migrants that started in the 1980s. Situating his paper in the social history of this migration, he goes on to focus on the micro level of interaction. He demonstrates how the analysis of discourse, in this case speaker choices of deictic centre, signalled by selection of deictic verbs in Zinacantec Tzotzil, can uncover and identify shifting positionings of the narrated self in space ('here' and/or 'there') which can be used flexibly to index shifting social relationships over time.

In chapter five, Blommaert explicitly addresses the impact of global-ization and mobility on locally available discursive resources, proposing an emphasis on speech, place and mobility in order to understand the im-pact of these globally available resources in local contexts. Using data from a Cape Town radio talk-show, he demonstrates how the language varieties deployed by the talk-show host index positions in social and dis-cursive space that in turn enable the deployment of "delicately organized packages of identity features indexed in talk". Blommaert treats narrative as part of the wider speech event, in this case radio deejaying and talk-back hosting.

In chapter six, McCormick discusses narratives of the forced reset-tlements that took place in Apartheid South Africa under the infamous Districts Acts, and demonstrates that the dynamics of dislocation and re-location do not need to involve moves across national borders. Internal borders can be invented or redrawn by legal whim. In his account of the beginnings of the Zinacantec migration process, Haviland writes of "the next logical step in the migratory process – a discursive step, an idea, a conceptual presence, a body of information about the north where one could go in search of work". In these narratives, told by those forcibly resettled from the fertile Protea suburb of Cape Town to a township on the Cape Flats, another important narrative drive emerges: the desire to use storytelling to look back not forward, to recreate a lost social space from which the narrators have been dispossessed.

The chapters in Section III address some issues that arise from narra-tives told in institutional settings, as part of legal, semi legal or bureaucratic processes. The ways that such narratives can be heard, in both the legal and the everyday sense, are radically constrained by the purposes of the speech events in which they are embedded. Narratives can be misunder-stood, discounted and silenced by the discursive routines of institutional procedures.

In chapter seven, for example, Maryns uses the theoretical constructs of contextualization and meta-pragmatics to analyze the mechanisms by which narrative re-tellings by asylum seekers in eligibility determination interviews can be systematically misunderstood and discounted within the institutional interview dynamics. Sketching out a theory of the mobility of repertoires reminiscent of that presented by Blommaert in chapter five, and proposing the idea that as difference increases between individuals, the more important discursive contextualization becomes, she examines a range of factors that systematically work against the ongoing effective contextualization of the asylum seekers' narratives.

In chapter eight, Jacquemet examines communicative practices in asylum seeker interviews in Kosovo. While Maryns demonstrated the consequence of missing/ignoring contextualization cues in the narrative re-tellings of asylum interviews, Jacquemet here describes a more radical scenario in which narratives themselves are consciously ruled out of the interview process in favour of a focus on local knowledge (place names, dialect features and terminologies) designed to identify whether the asylum seeker can effectively back claims about her/his origin. Here narratives are abruptly silenced by interactional moves typically initiated by the Kosovan interpreter.

In chapter nine, Barsky, drawing on the socio-legal concept of 'outsider law', life story research and discourse analysis, presents data from fictional accounts of migration, asylum seeker hearings and interviews with homeless men, all of which allow further exploration of the ways that institutional procedures such as appeal mechanisms fail to hear the stories of the displaced. The author shows how the claims of the displaced are somehow filtered out, not heard in a literal as well as a legal sense, because they fall outside the generic expectations of the appeal procedure as speech event. The Afterword by James Collins brings together the various contributions through a fascinating and comprehensive reflection on salient themes and threads in the volume and on central questions that remain open to investigation.

The narratives presented in this volume are the discursive traces of trajectories in space and time, from here to there (and sometimes back again) in ways that permanently reconfigure how 'here' and 'there' can be understood. These trajectories make and remake social spaces, identities and practices in ways that are always situated and contextualized, locally produced, yet globally indexed. The analytical challenge faced by contributors is to reconnect the microanalyses of discourse in local environments with such large-scale social processes of dislocation and relocation in the context of transnational flows. The contributors to this volume show how language choices, whether of grammatical items, sociolinguistic repertoire or genre are never neutral, autonomous or natural, but rather work dynamically to construct and respond to a social world that is characterized by mobility and flow more than it is by the relative stasis and permanence of the traditional sociolinguistic speech community. It is as a contribution to this dynamic re-thinking of sociolinguistic theory that we locate this volume.

References

Antaki, C. and S. Widdicombe (eds.) (1998) *Identities in Talk*, London: Sage.

Bamberg, M. (ed.) (2000) 'Theme Issue on Narrative Identity', *Narrative Inquiry* 10(1).

Bauman, R. and C. Briggs (1990) 'Poetics and Performance as Critical Perspectives on Language and Social Life', *Annual Review of Anthropology* 19:59-88.

Baynham, M. (2003) 'Narratives in Space and Time: Beyond "backdrop" Accounts of Narrative Orientation', *Narrative Inquiry* 13(2):347-366.

Bhabha, H. (1990) *Nation and Narration*, London: Routledge.

Blommaert, J. (2001) 'Investigating Narrative Inequality: African Asylum Seekers' Stories in Belgium', *Discourse and Society* 12(4):413-449.

Blommaert, J., J. Collins, M. Heller, B. Rampton, S. Slembrouck and J. Verschueren (eds.) (2003) 'Introduction. Ethnography, Discourse and Hegemony', special issue of *Pragmatics* 13(1):1-10.

Briggs, C. (ed.) (1996) *Disorderly Discourse: Narrative, Conflict and Inequality*, Oxford: Oxford University Press.

------ (1997) 'Sequentiality and Temporality in the Narrative Construction of a South American Cholera Epidemic', in M. Bamberg (ed.) *Oral Versions of Personal Experience: Three Decades of Narrative Analysis*, *Journal of Narrative and Life History* 7:177-184.

Brockmeier, J. and D. Carbaugh (eds.) (2001), *Narrative and Identity: Studies in Autobiography, Self and Culture*, Amsterdam: John Benjamins.

Chafe, W. (1994) *Discourse, Consciousness and Time*, Chicago: University of Chicago Press.

de Certeau, M. (1988) *The Practice of Everyday Life*, Berkeley: University of California Press.

De Fina, A. (2003a) 'Crossing Borders: Time, Space and Disorientation in Narrative', *Narrative Inquiry* 13 (2):367-391.

------ (2003b) *Identity in Narrative. A Study of Immigrant Discourse,* Amsterdam: John Benjamins.

Fabian. J. (2001) 'Time, Narration, and the Exploration of Central Africa', *Narrative*, 9 (1):3-20.

Fairclough, N. (1989) *Language and Power*, London: Longman.

Gal, S. (2001) 'Language, Gender, and Power: An Anthropological Review', in S. Duranti (ed.) *Linguistic Anthropology: A Reader*: (pp.420-430) Oxford: Blackwell.

Georgakopoulou, A. (2003) 'Looking Back when Looking Ahead: Adolescents' Identity Management in Narrative Practices', in J. Androutsopoulos and A. Georgakopoulou (eds.), *Discourse Constructions of Youth Identities*: (pp.75-91) Amsterdam/Philadelphia: Benjamins.

Hall, S. (2000) 'Who Needs Identity?' in P. Du Gay, J. Evans, and P. Redman (eds.), *Identity: A Reader*: (pp.15-30), London: Sage Publications and the Open University.

Harris, M. (1999) *Theories of Culture in Postmodern Times*, Walnut Creek: Altamira Press.

Herman, D. (2002) *Story Logic*, Lincoln: University of Nebraska Press.

Hill, J. (1999) 'Styling Locally and Styling Globally: What Does it Mean?', *Journal of Sociolinguistics* 3 (4):542-556.

Hymes, (1996) *Ethnography, Linguistics, Language Inequalities*, London: Taylor and Francis.

Labov, W. (1972) *Language in the Inner City,* Philadelphia: University of Pennsylvania Press.

------ and J. Waletzky (1967) 'Narrative Analysis: Oral Versions of Personal Experience', in J. Helm (ed.), *Essays on the Verbal and Visual Arts*: (pp.12-44), Seattle: University of Washington Press.

Mattingly, C. (1988) *Healing Dreams and Clinical Plots: The Narrative Structure of Experience*. Cambridge: Cambridge University Press.

Mishler, E. (forthcoming) 'The Double Arrow of Time', in A. De Fina, D. Schiffrin, and M. Bamberg, *Discourse and Identities*. Cambridge: Cambridge University Press.

Ochs, E. and L. Capps (2001) *Living Narrative*, Cambridge Mass.: Harvard University Press.

Rampton, B. (2003) 'Hegemony, Social Class and Stylization', in J. Blommaert, J. Collins, M. Heller, B. Rampton, S. Slembrouck and J. Verschueren (eds) 'Introduction. Ethnography, *Discourse and Hegemony, Special Issue of Pragmatics* 13 (1):1-10.

Riessman, C.K. (2002) 'Analysis of Personal Narratives' in J. F. Gubrium and J. A. Holstein (eds.) *Handbook of Interview Research, Context and Method*, pp.695-710, Thousand Oaks and London: Sage.

Wertsch, J. (1994) 'Historical Representation', Special Issue, *Journal of Narrative and Life History*, 4 (4): 247-255.

Wodak, R. and M. Reisigl (1999) *Discourse and Discrimination. The Rhetoric of Racism and Anti-Semitism*, London: Routledge.

Wortham, S. (2001) *Narratives in Action*, New York: Teachers College Columbia Press.

Section I

Orientation in Social Worlds

Orientation in Social Worlds

The three chapters that comprise this section analyze how individuals or groups orient themselves with respect to social expectations and norms regarding their role in society and their position in social space, their relationship to others and their participation in various domains of social life. The authors look at a variety of subjects and situations: Moroccan men and women who migrated to the UK. in Baynham's chapter, West Germans who moved East in Liebscher and Dailey-O'Cain's chapter, and Mexican women who migrated to the US. in Relaño Pastor and De Fina's chapter. In the three studies, however, the focus is on narrators' conscious reflection on their migration experience. Such reflection inevitably carries with it a confrontation with social expectations related to roles and places. Thus, in the case of Moroccans in London, expectations about roles are embodied in hegemonic narratives constructed and circulated by individuals and organizations that portray migration as centred on the achievements of young males who open the way for their families. For West Germans, social expectations have to do with an image of East Germany as an under-developed country, and therefore of East Germans as less efficient, able and successful than West Germans. For Mexicans in the US. expectations involve power relations that 'naturally' place those who are native speakers of Spanish and belong to immigrant groups in a position of inferiority with respect to those who are native speakers of English and belong to the dominant social group. All the authors look at challenges to these notions or, at least at contradictions and negotiations in which new self-definitions surface.

Two constructs emerge as important for the analysis of the representation and negotiation of social roles, relationships, and norms: *positioning* and *agency*. In Liebscher and Dailey-O'Cain (as in Haviland's chapter in this volume) positioning is related to place formulations that express empathy or distance with respect to sites of departure and arrival, and to narrators' linguistic management of time and space in storytelling. Thus, West Germans represent themselves in the stories they tell as centrally 'here' or 'there', as close to the West or to the East, as looking back or forward, or as 'in between' through linguistic choices involving verbs, adverbs and temporal expressions. They also use, and negotiate with their interlocutors, linguistic configurations of time and place and referential expressions to place themselves in certain ideological positions with respect to shared stereotypical notions about Eastern and Western Germany.

Agency is central to the studies by Baynham and Relaño Pastor and

De Fina. In both chapters, agency is related to self-representation and analyzed in terms of "the degree of activity and initiative that narrators attribute to themselves as characters in particular story-worlds". Baynham illustrates how Moroccan women show agency in their stories through the mobil-ization of their linguistic resources. Language choice allows them, in these narratives, to relocate themselves from a position of dependence and powerlessness to a central role in the shaping of their destiny, or to a combative position in difficult relations with others. In the narratives of language conflict told by Mexican women, agency is encoded through the presentation of self as a story protagonist who reacts in a multiplicity of ways to situations of injustice and discrimination. Agentive selves are also, in these stories, moral selves who foreshadow a different social order from the one accepted and presented as natural in the host society.

Looking at the kind of agency that emerges in the stories, we notice how immigrant women start claiming a role for themselves as agents in migration processes and are eager to tell narratives in which they are no longer an appendix to enterprising males, or the silenced participants of social encounters in which more powerful interlocutors express their domi-nance. On the other hand, we also learn that members of privileged groups, such as the West Germans in the conversations conducted by Liebscher and Dailey-O'Cain, do not necessarily accept received notions about who they and others are, but build nuanced and at times conflicting views of their positions in the social spaces between which they move.

With respect to narrative as a genre, the three studies confirm its cen-trality in the construction of agency and identity. However, the authors also offer new insights into the relationship between different types of narrative structures and discourse functions. In Baynham's chapter the ge-neric narrative specifically carries the function of conveying the typicality of the hegemonic account of migration. In Liebscher and Dailey-O'Cain's chapter, structural slots in narratives are shown to be crucial for inter-actional positioning: such is the case with story prefaces, orientation sections and evaluations that provide sites for the negotiation of stances and the expression of judgments about self and others. Finally, in Relaño Pastor and De Fina's chapter, complicating action sequences with their combinations of actions and reactions become the fundamental means of expression of agentive portrayals of characters. As well as narrative struc-tures, specific linguistic devices also appear to be instrumental in the expression of agency and social orientation: language shifts, reported speech, emotional language, and deictics all play a leading role in the po-sitioning of narrators with respect to characters, events and ideologies.

The three chapters in this section contribute to build a view from the inside about processes of identity formation and social orientation among members of groups that have been displaced (by choice or necessity) from their home countries. Thus, they contribute to an understanding of what migration processes mean to their protagonists and of their consequences on self-representations. These studies also contribute to narrative theory in that they propose ways of analyzing agency and positioning in stories and offer insights on the complex interactions between structure and function in narrative discourse.

Network and Agency in the Migration Stories of Moroccan Women

MIKE BAYNHAM, *University of Leeds.U.K.*

Introduction

The Moroccan community in West London, U.K. began its migration in the late 1960s and early 1970s at a time when, as Sassen (2000) points out, the need for additional foreign workers in European countries had led to their active and organized recruitment, to work for example in the hotel and catering industries. Joffe has this to say about the Moroccan migration to the U.K.:

> The British connection developed in the 1960s, as an offshoot of the sudden boom in the British tourism industry. Major hotel chains in Britain began to look for labour to staff new tourist hotels. Such labour, being required on a seasonal basis only, was often poorly paid and since the domestic market showed little interest, hotel and restaurant chains looked abroad. (Joffe, unpublished)

The recruitment processes for these chains is described in Z.T.'s narrative below. Generic narratives of this migration suggest a 'typical scenario' in which the (male) head of the family migrates, establishes himself in the new environment, then sends for his wife and family. Like all hegemonic narratives, this erases and excludes the experience of those who don't fit the pattern, for example the migration experiences of single woman like Z.T., young single men, or indeed of the wives and children of the male migrants.

In this paper I begin by characterizing the hegemonic, generic account of the migration process as told by a male Moroccan community worker, a newspaper article on the early stages of the Moroccan settlement and a case study from English language tutor training materials. I go on to examine narratives which take another perspective on the migration process, first through the experience of Mrs Tal., a wife united with a husband who migrated earlier. Her story is jointly constructed with her adult children. Mrs Tal. is driven to take on a powerful speaking position in the face of sustained harassment from her landlady. I then consider two narratives told by single women who migrated in search of work, the first (Z.T.) after quitting high school, the other (Mrs Tar.) after going through a painful divorce.

Z.T. is an educated and capable young woman who not only secures her own work permit, but also those of her friends through her own strategies by drawing on key figures in her network. Mrs Tar. is 'helped' to migrate through the intervention of a young male relative. She is not literate, having gone out to work as a child domestic at the age of eight, yet in her interactions with immigration officers on her arrival in the U.K., she demonstrates her agency and access to literacy knowledge when she challenges their attempt to deny her entry. Both these women, in different ways, demonstrate agency and enterprise in their migration, in ways that challenge the hegemonic account of the heroic male migrant/provider.

Personal Narrative and Generic Narrative
Issues of entitlement and right to speak

In Baynham (2003) I describe how a speaker, instead of recounting a unique and singular sequence of events, will sometimes recount one that happened regularly or repeatedly to a particular group of participants over time. If one of the conditions on 'canonical' narrative is that its sequence of events occurred once and once only to a determinate set of participants (a uniqueness condition), then, in such *generic* narratives the uniqueness condition is suspended. What is emphasized is typicality, iterativity. This creates a particular kind of truth claim in the narrative: the claim to represent not just one's own experience but also the experience of others.

In the following extract M.A., a community worker with a prominent position in the community at the time I carried out my fieldwork in the early 1980s, describes a typical pattern starting with the migration of the head of the family who, once established, brings his family over to join him.

> the head of the family works for a while sends the money to the family and the family arrives to london mostly to in a just a small room the husband sometimes has to go and work during the day he has got nobody to inform him the even if there was any leaflets in arabic or anything they could not read it most of them so they rely on word of mouth mostly and they try to get together it was very difficult for them but they did have a couple of cafes in the west end they were run by algerians and they used to get there and they used to get together and drink coffee and talk about various things that they can help them like for instance how do they communicate with their relatives back

in morocco how do they how can they send money back home erm what immigration what the home office think about the various things what er if there is any hassle of bringing families what is the cheapest fare etc.

The generic narrative raises interesting questions of authority, authorization and rights to speak: who has or claims the right to make such generalizations. Taking on the right to tell generic narratives means taking on a public speaking position, a resource in a sense made available by the genre itself, but bespeaking also a social role of leadership. In this chapter I develop the argument that these generic narratives produce a kind of hegemonic account that excludes other types of account, for example those of other family members, the single women, or indeed single men migrating which are evidenced in my data. All the men whose stories are drawn on in this chapter provide instances of the hegemonic account in that they migrated to the UK. as already married men, earning money to set up a base to bring over their families.

These first experiences of migration have also been dealt with from the angle of other family members in two autobiographical accounts by Moroccan teenagers. *My Life* by Mohammed Elbaja and *Families* by Zohra El Kssmi (English Centre, 1979). Mohammed Elbaja describes how his father leaves to work in the UK., first in Scotland and afterwards in London. He returns on holiday and brings his wife back to London leaving his children in the care of their grandmother. Finally, his parents return on another holiday, having made arrangements to bring their children back with them to London. Mohammed is reunited with his parents, but is to be separated from his school friends and extended family.

Another example of generic narrative can be found in the following extract from English language volunteer tutor training materials produced at the time of my fieldwork. Here a similar narrative sequence provides a fictionalized 'typical' account of the Moroccan migration, with the male bread winner migrating first, being joined by his wife once he establishes a base in the new environment and gradually bringing over the older children to reunite the family.

Omar: A Case Study

Omar comes from Larache, a small town on the coast of Morocco, not far from Tangier. His father died when he was young and he had to go out to work as a small boy. He received no schooling and is totally illiterate in Arabic. In 1970, Omar comes to London, having obtained a job and a work permit through an employment agency operating in Larache, recruiting workers for the hotel and catering industry in London. In 1972 his wife Fatima joins him. Omar in the meantime has been living in a bedsit in Queensway, working in a hotel, split shifts, almost entirely with non-English speaking people. In 1975, Fatima has a baby and Omar and Fatima bring over their eldest daughter Raquia aged 12 to help out. They do not realize that schooling is compulsory in the UK. Educational Welfare discover that she is not at school but is at home looking after the baby. They contact the Language Scheme for an interpreter to explain the situation to Omar and also to arrange tuition. Both Omar and Fatima are keen to learn, aware of their inability to communicate, and the acuteness of other problems like housing. A volunteer is assigned to them.

An article in the local newspaper provides another example of the 'typical' story. ('Investigation into the Plight of Moroccans in the Royal Borough', Kensington News and Post 21/9/73). This article is the first newspaper reference to the settlement of Moroccans in North Kensington, and it dates from the period in which we have suggested that awareness of the settlement began to emerge in statutory and voluntary organizations concerned with the area.

The article begins as follows:

> They work in hotels, restaurants and sometimes pubs doing jobs few Englishmen would touch. When their jobs are done they drift home to the tiny, overcrowded rooms they call home – at best a damp basement flat in north Kensington. They are the "invisible citizens" – the Moroccans.

Linguistically we note the use of the present simple as a strategy for asserting the general truth of a sequence of events. Notice also the postponement of the subject and topic (*'the Moroccans'*) and the consequent cataphoric reference (*'they... their... they...they... they.... the Moroccans'*) a stylistic device typical of journalism to involve the reader and build up tension: who are these invisible citizens, unnamed till the end of the paragraph? The tone of the paragraph gives a somewhat melodramatic tinge to themes addressed earlier in this chapter, albeit in a rather plainer manner: the type of work Moroccans were doing at that time, the type of accommodation they were liable to have, the level of awareness of the existence of their settlement in the institutions of the dominant culture. This tone is achieved partly lexically, through the use of marked lexical items like '*drift*', '*tiny*', '*overcrowded*', '*damp*' and through metaphor (how can citizens be invisible?). The article produces a 'representation'' in the sense that Grillo (1985) uses the term, of the typical life situation of newly settled Moroccans, at the bottom of the job market and the housing market, invisible to the services of the welfare state. This is, in Grillo's terms, a representation 'from the outside' while the extracts from interviews cited above have constituted representations 'from the inside'.

The narrative of Mr R. (discussed in more detail in Baynham, forthcoming) describes the first stage of such a 'typical' migration in which the husband migrates first and is later rejoined by his family:

1.	I/	how did you come here first when you came
2.	Mr R./	when I came here I came by uh from morocco to spain
3.		spain to London by aeroplane
4.	I/	yeah
5.	Mr R/	yeah because I got a contract and the contract is for
6.		one month then I was uh 'pply for my passport take me
7.		eight days take me eight days then I (give) then I till I
8.		prepare then I uh have to find some money and uh wife
9.		eh have to keep my family secure and
10.	I/	yeah
11.	Mr R/	and eh I reach here in heathrow I don't know where to
12.		go I don't got no friends

We will now explore how these 'typical' narratives, can be understood as hegemonic accounts, eliding the narratives of others: wives, children or indeed single women migrating alone.

Hegemony and Narrative Representations

Hegemony is a concept developed and refined by the philosopher and political activist Gramsci to account for the networks of representation that support and naturalize power relations, allowing a particular state of affairs to be treated as common sense or taken for granted. Gramsci elaborated the construct in relation to macro political structures, the state and the class system, in order to account for the persistence and authority of state power and the relationships of class domination. Here we consider it in relation to a 'micro politics of discourse'. It has been argued that rather than one hegemony there are many hegemonies, such as class hegemony, gender hegemony and geographical hegemony (Laclau and Mouffe, 1985). According to Litowitz (2000:519) hegemony "involves the subtle dissemination of the dominant group's perspective as universal and natural, to the point where the dominant beliefs and practices become an intractable component of common sense". It is clear that the term hegemony has evolved somewhat in the environment of cultural studies, to be applied to the ways in which cultural representations normalize and support power relations. In a definition of the term taken from the website *Anthrobase* hegemony is linked with the notion of discursive power from this cultural studies perspective and described as referring to "a system of meaning in a situation or society that overshadows or dominates other meaning systems".[1] In this chapter I am arguing that the account of the 'typical' process of migration, favouring an image of the heroic male provider blazing a trail in the new country to be followed afterwards by wife and family, can be seen as a hegemonic representation of a process in which male agency operates, ignoring the experiences of other family members and single women who have migrated for a range of reasons.

In doing this I am in no way trying to talk down the experience and struggle of these male migrants, described so powerfully in Taher Ben Jelloun's *La Plus Haute des Solitudes*, but simply to suggest that in the generic account something is elided. So is it using a theoretical hammer to crack a walnut, to describe these narratives as being in some way hegemonic? Surely hegemony is best adapted to characterize the powerful representations of the media and other cultural artefacts, the preserve of cultural studies. How can it make sense to talk of hegemonic discourses in these ordinary everyday narratives? It has always, on the contrary, seemed to me to be important to examine the operation of power relations in the everyday micro environments of conversation, since it is here that power relations are repeatedly played out. The notion of hegemony plays a useful role in characterizing how discursive representations are enlisted in support of power relations, even in these micro conversational environments: here we can see in detail the discursive operation of this hegemonic claim to represent in the generic narrative.

Generic narrative, as described above, is adapted to hegemonic discourses simply because its truth claim is to represent the experience not just of the speaker but of a group. In these narratives the speaker claims a particular right both to speak and also to generalize on behalf of others. I will go on to consider narratives that diverge somewhat from the typical

---

[1] http://www.anthrobase.com/Dic/eng/index.html

scenario of the agentive, trail-blazing male migrant, in which three Moroccan women describe their experiences of migration. In the first, the narrator and her grown up children, describes from her own point of view the 'typical' scenario, in which she (the narrator) comes to London to rejoin her husband who has migrated before her.

Different Perspectives on a Family Migration Process

The interview with Mrs Tal., during which this narrative was told, took place with her teenaged daughter and son present. The autobiographical account of her upbringing in Morocco and her settlement in London were at many points constructed interactionally between them. In this narrative extract she describes her arrival at London airport with her children, and an early conflict with her landlady who objected to her bringing her children with her. Her daughter, S., provides interpretation and orientation of the story in a jointly constructed telling:

(In the transcription, Arabic is in *italics*, French in **bold**, Spanish underlined)

13.	Mrs T/	I remember when I come first time london 1974 'member
14.		that your father meet me airport so we come down just
15.		when I come I'm straightway (tell) lady ermwhat you
16.		call her eh *škun hadik* [Who was that] eh
17.	S/	*škun* [Who?]
18.	Mrs T/	*jaryatna hadik italyanya* [that italian neighbour of ours]
19.	S/	ah the italian woman she was the landlord landlady
20.	Mrs T/	yeah
21.	S/	who lived on the first floor and we lived in the basement
22.	Mrs T/	and when she's gone he said lady come all the four
23.		children she come straight away down she said to my
24.		husband yeah wanted to speak to him in spanish not
25.		in english how dare you to bring your children here I
26.		hate ( ) children he said you hate your children too if
27.		you don't like my children you throw your children
28.		outside and I throw my children too like you like your
29.		children with you my children ( ) I pay rent so I bring
30.		my children she said no so I have really hard time with
31.		her I don't speak eh I couldn't speak to her I couldn't
32.		say nothing to her because only understand nothing but
33.		she's very horrible lady all the timecome down fight-
34.		ing and one day I been cleaning outside the door like

35.		that and she just bring teapot with the leaves put on my
36.		head
37.	I/	yeah
38.	Mrs T/	yeah she live upstairs I'm downstairs put down and
39.		shout
40.	I/	god
41.	Mrs T/	how can he do that lady so just speak to her you /**sagas**/
42.		[? = Ça m'agace = that enfuriates me?]
43.	I/	what
44.	Mrs T/	**viens ici** [come here] just I speak to her in French/ ah
45.		just I bring a bottle and I go straight away to her said
46.		just come here

(LAUGHTER)

47.	S/	( )
48.	Mrs T/	come here down I'm fed up of you
49.	I/	and what did she say
50.	Mrs T/	well she just said close the door and her husband said
51.		oh my dear don't go out don't go out

(LAUGHTER)

| 52. | | from that day she stop talking no more |

(LAUGHTER)

53.		really
54.	Y/	you picked up a bottle
55.	Mrs T/	yes empty bottle and

(LAUGHTER)

| 56. | Y/ | Jesus |
| 57. | Mrs T/ | you/**sagas**/**viens ici** [....come here] |

(LAUGHTER)

| 58. | | **j'en ai marre** [I've had enough of it] god |

The narrative describes the harassment to which the newly reunited family is subjected by the landlady, who objects to the fact that they have brought their children to live with them. In the first episode, Mrs Tal.'s husband turns on the landlady and, in Spanish, eloquently defends his right to bring his children into the flat. Interestingly, Mrs Tal. in the narrative emphasizes the landlady's choice of Spanish as the language of confrontation, perhaps because it affords her a more powerful speaking position: "she said to my husband yeah wanted to speak to him in Spanish not in English how dare you to bring your children here I hate ( ) children" (Lines 23-26). In this, her husband is the heroic male defender of the family. Mrs Tal. is rendered voiceless by the fact she can't speak English (or indeed Spanish, the lingua franca shared by her husband and the Italian landlady): "I don't speak eh I couldn't speak to her I couldn't say nothing to her because only understand nothing" (Lines 26-27). In the second episode, Mrs Tal. is at last driven to desperation and action by the landlady's continued harassment, culminating in her tipping tea leaves over the stairs onto Mrs Tal. Her anger explodes both verbally and physically and the language she chooses to express it in is French. Brought up in Oujda, in what was formerly French Morocco, she had grown up speaking French as well as Arabic.

We can see here how, in this multilingual sociolinguistic space, language choice plays a significant role in taking up a powerful speaking position and that, in the cases of Mrs Tal. and indeed the Italian landlady, the languages chosen in which to argue were not English, but Spanish and French. Later on in the interview, Mrs Tal. and her grown up children describe rather poignantly, how they were initially impressed by her husband's English only to discover, as they themselves grew more fluent, that his English was in fact very restricted.

59.	I./	but did your husband, he spoke better english didn't he?
60.	Mrs T./	yeah first time when I come I think he's very good but
61.		after (laughter) after find it very horrible
62.	I./	why?
63.	Mrs T./	speak very badly
64.	S./	when we came and he know some words we thought
65.		he was brilliant
66.	Mrs T./	mmm
67.	S./	afterwards when we came and got used to learn english
68.		we found that his english was really terrible I think the
69.		reason why my mother picked up english better than
70.		him it's because he's involved in the catering world and
71.		you know one tends to learn spanish and italian instead
72.		of english because of all the different immigrants work-
73.		ing there
74.	I./	yeah
75.	S./	while she was working the only per- the only foreign
76.		lady there in a small commun- advisory
77.	Mrs T./	(................................)
78.	I./	where were you working in the marriage advisory
79.	Mrs T./	yeah
80.	S./	and they all spoke clearly
81.	Mrs T./	nice people

It seems that after an initial stage of admiration other family members, whose competence in English starts to overtake his, begin to see through the heroic male provider, developing skills and capacities adapted to their new situation.

It is interesting to note the embedding of a strip of generic narrative in S.'s speech in Lines 71-73, in which she explains the reason why her father's English remained poor: "you know one tends to learn Spanish and Italian instead of English because of all the different immigrants working there".

The choice of the pronoun 'one' as well as of the general present, signals this as a generalization (cf. Laberge and Sankoff, 1979) typifying the multilingual sociolinguistic space of these London hotels and restaurants. S.'s mother, working as a cleaner in the Marriage Advisory Bureau, is in a work environment where only English is spoken. It seems that her capacity in English begins to exceed that of her husband. It seems that S. who at the time of the interview was just starting out in her career as a community worker, is prepared to take on the powerful generic speaking position that involves speaking for a *group* not just for oneself.

The following narrative is told with a great deal of laughter and recounts how, in the early stages of their life in London, Mrs Tal. and her children join her husband in an overcrowded flat. Their two bedroomed accommodation, in a run down area of North Kensington, is part of a multiple occupancy house and mice run around the floor as soon as the lights are turned out at night. Here Mrs Tal. is describing how, after the difficult birth of her younger daughter, the family was rehoused:

82.	Mrs T./	so the doctor said that baby still in hospital couldn't
83.		take him that house really have very old house and
84.		(laughs) mouses)
85.	S./	(Laughter) remember that!
86.		(...)
87.	Mrs T.	only two rooms two bedrooms and little kitchen and
88.		bathroom next to the kitchen really very old house
89.	S./	and damp
90.	Mrs T./	yes and the bedroom just two bedroom two bed double
91.		bed so I put S. and Mo. And Mi. altogether in bed and
92.		(laughs) me and my husband one bed in bedroom and
93.		Y. one single bed for him and when I switch the light off
94.		the mouses come
95.		(.....................................)

96. S./   a Royal Marine troops
97. Mrs T./   was Y. was fighting with the mouses (laughter) all night
98.   fighting with the mouses

This narrative shows how the account of a 'typical' migration process, in which the father of the family goes ahead and creates a base where his family can join him, can be constructed in a completely different way by other members of the family, such as his estranged wife and grown up children. In the previous narrative extract, we saw how Mrs Tal., initially feeling helpless and deprived of the ability to communicate, is driven by her landlady's harassment to make use of her ability to speak French in order to challenge her. Initially the family has confidence in their father's ability to speak English, but as their English improves and apparently his doesn't, they begin to see the limits in his ability. Perhaps the fantasy of the heroic male provider ends in disillusion, with both wife and children developing a wider range of adaptive skills in the new context. However, in this multilingual environment powerful speaking positions can be taken up not just in English, but also in other lingua francas available to the migrant communities such as French, Spanish, Italian.

Experiences of Single Women Migrating

Two contrasting cases

The experience of single women migrating for work falls outside the scope of the typical narrative we have been examining so far, of the male migrant migrating in advance of his family. In the two cases we shall consider, there are striking differences in the level of education and opportunity that was available to Z.T. and Mrs Tar., and these factors have considerable bearing on how they approached the process of migrating. In both cases I will use their autobiographical narratives to demonstrate the differences in life chances in their upbringing, before considering the narratives in which they recount their process of migration.

Z.T.: agency and networking and an opportunity to migrate

At the time that this interview took place, Z.T. was a young woman bringing up her two younger brothers single handed after the death of her parents.

She attended school until the end of her secondary education and in the following narrative recounts how her widowed mother, advised by her dead father in a dream, supported her in going to school to gain the education, including literacy in French, that would help her to migrate:

99. Z.T./	but my mother was erm well she wasn't educated of
100.	course but she was very erm I think very educated inside
101. I/	yeah
102. Z.T./	you know she was really inside educated
103. I/	she had a good understanding of things
104. Z.T./	very very good because once she said to me that well
105.	look ah we don't have erm no money for the next year
106.	because I'm going to **troisieme année secondaire** you
107.	know to have my brevet and it was very hard year for
108.	me and erm so do you have to quit and erm she was
109.	dreaming that my father said don't don't let her to quit
110.	her school
111. I/	she dreamed . . .
112. Z.T./	yes and next morning said well never mind you can go
113.	I said who changed your mind then later she told me
114.	after I pass my class
115. I/	yeah
116. Z.T./	she didn't tell me in that time but after I pass my class
117.	failed in the exam in the first time but we always we erm
118.	in September we do have a second chance all of us and
119.	we pass the exam then I I passed
120. I/	and she told you afterwards
121. Z.T./	yes that day she told me that ( ) you are very lucky I
122.	was dreaming that day when I told you that you have to
123.	quit I was dreaming that your dad comes to me and said
124.	don't let her to quit and don't let her to stop eh stopping
125.	her from anything
126. I/	yeah
127. Z.T./	and she never did M. believe me she never did

In the following narrative, analysed in terms of time space orientation in Baynham (2004), she describes how, after leaving school she couldn't find a job and decided to migrate. She is recruited to work in the Grand Metropolitan hotel chain in London:

| 128. I/ | what made you decide to come to England |

129.	Z.T./	erm well really not eh to England but somewhere abroad
130.	I/	yeah
131.	Z.T./	and eh of course umm I quit my high school and I was
132.		looking for a job actually
133.	I/	yeah
134.	Z.T./	couldn't find any so erm we had eh local whaddycallit
135.		eh the man who does eh typewr- erm whaddyoucallit I
136.		forget now who does writing b the machine you know
137.		for the public
138.	I/	ah hah
139.	Z.T./	and I think because he told me that someone in england
140.		came to meknes
141.	I/	yeah
142.	Z.T./	and he knew this man but he's very very very nice very
143.		educated and he gave him the address of grand metro-
144.		politan hotel
145.	I/	ah hah
146.	Z.T./	so friend of mine know him and she said I wanted to go
147.		to see mr n so and so and can you go with me says all
148.		right so we we went.
149.	I/	yeah
150.	Z.T./	and erm we were talking and he said do you want to go
151.		abroad said oh yes I'd love to but how well I have got the
152.		address and you can write to them yourself
153.	I/	uh huh
154.	Z.T./	and send them two picture of yours but you're going
155.		to get reply in English so who's going to read it for me
156.		(LAUGHTER) I don't know English at all so erm we
157.		really did it is erm eh not a seriously
158.	I/	yeah
159.	Z.T./	but just through our luck maybe yes or no
160.	I/	uh huh
161.	Z.T./	so I did and I wrote a letter for my friend as well
162.	I/	yeah because you could write in
163.	Z.T./	yes I wrote in eh in eh in French and we send two
164.		picture of each and then in four weeks we get a reply
165.	I/	yeah
166.	Z.T./	in English but I and a friend of mine very old woman she's
167.		French and she works at the co- uh French consulate
168.		so I took it to her and she told me that you're going to
169.		get your work permit within four to six weeks but I
170.		didn't..I know I I wasn't lucky but eh I didn't take it eh

171.   that much so I waited
172. I/   yeah
173. Z.T./   well that time three of us wrote letters already myself
174.   and Fatima then another Fatima which I told her to do
175.   so and she did but when we did getwork permit the last
176.   one was the first my friend was the second and I was
177.   three days behind them
178. I/   Yeah
179. Z.T./   so I says well I know my luck is my sign is good go to
180.   work so um so it did so I get my work permit

Z.T. is a young woman who finished secondary schooling. We see in this narrative how she actively deploys her schooled knowledge and network contacts to make something happen for both herself and her two friends. Again we note that Z.T. and her friends are operating in a multilingual, multiliterate environment: her schooled capacity to write in French enables her to write the letter of application on behalf of herself and her friends to the Grand Metropolitan chain. However, when the reply arrives in English she is thrown back into incapacity: "you're going to get reply in English so who's going to read it for me (LAUGHTER) I don't know English at all" (Lines 154-156). All is not lost, though, since through her network contacts "a friend of mine very old woman she's French and she works at the co- uh French consulate" (Lines 166-167), she is able to get the letter translated. It seems that Z.T. is active in two sorts of ways: she can use her own multiliterate capacities to set the process of getting a job in London in motion. Where she is blocked by some obstacle she can find a solution using network contacts. She also acts for herself and her two friends, though later on she is indeed joined by her two younger brothers. Thus there is a parallel process to the migration of the father/husband and hers: by taking responsibility for the migration process, Z.T. creates the possibility of a home for her orphaned brothers.

Network, agency and mediation: Mrs Tar.'s migration

In this narrative, Mrs Tar. describes how her divorce provided the catalyst for her decision to migrate. She is in a very different position than Z.T. who deploys her school gained knowledge and confident networking skills to achieve her purposes. Mrs Tar. had never been to school and had worked as a child domestic in a Spanish family in Morocco. In response to a question from the interviewer:

"and did you go to school"

she replies with a recounting of the events which followed the death of
her father when she was eight.

181. Mrs Tar/ I'm tell you about this problem my father dead died
182.   because I have eight years me just my mother my mother
183.   all because she can't works he couldn't because she
184.   never work you know all take it all furniture no clothes
185.   nice clothes you know 'spensive all selling this time
186.   this time () have spanish spana spain *aš kayaquli l guerra*
187.   [How do you say war?]
188. A/   war
189. Mrs Tar/ war
190. I/   a war
191. Mrs Tar/ yes all my mother can't work she don't know you know
192.   because is never work in her life you know all the furni-
193.   ture all everything just the floor n the n the *aš ka* . . .
194.   [How do....]
195. I/   the carpets
196. Mrs Tar/ the carpet just the carpet n the *aš kayaqulu mantat* . . .
197.   [How do you say blankets]
198. A/   blanket
199. Mrs Tar./ just blanket for sleep on the floor (that's) everything
200.   gone I remember I'm been school this time I remember
201.   my mother I can't remember because you now I don't
202.   like remember this time my mother e take me the mm the
203.   doctor you know the doctor Spanish doctor you know
204.   because my my family this eh T wife T sister is work eh
205.   nurse in hospital you know for the doctor.......I'm little
206.   girl me eight years well nine years like this this time
207.   you know I'm I'm I'm go work for the doctor you know
208.   I'm look after the baby I'm nanny
209. I/   nanny
210. Mrs Tar/ I'm nanny too look after me you know this time e give me
211.   five pound eh no no no five pound no erm twenty five
212.   penny a month
213. I/   blimey
214. Mrs Tar/ twenty five penny I remember twenty five penny month
215.   ....
216.   that's it I'm no I can't read I can't do nothing you know

This narrative, told by Mrs Tar. in response to the interviewer's question about whether she went to school, ends with a declaration of incapacity "I can't read I can't do nothing you know" (Line 216), which is similar to the feelings about English expressed by Mrs Tal. in her early days in London, and indeed those of Z.T. faced with the letter from Grand Metropolitan in English.

217. I/   why did you come to england why england
218. Mrs Tar/   I'm tell you before because I'm fed up for myself you
219.   know
220. I/   why not france, spain
221. Mrs Tar/   well you know why because I'm working nn when me
222.   divorce I'm working for the embassy spanish you know
223. I/   Where
224. Mrs Tar/   in () morocco in rabat
225. I/   uh huh
226. Mrs Tar/   the boyfriend <u>de</u> [of] my niece just joking he told me
227.   because sometime I'm cry I remember my husband re-
228.   member my home he told me You want to go london tell
229.   her you must joking. I me yes <u>si</u> [if] you want to go I I
230.   give you uh write for you he give you a <u>contrato</u> [con-
231.   tract] ( ) oh you must joking well she do it she did it you
232.   know one day in one week he answer me he tell me yes
233.   you have a job in a in hotel

In the earlier part of this narrative, we saw Mrs Tar. in the aftermath of a painful divorce, responding to an opportunity put her way by a relation. The migration arrangements are here achieved by her niece's boyfriend "si [if] you want to go I I give you uh write for you he give you a contrato [contract]" (Lines 229-231), so that we do not see Mrs Tar playing an active role in setting up the migration process. Owing to her lack of basic literacy in Arabic or any other language, she must fall back on family and friends to achieve her objectives.

234. Mrs Tar/   when me going (in) hotel well I have my <u>contrato</u> with
235.   my passport n everything when me come back here I
236.   can't speak english very well because I'm I speak
237.   spanish last day is finished the eh <u>contrato</u> just one
238.   day like today when me come here in the airport they
239.   told me no no you can't come in london because you

240.   look is too late I'm tell him no I'm sorry today last day
241. I/   of the contract
242. Mrs Tar/   yes the contract he told me no no he told me what you
243.   speak () french I'm tell him no I'm speak spanish he
244.   look somebody else he can speak spanish he told me
245.   <u>mira que dice la policia hoy no puede entrar ya muy</u>
246.   <u>tarde 1 ultimo dia entonces yo le dije no yo puedo</u>
247.   <u>entrar porque este l ultimo dia yo puedo entrar yo tengo</u>
248.   <u>que entrar aqui hoy porque hoy 1 ultimo dia si vengo</u>
249.   <u>manana no</u> [look the police say that you can't come in
250.   today, it's too late, the last day then I said no I can
251.   come in because today is the last day I can come in
252.   I've got to come in because this is the last day if I come
253.   tomorrow no]
254. I/   what did they say
255. Mrs Tar/   yes
256. I/   <u>i que dijeron</u>? [what did they say?]
257. Mrs Tar/   is talking together <u>esta hablándolo los mismos y dice si</u>
258.   <u>si</u> [they are talking among themselves and say yes yes]
259.   is all right <u>yo me acuerdo y dicen</u> [I remember and they
260.   say] english yes is all right all right
261. I/   yeah
262. Mrs Tar/   yes <u>yo me acuerdo entonces ya pasé</u> [I remember and
263.   then I passed through] yes

As is demonstrated in the latter part of the narrative Mrs Tar. does however speak a variety of Spanish, learnt orally during her period working as
a domestic with the Spanish family. She is able to draw on this resource in
the episode when she successfully challenges the passport control at
Heathrow to let her enter the UK. Again we see the relevance of a multilingual repertoire in taking up a strong speaking position, just as we did in
the narrative of Mrs Tal.'s confrontation with her neighbour/landlady. When
it is clear at the passport control that Mrs Tar. does not speak English
there is a process of negotiation to allow the intervention of an interpreter
"he told me what you speak () French I'm tell him no I'm speak Spanish"
(Lines 242-2433). Once the Spanish interpreter is available, Mrs Tar. is
able to make use of her fluency in Spanish to speak authoritatively about
the data on her work permit. As I have argued elsewhere (Baynham, 1995),
Mrs Tar. is participating and acting in a literate world, even though she is
not technically literate, she has access to literate knowledge and it is this
that she deploys to such effect in Spanish.

On the other hand, in the narrative of her early years, she regularly switches to Moroccan Arabic to involve her young son, A., and indeed on other occasions such as with the interviewer who speaks Spanish, to provide words she doesn't know (Lines 156-158:

Mrs Tar,/	*aš kayaqulu l guerra* [How do you say war?]
A/	war
Mrs Tar/	war

She is using him as a mediator (cf. Baynham and Masing, 2000) to get the story told. Again we have similar patterns of both knowledge (literate knowledge) and networking to achieve communication purposes to those we observed in Z.T.'s narrative. Where they differ is in the ways that Z.T. can initiate and lead a migration process through her multilingual literacy abilities.

Discussion

In this chapter I have shown how generic narratives, characterized by the truth claim that they represent something typical and recurring, are used to create a hegemonic account of the process of migration in which a heroic male migrant goes on ahead to trail blaze and organize a place where his family can follow. We have seen examples of this from media representations and in the accounts of M.A. who lays claim to speaking authoritatively that is representatively about the experience of the group. We have also seen this scenario typified in the case study from training materials. We have also seen evidence of this 'typical' account in the narrative of Mr R., which echoes other narratives told to me by Moroccan males in my fieldwork. Similarly, in *My Life* Mohammed Elbaja tells the story of his father's 'heroic' migration from a child's perspective. The background for the narrative of Mrs Tal. and her family is the heroic migration of her husband.

By considering the perspectives of other family members, I have shown that there is not just one story but many stories: Mrs Tal. has to fight her own battles with an abusive neighbour/landlady and, drawing on her ability in French, finds a voice and takes up a powerful speaking position. It is indeed a cross cutting theme in these narratives that the narrators draw on multilingual language capacities: Mrs Tal.'s husband and the landlady argue in Spanish, Mrs Tal. herself uses French. In Mrs Tar.'s story of her encounter at Heathrow, it is through Spanish that she is able to argue her case, successfully and is allowed to enter the UK. It is Z.T.'s competence in French that enables her to act as a mediator or cultural broker for her two friends. When she is linguistically challenged by the letter in English, she locates someone on her network who can solve the problem. Mrs Tal. and her children recount how they eventually saw through the skills in English of her husband, which had so impressed them earlier on, as their own fluency in English surpassed his.

In terms of the interactive telling of the narrative, speakers may draw on their multilingual resources to resolve a lexical problem or to mobilize some element of the narrative re-telling: Mrs Tar. draws on her son's linguistic resources to resolve lexical items in her narratives, switching into Moroccan Arabic to do so "aš kayaqulu mantat? [How do you say blankets?]" (Line 196). Mrs Tal. switches to Moroccan Arabic in Line 18 to activate the persona of "jaryatna italyanya" [our Italian neighbour] as she begins to tell her story.

So these are narratives in which agency is demonstrated through the strategic deployment of multilingual resources. (There are of course other forms of agency in these narratives, as when Mrs Tal. sees off her abusive neighbour with a bottle or indeed as her son Y. sees off the 'mouses'). The Linguistic Minorities Project (LMP 1985) described London as a multilingual setting characterized by immigrant bilingualism, however these narratives show that the sociolinguistic space portrayed in these narratives is richer and more complex: it is a multilingual setting characterized by immigrant *multilingualism.*

The narrative of Mrs Tal. and her children supplements and extends the narrative of the heroic male migration, providing the perspectives on this process of other family members. In this family story, jointly told by Mrs Tal and her children, we find a richer and more nuanced account than that provided by the generic narrative which of its nature elides specificities and different perspectives. The migration stories of Z.T. and Mrs Tar. are also outside the frame of the hegemonic generic narrative of the heroic male migration, although there are significant differences between them. Z.T. is able to draw on the cultural capital provided by her education and contacts to be an active player in the migration process, both on her own account and as an enabler of the migrations of her two friends. Mrs Tar. is dependent on the support of a male family member to complete the necessary paperwork for her migration. Completely uneducated, a domestic

servant from the age of eight or nine, she nevertheless is able to participate actively in the literate world when she correctly identifies that her
work permit has not yet expired, and takes up a powerful speaking position, using her Spanish to make her case.

The hegemonic, generic narrative of migration creates a generalization: while this generalization may indeed be largely true (we have seen in
the course of this paper, a number of instances of its typicality), it necessarily elides both other versions of the same story and indeed other stories.
I have focused here mainly on how the generic account sidelines the migration stories of women migrants. Another neglected aspect in studies of
the narratives of migration is undoubtedly the migration experience of
children. A complex and adequate account of migration from the inside
will necessarily address this diversity of perspectives.

References

Baynham, M. (1995) *Literacy Practices*, London: Longman.
------ (2003) 'Narrative in Space and Time: Beyond "Backdrop" Accounts of
    Narrative Orientation', *Narrative Inquiry* 13 (2):347-366.
------ (forthcoming) 'Lifestories/Lifeworlds: Representations and Representa-
    tions of Self, Family and Community in Narratives of Migration and
    Settlement', in A. De Fina, D. Schiffrin and M. Bamberg (eds.) *Discourse
    and Identity,* New York: Cambridge University Press:
------ and H.L. Masing (2000) 'Mediators and Mediation in Multilingual Lit-
    eracy Events', in M. Martin-Jones and K. Jones (eds.) *Multilingual
    Literacies,* Amsterdam: John Benjamins:189-207.
Ben Jelloun, T. (1997) *La Plus Haute des Solitudes: misère affective et sexuelle
    'émigrés nord-africains* [The Deepest of Solitudes: Emotional and Sexual
    Misery of North African Emigrants], Paris: Éditions du Seuil.
Crehan, K. (2002) *Gramsci, Culture and Anthropology,* Berkeley: University
    of California Press.
Elbaja, M. (1979) *My Life,* London: English Centre.
El Kssmi, Z. (1979) *Families,* London: English Centre.
Grillo, R.D. (1985) *Ideologies and Institutions in Urban France: The Repre-
    sentation of Immigrants,* Cambridge: Cambridge University Press.
Joffe, E.G.M. (unpublished) *The Moroccan Community in Britain.*
Laberge, S. and D. Sankoff (1979) 'Anything you can do', in T. Givon (ed.)
    Syntax & Semantics Vol. 12, Discourse and Syntax, New York: Academic
    Press: 419-440.
Laclau, E. and C. Mouffe (1985) *Hegemony and Socialist Strategy: Towards*

a Radical Democratic Politics, London: Verso.

Linguistic Minorities Project (1985) *The Other Languages of Britain,* (London: Routledge and Keegan Paul.

Litowitz, D. (2000) *Gramsci, Hegemony and the Law,* Brigham Young University Law Review 2:515-551.

Sassen, S. (2000) *Guests and Aliens*, New York: The New Press.

Contesting Social Place
Narratives of Language Conflict[1]

ANA M. RELAÑO PASTOR, *University of California San Diego, U.S.*
ANNA DE FINA, *Georgetown University, U.S.*

Introduction

This chapter focuses on narratives of language difficulties or conflicts told by a group of Mexican first generation immigrant women in the San Diego California area. Our main interest lies in the analysis of narrators' self-representations in story worlds, as a tool to understand identity construction in the context of migration.

Among the questions that we discuss are the following: how do women talk about language difficulties and lack of access to language resources? What kinds of agency do they project for themselves as characters in represented story worlds and as participants in interactional worlds? Do they perform acts of resistance to language discrimination through the telling of stories? Is there a gender specificity in the way they talk about language and identity issues?

We examine both action structure and performance devices in the narratives in order to answer these questions. We argue that the strategies and narrative resources used by women to present themselves as protagonists in the story world point to a type of self construction in which the stress is on resistance to dominant exclusionary practices and on the configuration of a different moral order from the one established and experienced by them in the host society.

Before presenting and analyzing the data, we introduce some of the theoretical considerations that have guided us, explain the rationale for our methodological choices, illustrate the links between our work and the objectives and main questions proposed in the volume, and give some background on the contexts that frame the narrative discourse produced by these women.

---

[1] Ana M. Relaño Pastor wants to thank the postdoctoral programme fellowship of the Spanish Ministry of Education, Culture and Sport *(Programa de becas postdoctorales en el extranjero del Ministerio de Educación, Ciencia y Deporte),* for funding and making the writing of this article possible during the academic year 2002-2003 at the University of California, San Diego.

Narratives, Displacement and Identity

The use of narratives as a tool for the study of identity has become more and more of an established practice among linguists. Narrating is seen as a discourse practice (Fairclough, 1989) of self-construction in that it does not simply convey images and conceptions about the self that pre-exist the occasion of discourse in which narratives are generated. Instead it enacts, performs, shapes and also represents identities within specific interactional contexts, while at the same time building upon, reflecting and conveying social experiences related to other practices. In this sense narrative identity has been linked in recent sociolinguistic and anthropological research, to discursive work and practice both in the field of autobiographical tellings (Bruner, 1993; Mishler, 1999; Brockmeier and Cardbaugh, 2001; Wortham, 2001) and in the area of narratives of personal experience in interview contexts (De Fina, 2000 and 2003; Lucius-Hoene and Deppermann, 2000; Schiffrin, 1996) and in conversation (Goodwin, 1997; Ochs and Capps, 2001; Georgakopoulou, 2002).

Narrative activity becomes particularly illuminating in the case of 'displaced' groups such as immigrants, in that it is through the process of retelling and reconstructing past experience that members of these groups often make sense of social encounters and conflicts and foreground an emerging sense of their identities, a process that in many cases implies contesting established roles and claiming social space. As argued in the introduction to this volume, narratives give us both a view from 'the inside' of silenced groups about displacement, settlement and about the conflicts that accompany such processes, and allow members of these groups to enact or perform social and moral relocation.

We have chosen narratives centred on language difficulties and conflicts as an object of analysis because we believe that dominance and access to power are crucially played around language issues. 'Symbolic domination' (Bourdieu, 1977), understood as control over accepted representations of reality and social relations, is firmly tied to language domination. Thus, investigation of discourse around language access allows us not only to understand the dominant culture, but also to make sense of how minorities position themselves with respect to lack of access to symbolic and material resources. Furthermore, we study narratives told by women because, given their social role as main agents in socialization processes, their discourse on language issues is crucial to, and has concrete consequences for, the way immigrant groups behave, come to view themselves and socialize their children (Relaño Pastor, forthcoming).

Studies on gender and migration agree on the active role that female immigrants play in the settlement process in the U.S. Hondagneu-Sotelo (1994) and Chavira (1988), for example, have shown that women have a prominent function in everyday social transactions in shops, schools and places of employment, in the use of public and private financial support as well as in the development of community activities. Ruiz and Tiano (1987) have found that women also play an active role in directing their own destinies in the economic and cultural fabrics of the borderlands.

Insights from studies about immigrant women are enriched by recent research on gender and discourse that rejects an essentialist paradigm looking for women's 'natural' identities, in favour of a constructionist perspective in which women build gender specific discourses in response to particular historical and local contexts (Bucholtz, 1999; Sawin, 1999; Gal, 2001). Thus, the specific role of immigrant women in the migration process and in the family settlement are factors that impinge on the shape of the narrative discourse produced by them together with the type of story world evoked and the circumstances of the interview.

The identity constructions that emerge in these circumstances are therefore not part of an essential feminine positioning, but are historically and socially determined. As narratives build and reflect social realities, they should be regarded as 'multiply contextualized' (Sawin, 1999: 254). In this case, among the pertinent contexts for the production and analysis of the narratives, we need to consider the wider frame of dominant language ideologies and practices in the United States (particularly in California) on the one hand, and the local frame of the interview on the other.

Language Ideologies and Practices in the U.S.

According to last Census 2000 data, Hispanic/Latinos constitute 33% of the total population in California, and 77% of them are Mexicans. Out of the total 31, 416, 629 Californians five years and older, 12,401,756 speak languages other than English at home. 8,105,505 of these are Spanish-speaking, and more than half of them, 4,303,949, are labelled as speaking English 'less than very well'.

This is the case with most first generation Mexican immigrant women, who do not speak English when they migrate to the U.S. Lack of language proficiency faces them with a host of difficulties at school, work, in other important institutions such as hospitals and public services, and often also at home. Such difficulties derive not only from the objective inability to communicate and make themselves understood in everyday situations, but also from the hostile language ideologies and practices that support and are, in turn, supported by symbolic domination.

Mainstream language ideologies are built around basic beliefs about minorities and linguistic diversity. According to these, linguistic diversity is a cause not only of cultural disintegration, but also of social, educational, and economic conflicts whose solution lies in the reestablishment of the supremacy of the dominant language variety (Baker, 2001). These ideologies have led to 'blatant Hispanophobia' (Zentella, 1997), and to the growth of xenophobic power groups such as the U.S. English-only movement, a political organization aimed at fighting multilingualism and the use of Spanish. Among the association's most important projects, has been the implementation of *Proposition 63* proclaiming English as the only official language of California, and the approval of *Proposition 227* aimed at eliminating bilingual education in schools. These ideologies and practices emphasize the status of Spanish as a dis-preferred variety and of Spanish speakers as a low-prestige minority group.

Being unable to speak English makes immigrants vulnerable to acts of aggression and discrimination and to open or implicit acts of 'disrespect' since "the more unequal the situation, the more one is held to a measure of behaviour that does not come into play among equals" (Urciuoli, 1996:160). Asymmetry of power and lack of access to symbolic resources are important elements of the context within which Mexican women in California experience everyday interactions in public and private spaces and therefore of their retelling of those experiences. However, domination often breeds resistance on the part of dominated groups. According to Gal:

> Resistance to a dominant cultural order occurs in two ways: first, when devalued linguistic forms and practices (such as local vernaculars, slang, women's interactional styles or poetry, and minority languages) are practised and celebrated despite widespread denigration and stigmatization. Second, it occurs because these devalued practices often propose and embody alternate models of the social world. (2001:424-425)

We will see that resistance is embodied in Mexican women's stories of language conflict through recourse to strategies and narrative resources that allow them to contest public discriminatory discourse, to construct themselves as agents of change, to propose alternatives to the existing moral order and to engage in an activity of moral relocation.

The Interview

The narratives analyzed here were told during sociolinguistic interviews with eighteen first generation Mexican immigrant women. The interviewer was also a woman and an Andalusian Spanish speaker. The interview log focused on language experiences at home, at work, and in social life. All the interviews were elicited in the language chosen by the subjects. Since the research focus was on language experiences, the interview became a locus of ideological exchange in which the women and the interviewer shared views and perspectives on issues having to do with language rights, language tolerance, respect, prejudice and discrimination. Thus self rep-resentations and self reflection were elicited and they took shape within an interaction that can be described as 'sympathetic' and involved.

Some consequences of the presence of an interviewer sharing the wom-en's concerns about their position in society were the high involvement of the narrators and the use of emotional language, the effort to co-construct explanations and evaluations, and the focus on topics such as discrimina-tion, family conflicts and problems. As Capps and Ochs (1995) notice in their study of agoraphobic women's discourse, individuals need to tell their stories to authenticate and validate their past experiences. The inter-view is one of the possible contexts in which this kind of work can be done, but in the case of immigrants it is particularly important since it allows the expression of perspectives on identity from the inside. For this reason narratives told in interviews should not be regarded as 'artificial' but rather as a kind of narrative more centred on reflexive activity than conversational ones.

Data and Subjects

We have selected for analysis a corpus of 20 narratives on language diffi-culties and language conflicts told by eighteen first generation Mexican immigrant women participating in a bilingual/bicultural after-school com-puter programme called 'La Clase Mágica' (LCM).[2] The programme, addressed to different age groups, including adults, was developed to suit the linguistic and cultural needs of the Mexican/Latino community in San Diego. Its goal was to provide the participants with educational resources and institutional support through a computer-based curriculum designed for different age groups. LCM runs under the direction of a working class

---

[2] La Clase Mágica was designed in 1989 by Professor Olga Vásquez and her team at the Laboratory of Comparative Human Cognition (LCHC) at the University of California, San Diego. It currently serves as a research and community oriented educational setting for Mexican/Latino families in San Diego County. For more information see Vásquez (2003).

Mexican community. The curriculum is bilingual and designed and re-shaped continuously to meet the daily linguistic and cultural realities of the community. Seven women of Mexican origin currently work as site coordinators in the locations where LCM operates.

The group of Mexican female immigrants interviewed includes the seven female site coordinators of La Clase Mágica project and a group of eleven mothers and participants in the program. All the participants had been in the U.S. for a range of one month to more than thirty. They were from the Mexican states of Jalisco, Guanajuato, Guerrero, Morelos, Durango, Baja, California and from Mexico City. They had all received either primary or secondary education and worked in domestic services, as administrative staff in community services, as site coordinators of the LCM's program, in restaurants, and janitorial services. As for their reasons for coming to the U.S., these participants quote economic and social networks as motives, thus confirming Cornelius' (1992) findings about the main factors that explain Mexican settlement in California. The degree of English proficiency correlated in most of the cases with the period of residency in the United States, ranging from none to full bilingualism and ability to code-switch in English and Spanish. Three of the women grew up bilingual after coming to the U.S. at a very young age. One had received some language instruction in Mexico and had just arrived in the U.S. The rest had received some language instruction at some point in their stay in the U.S. and had different degrees and personal assessment of their English proficiency.

Categories of Analysis

Agency

Our analysis of self-representation in story worlds focuses on the projection of agency. We define *agency* as "the degree of activity and initiative that narrators attribute to themselves as characters in particular story worlds" (De Fina, 2003:93). We relate agency in story worlds to characters' reactions to troubles and difficulties, and regard it as defined on a continuum. On the lower end of the continuum there is lack of reaction to conflicts, while on its higher end there are characters' active attempts to solve problems. To operationalize the concept of agency we designed coding categories that are based partly on Labov and Waletzky's (1967/1997) and partly on Ochs and Capps' (2001) models of narrative analysis. Following Labov and Waletzky, we divided narratives into clauses and coded them as:

1   Orientation clauses (OR)
2   Complicating action clauses (CA)
3   Evaluation clauses (and sections) (EVAL)

According to their definition, orientation clauses give indications about the setting of the story and its protagonists, complicating action clauses present the main action and evaluation clauses give the narrator's view of what the point of the story is.

For a more detailed analysis of complicating action clauses, we took into account Ochs and Capps' (2001) model that lists among story components (173):

1   *Unexpected events/complicated action*, i.e. unanticipated, usually problematic, incidents.
2   *Psychological/physiological response*, i.e. change in a person's thoughts, emotions, or somatic state, provoked by an unexpected event, unplanned action, attempt, physical response, and/or another psychological/physiological response.
3   *Attempt*, or behaviour initiated to attain a goal and resolve a problematic unexpected event.

Based on this model we further subdivided Complicating Action clauses into:

1   Complicating events (CE)
2   Reactions (RE)
3   Resolution (RES)

Complicating Events consist of problems related to language and communication difficulties in different social settings: from having no English proficiency, to instances in which protagonists struggle to make themselves understood or to obtain respect and attention. *Reactions* include different kinds of responses to complicating events. *Psychological* responses are reactions involving emotional states such as anger, shame, and sadness. *Verbal* responses are linguistically represented verbal reactions commonly introduced by the quotation formula "LE DIJE" (I TOLD HER/HIM). *Action* responses are reactions represented by specific acts such as calling or getting the attention of a third party, leaving, or other measures taken to face a difficult event. *Resolutions* include actions that bring about a solution to the complicating event.

At this point a clarification about evaluation is in order. As mentioned above, *evaluation* (EV) clauses and sections encompass moral reflections and moral re-locations in social spaces. As pointed out by Labov (1972), evaluation devices are found throughout narratives and it is therefore not possible totally to distinguish evaluative clauses from other types of clause. For example, clauses classified as expressing 'reactions' are often evaluative in nature. In the coding of evaluative clauses we concentrated on clauses inserted into sections that interrupted the main action, or were placed at the end of the narrative, where narrators were clearly engaged in the work of making the events meaningful to the interviewer.

Besides explicit evaluation, narrators use other linguistic strategies to express their point of view on events and to convey moral stances. The most salient in our corpus are the uses of reported speech and of emotional language.

Emotion

In this paper we understand emotions and emotional language as 'being done' in conversation through multiple linguistic and paralinguistic devices such as facial expressions, body postures, prosodic features, lexical and syntactic forms. Besnier (1990:437) points out that it is important to recognize the multifunctionality of many affect-encoding linguistic categories and to look at the semiotic status of affect in language, which "permeates all levels of linguistic and communicative structures, all utterances and all communicative contexts in more or less transparent ways". Ochs and Schiefflin also use the expression 'affect', arguing that it is "a broader term than emotions, (which includes) feelings, moods, dispositions, and attitudes associated with persons and /or situations" (1989:7). Affect is, according to these authors, expressed through 'affect keys', i.e. "those linguistic features that intensify or specify affect functions" (ibid.:13). Such keys can index different kinds of emotions and affective meanings such as anger, sarcasm, disappointment, sadness, pleasure, humour, surprise, etc, related to different kinds of positioning towards the events portrayed in the narratives. Ochs and Schiefflin's list of affect keys includes: "pronouns, determiners, tense/aspect, verb voice, case marking, number/gender/animacy marking, affixes and particles, reduplication, intonation, voice quality, sound repetition, sound symbolism, lexicon, verb variants, word order, code-switching and affective speech acts and activities" (ibid.:129). Among the affect keys commonly used in the narratives analyzed we found the following:

1. Intonation:
   a. Changes in pitch   le digo, "Esta persona no tiene cuidados"

	and I tell her, "*This person has no care*"
b. Changes in loudness	luego en la casa le dije, "NUNCA TIENES QUE SENTIR VER- GÜENZA PORQUE TÚ HABLAS ESPAÑOL"
	and then at home I told him, "YOU NEVER HAVE TO FEEL ASHAMED BECAUSE YOU SPEAK SPANISH"
2. Lexicalization of emotions:	AY:: ↑ ME DIO CORAJE↑ Me dio tristeza por la señora
	AY:: ↑ I GOT SO MAD↑ I felt bad for the lady
3. Description of emotional state:	y me sentí tan mal que me puse a llorar
	and I felt so bad that I started to cry
4. Use of lexical elements or expressive morphology:	A usted le gustaría que le dijeran, "Tú eres un *pinche* americano↑"
	Would you like it if they told you, "You are a fucking American↑"
	Y un día mi niño llegó llorando y me dijo,"Mami, por qué yo soy oscurito[3]↑"
	And one day my little boy came crying and said, "Mom, why am I *dark*↑"

These devices allow us to identify emotional language and to characterize 'emotional narratives' as those stories in which emotion is displayed throughout the narrative structure through a variety of affect keys. As we will see, affect is a central device in the construction of moral stances.

Analysis

The data analyzed here consist of twenty narratives related to language conflicts. In these narratives 'complicating events' have to do with story

---

[3] The affect key in this case is the suffix – *ito* which is attached to the word *oscuro* (*dark*). The suffix denotes something small and is usually associated with positive affect.

world situations in which Mexican women narrate incidents and problems related to language difficulties in a variety of social settings: hospitals, shops, workplace, school, home, church. Complicating events included not only incidents in which narrators/protagonists or other characters were unable to understand what was said to them and could not communicate, but also incidents in which antagonists used language identity as a basis for discrimination or aggression. These settings also represent specific social spaces where roles are often perceived by participants and established on the basis of power relationships within which immigrant women are clearly at a disadvantage. Below (Chart 1) we present some examples of our narrative analysis, which include language experiences in hospitals, in the workplace and at church. These examples are schematic in the sense that we have included only the utterances that carry out the narrative functions examined.

CHART 1: NARRATIVES OF LANGUAGE CONFLICTS

COMPLICATING EVENTS	REACTION	EVALUATION	RESOLUTION
HOSPITAL nadie hablaba español *nobody spoke Spanish*	**PSYCHOLOGICAL** me sentí horrible *I felt horrible* **ACTION** pero rellené los papeles como pude *but I filled out the documents as I could*	fue mucho problema, mucho problema *it was very problematic, very problematic*	pero la doctora hablaba un poco español entonces ya me pude comunicar con ella *but the doctor spoke a little Spanish so I was able to communicate with her*
WORKPLACE y yo les dije "¡Ay! Una spidermen!!" y todo el mundo se rió de mí. *and I told them, "Oh! A spiderman!" and everybody laughed at me.*	**PSYCHOLOGICAL** y yo me sentí horrible *and I felt horrible*	pero yo nunca olvidaré ese trabajo porque nos ayudaron a mi amiga y a mí superar un poquito el miedo y a que no te importe nada de lo de aquí ni nada de lo de allá *but I will never forget that job because they helped my friend and me overcome fear not to care about things here and there*	No resolution

COMPLICATING EVENTS	REACTIONS	EVALUATION	RESOLUTION
CHURCH	**ACTION**		
y me di cuenta de que todo lo que estaba pasando allí era puro inglés *and I realized that all that was happening there was in English*	y no llegué a la mitad porque me salí *and I did not even go through half of it because I left* **PSYCHOLOGICAL** me salí bien enojada *I left really angry* **PSYCHOLOGICAL + VERBAL** me salí tan enojada que les dije a mis hijos"Vámonos, vámonos!" *I left so angry that I told my children 'Let's go, let's go!'*	me sentí que era una celebración ridícula, porque sentí que era un insulto para la raza y así como que tú no eres importante, me sentí que esa celebración no era para nosotros por eso la dieron en inglés. *I felt it was a ridiculous situation, because I felt it was an insult for our race like saying you are not important, I felt that was not a celebration for us that is why they gave it in English* no se me hace justo que hay mucha gente que no habla inglés que no entiende el inglés y nomás están ahí. *I do not think it is fair because there are a lot of people who do not speak English and do not understand English and they are just there.*	No resolution

This general analysis shows some common trends in the narratives. One is the widespread use of emotional language. Of the twenty narratives analyzed, sixteen use either lexicalisation of emotions or descriptions of emotional states. In the case of two more stories, affect is conveyed through reported speech as characters are depicted engaging in emotionally charged dialogues. The fact that 90% of the narratives present use of emotional language confirms the significance of language related incidents in the life of Mexican immigrant women and the centrality of the language problem in everyday interactions in which they engage. Communicative difficulties and/or language related prejudice appear to stir a variety of sentiments that range from anger to sadness to shame both in the story world and in the storytelling world evaluation. Among the narratives, some stand out as highly emotional both because of the intense use of affect keys and of the emphasis on moral issues in the evaluation section. These narratives report incidents where basic rights such as the right to healthcare or to proper treatment in public services have been violated, or people's dignity has been overlooked. Such scenarios are often the ones that elicit agentive reactions represented by what we have called 'moral relocations'. In such cases, narrators redefine social space by placing themselves, other immigrants, and their interlocutors as story characters and as present interlocutors in social roles that contest power relationships and affirm their agency. In some cases moral relocations do not simply imply changing one's social role, but even conquering a role: becoming socially visible as opposed to invisible. Narrators often achieve such relocations in social space by presenting themselves as moral agents and bearers of alternative values both in the story world and in the interactional world. Thus emotional language is not only indicative of the significance of the incidents narrated, but it also constitutes a central strategy for the communication of moral indignation and therefore also for the elicitation of the listener's alignment.

The action structure of the narratives presents another common trend, which is the lack of resolution to the conflicts presented in the story world. In most of the narratives (fourteen out of twenty) complicating events lead to conflicts and problems that do not get resolved at the end. However, it is interesting to notice that of the six narratives in which narrators report a resolution brought about through their action as characters in the story world, three have to do with problems in which children are involved, such as discrimination at school or in the neighbourhood. Thus, it appears that women construct themselves as particularly active and combative when it comes to family matters.

If we look more closely at agency in these narratives, we find that in most of the stories narrators describe themselves as reacting to complicating events. Only in a minority of narratives (four out of twenty) do narrators/protagonists depict themselves as doing nothing to overcome a language related problem. Three of these stories do not deal with basic violations of rights, but rather with antagonists' minor acts of aggression such as making fun or laughing at the protagonists' inability to speak the language or to express themselves correctly. In the rest of the narratives protagonists are presented as reacting not only psychologically but also verbally and/or through different endeavours in order to face, correct, or overcome a language related problem. Again, emotional language plays a central role in depicting reactions since characters are often presented as responding to language difficulties not only with sentiments of anger, frustration or shame, but also with words or actions that are emphasized through the use of affect keys.

Thus, agency in the narratives examined is emphasized through the presentation of protagonists' reactions to difficult situations, and moral stances are constructed with the aid of discourse strategies, among which emotional language and reported speech stand out as central. As we will see, character reactions and story evaluations give substance to acts of resistance by these immigrant women to discriminatory ideologies and practices.

Contesting Social Place

In this section we analyze in detail one narrative about a language centred conflict in order to illustrate the type of narrative resources used by the Mexican immigrant women interviewed to contest their place in U.S. society and to realize acts of resistance. We look at the enactment of moral relocation through different performance devices allowing the narrator to describe herself "relative to a moral ideal of what it is to be a good person" (Rymes, 1995:498).

Marina's story

One of the biggest challenges for Mexican immigrant women is access to health resources. Experiences at the doctors' or in hospitals were related to the frustration of not having the language to communicate, unsuccessful translation attempts, and unfair treatment that resulted in being ignored and discriminated against for not having an adequate command of English. In the following narrative Marina reports on an incident that took place at a local hospital and that involved someone from her village. Marina is a first generation immigrant who has lived in the U.S. for fifteen years. She spoke no English when she arrived, however, spurred by her husband, she learned it over the years. Her narrative was told as a response to a question by the interviewer on problems with the language:

R[4]:   ¿Se ha sentido usted alguna vez que no le han ayudado con el idioma?
M: Pues tal vez sí pero porque uno no quiere ¿verdad?, porque si uno habla y pide ayuda, es así como se va abriendo paso.
R: ¿Y alguna experiencia con el idioma?

[4] 'R' stands for researcher. The abbreviations to identify the clauses in the transcript are: OR (Orientation); CA (Complicating Action); EV (Evaluation); CE (Complicating Event); RE (Reaction).

	M:	Pues, yo creo que sí que estos casos se dan en todo Estados Unidos, principalmente con los Latinos que no hablan inglés o que vienen de otro país. Yo no sé personalmente pero por lo que yo he observado en otras personas es que lo ignoran más si uno no sabe y tengo un caso más reciente.
1	M:	Una persona que es de la misma comunidad de dónde yo vengo[(.) de un pueblo *OR*[4]
2	R:	[aha
3	M:	se enfermó *OR*
4		llegó al hospital *CA*
5		uhm:: y: esta persona no sabe inglés (.) nada *OR*
6		y entonces lógicamente que uno se siente incómodo de estar todo el tiempo de una sola posición si no se puede mover *EV*
7	R:	claro
8	M:	y más si no puede hablar inglés *EV*
9		y cómo decirles, "Cámbiame [ayúdame" o
10	R:	[aha "falta algo", no? *EV*
11	M:	aha (.2)
12	M:	uh:: las camas deben de tener (.) un botón= *EV*
13	R:	=aha
14	M:	para que si hay alguna emergencia (.) que salga la:: (.) en dónde se encuentra el la que sé yo la cabeza (.2) *EV*
15	R:	aha
16	M:	o yo no sé como le llamen *EV*
17	R:	aha sí
18	M:	no se me viene el nombre ahorita *EV*
19	R:	sí
20	M:	okay esta persona nunca le hacían caso *OR* (.2)
21		<u>no</u> le hacían caso (.2) *OR*
22	M:	eh:: [que este que no podía- *OR*
23	R:	[estaba sola.
24	M:	estaba sola y su esposo *OR*
25		creo que no (.) quería ir al baño *CE*
26		y no la llevaban *CE*
27		o:: yo no sé ni como estuvo eso *EV*
28		a mí eso, eso <u>a mí me dio coraje</u>↑ *RE* (*psych.*)

29	R:	aha
30	M:	okay está bien que estemos mal vestidos que no tengamos (.1) *EV*
31		pero son personas *EV*
32		[y se va a pagar↑ *EV*
33	R:	[aha
34	M:	de alguna forma van a pagar ¿verdad? los ((inaudible)) *EV*
35	R:	aha
36	M:	voy y que me dirijo con alguna de las enfermeras *RE (action)*
37		y le dije, "esta persona no tiene cuidados" ((raising her finger at R.)) *RE (verbal)*
38	M:	aha
39		y le digo, "NO TIENE"
40		le digo, "Por qué↑" *RE (verbal)*
41		o sea ya tenía como dos o tres días *EV*
42	R:	aha que no tenía la ayuda
43	M:	que no tenía la ayuda *EV*
44		y por qué no se la habían dado↑ *EV*
45		y entonces en ese momento [vi como este (.)
46	R:	[uhm (.2)
47	M:	por solamente hablar y decir, *EV* o sea vienen y ayudan pero si hablan inglés *EV*
48		y que si no hablan español [(.) no les
49	R:	[aha
		ayudan? *EV*
50		Ay: ↑ eso sí me dio [coraje no?[y *EV*
51	R:	[sí [sí
52	M:	y me dio tristeza por la señora *EV*
53	R:	aha aha
54	M:	y en ese momento me sentí satisfecha por haberla ayudado *EV*
55	R:	aha
56	M:	porque, pues le cambiaron la cama, *RES*
57	R:	aha y usted[habló con la enfermera en=
58	M:	[yo hablé con la enfermera y en
		= inglés
		inglés sí
59		y yo les dije bien o sea *EV*
60	R:	ahah
61	M:	que necesitaba ayuda *EV*

62	R:	ahah
63	M:	porque no sabía como se llamaba el botón *EV*
64		pero traté de darme a entender porque necesitaba ayuda *EV*
65		y sin miedo *EV*
66	R:	ahah sin miedo

Translation

	R:	Have you ever felt that people have not helped you with the language?
	M:	Well, maybe but (it is) because one does not want to, right?, because if one speaks it and asks for help, that is how you make your way.
	R:	And any experience with the language?
	M:	Well, I think that these cases happen all around the United States, mainly with Latinos who do not speak English or who come from another country. I do not know personally but from what I have observed from other people is that they ignore you more if one does not know and I have a more recent case.

1.	M:	A person who is from the same community I come [(.) from a village *OR*
2.	R:	[aha.
3.	M:	she got sick *OR*
4.		she arrived at the hospital *CA*
5.		uhm::and: this person does not know English (.) <u>nothing</u> *OR*
6.		and then obviously one feels uncomfortable being all the time in the same position if one cannot move *EV*
7.	R:	of course
8.	M:	and especially if one cannot speak English *EV*
9.		and how to tell them, "Change me [help me"
10.	R:	[aha
		or, "I need something" no? *EV*
11.	M:	aha (.2)
12.	M:	uh:: the beds should have (.) a button= *EV*
13.	R:	=aha
14.	M:	so that if there is an emergency (.) the:: can come (.) where the the I don't know, the head is *EV* (.2)
15.	R:	aha
16.	M:	I mean I do not know how they call it *EV*

17.	R:	aha yes
18.	M:	the name does not come to my mind right now *EV*
19.	R:	yes
20.	M:	okay nobody ever paid attention to this person *OR* (.2)
21.	M:	they _did not_ pay attention to her *OR* (.2)
22.		eh::[that she she could not-
23.	R:	[she was by herself *OR*
24.	M:	she was alone and her husband *OR*
25.		I think that she did not (.) she wanted to use the toilet *CA*
26.		and nobody helped her *CE*
27.		or:: I do not even know how that was *EV*
28.		that to me, _that got me mad_↑*RE (psych.)*
29.	R:	aha
30.	M:	okay it is okay that we are badly that we do not have (.1) *EV*
31.		but they are persons *EV*
32.		[and it is going to be paid for- *EV*
33.	R:	[aha
34.	M:	somehow they are going to pay right? the ((inaudible)) *EV*
35.	M:	aha
36.	M:	I go and I address some of the nurses *RE (act.)*
37.		and I told her,"_This person has no care_" ((raising her finger at R)) *RE (verb.)*
38.	R:	aha
39.	M:	and I tell her "SHE DOES NOT" *RE (verb.)*
40.		I tell her, "Why↑" *RE (verb.)*
41.		I mean it was already two or three days *EV*
42.	M:	aha that she was not helped out *EV*
43.	M:	that she did not have the help *EV*
44.		and why had not they given it to her↑ *EV*
45.		and then at that moment [I saw how it is
46.	R:	[uhm (.2) that (.) by just speaking and saying something
47.		I mean they come and help but only if they speak English *EV*
48.		and what, if they do not speak Spanish, [(.)they do not help them? *EV*
49.	R:	[aha

50.	M:	Ay: ↑ I mean I got [mad no.[and *EV*
51.	R:	[yes [yes
52.	M:	I felt sad for her *EV*
53.	R:	aha aha
54.	M:	and at that moment I felt satisfied that I helped her out *EV*
55.	R:	aha
56.	M:	because they changed her bed *RES*
57.	R:	aha and you [spoke English with the nurse
58.	M:	[I spoke with the nurse and English yes
59.		and I told them right I mean *EV*
60.	R:	aha
61.	M:	that she needed some help *EV*
62.	R:	aha
63.	M:	because she did not know what the name of the button was *EV*
64.		but I tried to make myself understood that she needed some help *EV*
65.		and without fear *EV*
66.	R:	aha without fear

Marina's narrative is told in response to the interviewer's question on language difficulties, as an exemplum (Martin and Plum, 1997) to support the argument that people get ignored when they cannot speak English. It is a story of neglect perpetrated in a hospital against a Mexican woman who is unable to communicate with the staff. The complicating event around which the story is built is described between lines 25 and 26 where the narrator relates that the woman wanted to use the toilet but nobody paid attention to her. Marina gets to the complicating event through a series of orientation clauses in which she gives background on who the woman was (line 1), her lack of English proficiency (line 5) and her reasons for going to the hospital (line 3). Orientation clauses combine with evaluation clauses to give the listener a feel of the protagonist's situation of neglect once she arrived at the hospital. In lines 6, 8 and 9 the information that the woman was alone, could not explain her discomfort, and could not ask for help, is embedded in evaluative comments that present such an experience as potentially significant to any person who cannot speak English, not as a specific problem of the protagonist. Marina achieves this through the shift from definite reference: "this person does not know English" (line 5), to indefinite reference through the pronoun *one*: "*One* feels uncomfortable being all the time in the same position if *one* cannot move" (line 6), "Especially if *one* cannot speak English" (line 8), but also through the use of an impersonal construction with no subject: "And how *to* tell them, 'Change me, help me', or 'I need something'" (line 9).

In the following orientation lines Marina focuses on the problem of 'invisibility' that is at the centre of the story conflict, since the protagonist could not speak English or call for help: "Nobody ever paid attention to this person" (line 20). The problem is underlined through repetition (line 21) and emphasis (use of negative evaluative devices '*nunca*' (never), and stress on the word '*no*' (did not)) in both utterances, thus drawing attention to its importance in the story.

The orientation has prepared the Complicating Event, depicted in lines 25-26, where the woman wanted to use the toilet but no one helped her. Marina's reaction as a story character, described in lines 28, 36, 37, 39 and 40, is presented both in emotional and personal terms. The narrator emphasizes her personal involvement through her stress on the utterance "*a mí me dio coraje*" (it got me mad), and her feelings of anger through direct lexicalization in line 28. However, anger is also performed through other narrative strategies. The evaluation in lines 30-34 has the form of an emotional argument, not only against common perceptions about Latinos, but also against a moral order based on the visibility of the wealthy and the invisibility of the poor:

30. M: okay it is okay that we are badly that
           we do not have (.1) *EV*
31.   but they are persons *EV*
32.   [and it is going to be paid for↑ *EV*
33. R: [aha
34. M: somehow they are going to pay right? the
           ((inaudible)) *EV*

We can notice that in this fragment there are significant pronoun switches that underline Marina's involvement in the story events and her identification with the protagonists. Although she refers to the protagonists as 'they' in lines 31 and 34, she uses 'we' in line 30 to identify with people who are 'badly dressed'. It's also important to underline that the apparent concessive utterances "it's ok that we are badly dressed, that we do not have", is indeed a polemic response to the implicit argument that badly dressed people (i.e. the poor) do not pay their hospital bills. At the same time the argument 'they are people', underlines the rebellion against being invisible because of presumed poverty.

The emotional character of the response is intensified in the reported act of taking personal responsibility and complaining to the nurses (lines 36 and 37). In line 37, the narrator introduces her own reported speech with the quotation formula 'Le dije' (I told her), in which the clitic LE (to her) has the effect of explicitly pointing to the person addressed. According to Longacre (1994:132), the mention of speakers and addressees in pronominal forms is indexical of the intensity of interactions. In this case, the clitic 'LE' emphasizes the narrator's disagreement with the unfair treatment described in the quote. Marina accentuates the emotional intensity of the telling by mimicking some aspects of the story world: when she raises her finger at the interviewer she is also 'acting' what she did with the nurse, and by emphasizing the utterance "this person has no care" (line 37) she is performing her anger.

This emotional tone also characterizes the following lines of reported speech in which repetition, emphatic intonation (39) and the questioning 'why↑' (line 40) contribute to Marina's performance of her own angry self. The moral indignation enacted in the reported speech is then proposed again in the storytelling world, through explicit evaluation (lines 41- 44) when Marina underlines the reasons for her anger and emphasizes them through repetition of the problem: "she was not helped out, she did not have the help" (lines 41- 42). These comments give further reasons for her reaction and also allow Marina to position herself in the storytelling world through polemic questioning of the nurses' behaviour. The evaluation gives substance to the moral indignation enacted in both storytelling and story world. In lines 45, 47 and 48, Marina takes up her initial thesis according to which people neglect immigrants who do not speak English, and questions the morality of such behaviour. Notice how she uses a rhetorical question in line 48 to express her disagreement and how she introduces new affect keys in lines 50 (see for example the interjection 'Ay: ↑') and 52 to express her feelings of anger and sadness for the woman in hospital.

The resolution to the conflict – an act of reversal of the neglect demonstrated by the nurses who finally fix the patient's bed – is embedded within an evaluation clause that once again is expressed in emotional terms. Marina was *satisfied* for having obtained some attention for the patient. The resolution is constructed in agentive terms since it is presented as the product of Marina's effort through her emphasis on personal involvement, both emotionally and actionally. Such emphasis is present in the last evaluation section where the narrator uses linguistic devices that enhance her agency: the verb *tratar* (I tried to) and the adverbial construction: *y sin miedo* (without fear). Thus, Marina not only reacts, but also confronts her own fear to speak up (line 63) in order to solve the problem.

This narrative is an example of how women in this group represent themselves as agents of change in society, but also as individuals who fight to establish a moral order in which they believe. In that sense it illustrates how resistance and moral relocation are enacted through story-telling. In this case Marina opposes an ideology that reduces people who do not speak English and are perceived as poor, to a social status of 'non personae', and resists consequent social practices that encourage neglect of immigrants who only speak Spanish.

We have shown how this discourse of resistance is achieved through the use of narrative resources. Evaluation allows Marina to present the moral order accepted at the hospital (and in society) and oppose her own moral rules to it, thus claiming a moral space. Story world actions and reactions allow her to represent herself as a character who agentively re-sists injustice and achieves a relocation of herself as protagonist in the particular social space of the hospital from inhabiting an invisible place to occupying a visible one. Thus both narrator and character stand up against stereotypical views of Latinos as humble, quiet and afraid to fight for their rights. The conveying of moral evaluation and agentive self-repre-sentation are based on the skilful use of emotional language.

Emotional language is also crucial to Marina's attempt to achieve a positive alignment with the interviewer. As we pointed out earlier in this paper, the interview constitutes a 'facilitating' context for the moral relo-cation that Marina strives for. We can observe throughout the transcript that the interviewer does indeed co-construct Marina's reaction to the in-cident by showing her alignment through continuous back channelling (see for example lines 2, 7, 10, 13, 15, 17, 19), collaborative interventions such as reformulations and or positive overlaps (line 23, 57), and rein-forcement of Marina's emotional states. Marina achieves the recognition and validation of her stance within the interview framework through her management of emotional language, since the interviewer's alignment is often elicited by her emotional displays. See a clear example of this align-ment in line 51, where the interviewer warmly responds to Marina's reported anger, and her last intervention in line 66 where she acknowl-edges Marina's bravery, '*aha y sin miedo*' ('aha and without fear'). With this narrative Marina has not only reported how she relocated herself and other characters in social space, but she has also positioned herself in the interaction as an agentive person and a moral character, thus she has achieved moral relocation.

Conclusions

In this paper we have discussed Mexican immigrant women's narratives of language conflicts looking at agency as it emerges both in story structure and in the storytelling. Our analysis shows that women represent themselves as actively engaged against social language practices that they consider unfair or unacceptable. Such engagement is embodied in the presence of a great number of characters' reactions to story-world situations of discrimination or aggression, and in the management of emotion as a strategy to express moral stances and to involve the listener in the defence of alternative values. Such narrative strategies are also resistance strategies in so far as they allow these women to struggle against social invisibility and to propose their own moral rules.

We have also shown that the study of narratives provides a view 'from the inside' on processes of language displacement and relocation lived by minority groups. In this case narrative analysis reveals how, contrary to stereotypical views, Latinas are not submissive and passive, but come to terms with difficult new experiences by resisting the roles assigned to them by dominant ideologies in U.S. society.

Appendix 1: Transcription Conventions

(adapted from Sacks, Jefferson, and Schegloff, 1974)

↑	rising intonation
↓	falling intonation
CAPS	louder than surrounding talk
.	at the end of words marks falling intonation
,	at the end of words marks slight rising intonation
-	abrupt cutoff, stammering quality when hyphenating syllables of a word
!	animated tone, not necessarily an exclamation
> <	speech faster than normal
___	emphasis
:::	elongated sounds
• hh	inhalations
ha ha	indicates laughter
uhm uh	shows continuing listenership
° °	soft talk
(0.3)	time elapsed in tenths of seconds
(.)	micropause
[ ]	overlapping speech
(( ))	nonverbal behaviour
( )	non audible segment
=	no interval between adjacent utterances

References

Baker, C. (2001) *Foundations of Bilingual Education and Bilingualism,* New York: Multilingual Matters.

Besnier, N. (1990) 'Language and Affect', *Annual Review of Anthropology,* 19:419-415.

Bourdieu, P. (1977) *Outline of a Theory of Practice,* Cambridge: Cambridge University Press.

Brockmeier, J. and D. Cardbaugh (eds.) (2001) *Narrative and Identity: Studies in Autobiography, Self and Culture,* Amsterdam: John Benjamins.

Bruner, J. (1993) 'The Autobiographical Process', in R. Folkenflik (ed.) *The Culture of Autobiography* (pp. 38-56), Stanford: Stanford University Press.

Bucholtz, M. (1999) 'Bad Examples: Transgression and Progress in Language and Gender Studies', in M. Bucholtz, A.C. Liang and L.A. Sutton (eds.), *Reinventing Identities: The Gendered Self in Discourse* (pp. 3-23), Oxford: Oxford University Press.

Capps, L. and E. Ochs (1995) *Constructing Panic: The Discourse of Agoraphobia,* Cambridge, Massachusetts: Cambridge University Press.

Chavira, A. (1988) '"Tienes que ser valiente" Mexicana Migrants in a Midwestern Farm Labour Camp', in M. Melville (ed.), *Mexicanas at Work in the United States* (pp. 64-75), Texas: University of Houston.

Cornelius W. (1992) 'From Sojourners to Settlers: The Changing Profile of Mexican Immigration to the US', in J.A. Bustamante, W. Reynolds and R. Hinojosa-Ojeda (eds.), *US-Mexico Relations: Labour Market Interdependence* (pp.155-195), Stanford, CA: Stanford University Press.

De Fina, A. (2000) 'Orientation in Immigrant Narratives: The Role of Ethnicity in the Identification of Characters', *Discourse Studies* 2 (2):131-157.

------ (2003) *Identity in Narrative: A study of Immigrant Discourse,* Amsterdam: John Benjamins.

Fairclough, N. (1989) *Language and Power,* London: Longman.

Gal, S. (2001) 'Language, Gender, and Power: An Anthropological Review', in S. Duranti (ed.) *Linguistic Anthropology: A Reader* (pp. 420-431), Oxford: Blackwell.

Georgakopoulou, A. (2002) 'Narrative and Identity Management: Discourse and Social Identities in a Tale of Tomorrow', *Research on Language and Social Interaction,* 35:427-451.

Goodwin, M.H. (1997) 'Towards Families of Stories in Context', in M. Bamberg (ed.) 'Oral Versions of Personal Experience: Three Decades of Narrative Analysis', *Journal of Narrative and Life History,* 7(1-4):107-112.

Hondagneu-Sotelo, P. (1994) *Gendered Transitions: Mexican Experiences of Immigration,* Berkeley: University of California Press.

Labov, W. (1972) 'The Transformation of Experience in Narrative Syntax', in

W. Labov (ed.), *Language in the Inner City* (pp. 354-396), Philadelphia: University of Pennsylvania Press.

------ and J. Waletzky (1967/1997) 'Narrative Analysis: Oral Versions of Personal Experience', in J. Helm (ed.) *Essays on the Verbal and Visual Arts* (pp. 12-44), Seattle/London: University of Washington Press. (Reprinted in *Journal of Narrative and Life History*, 7/97, 3-38).

Longacre, R. (1994) 'The Dynamics of Reported Dialogue in Narrative', *Word* 45(2):130-147.

Lucius-Hoene, G. and A. Depperman (2000) 'Narrative Identity Empiricized: A Dialogical Positioning Approach to Autobiographical Research Interviews', *Narrative Inquiry,* 10(1):199-222.

Martin, J.R. and G. Plum (1997) 'Construing Experience: Some Story Genres', in M. Bamberg (ed.) 'Oral Versions of Personal Experience: Three Decades of Narrative Analysis', *Journal of Narrative and Life History*, 7 (1-4):299-308.

Mishler, E. (1999) *Storylines: Craftartists' Narratives of Identity,* Cambridge: Harvard University Press.

Ochs, E. and B. Schieffelin (1989) 'Language has a Heart', *Text,* 9(1):7-25.

------ and L. Capps (2001) *Living Narrative*: *Creating Lives in Everyday Storytelling*, Harvard: Harvard University Press.

Relaño Pastor, A.M. (Forthcoming) 'The Language Socialization Experiences of Latina Mothers in Southern California' in A.C. Zentella (ed.) *Building on Strength: Language and Literacy in Latino Families and Communities*, New York: Teachers College Press.

Ruiz, V. and S. Tiano (1987) *Women on the U.S.-Mexico Border*, Boston: Allen & Unwin.

Rymes, B. (1995) 'The Construction of Moral Agency in the Narratives of High-School Drop-Outs', *Discourse & Society,* 6(4):495-516.

Sawin, P. (1999) 'Gender, Context and the Narrative Construction of Identity: Rethinking Models of "Women's Narrative"', in M. Bucholtz, A.C. Liang and L.A. Sutton (eds.) *Reinventing Identities: The Gendered Self in Discourse* (pp. 241-258), Oxford: Oxford University Press.

Schiffrin, D. (1996) 'Narrative as Self-portrait: Sociolinguistic Constructions of Identity', *Language in Society* 25:167-203.

Urciuoli, B. (1996) *Exposing Prejudice: Puerto Rican Experiences of Language, Race, and Class,* Boulder Colorado: Westview Press, Inc.

Vásquez, O. (2003) *La Clase Mágica : Imagining Optimal Possibilities in a Bilingual Community of Learners*, Mahwah, N.J.: Lawrence Erlbaum Associates.

Wortham, S. (2001) *Narratives in Action*, New York: Teachers College Press.

Zentella, A. C. (1997) 'The Hispanophobia of the Official English Movement in the U.S.', *International Journal of the Sociology of Language*, 127:71-86.

West Germans Moving East
Place, Political Space, and Positioning in Conversational Narratives

GRIT LIEBSCHER, *University of Waterloo, Canada*
JENNIFER DAILEY-O'CAIN, *University of Alberta, Canada*

The end of the Cold War had implications for the entire world, and one of the most visible symbols of that period was the fall of the Berlin Wall. Leading up to this event was a wave of migration in 1989 from East Germany to West Germany,[1] a phenomenon which only grew stronger after the borders were opened in November of that year. This group of migrants has been studied from the point of view of sociology (Grundmann, 1993), human geography (Ganz and Kemper, 2003), political science (Werz, 2001), and sociolinguistics (Barden and Großkopf, 1998; Auer, Barden, and Großkopf, 1998). Although they have been less visible, a second wave of migrants also moved from West to East after reunification in 1990, often to take on roles that did not exist in East Germany (in banks or in business), to fill positions left vacant by ousted socialists (in academia or the legal system), and to buy properties unaffordable or unavailable in the West. Far less scholarly attention has been paid to this group of migrants however, and the project of which this chapter is a part[2] is an attempt to fill this gap. By presenting migration stories of two western Germans who have settled in the East, this chapter studies some of the ways in which migrant identities are played out in conversational narrative.

---

[1] In this paper, the terms 'East Germany' and 'West Germany' refer to the two separate countries prior to October 3rd, 1990. The terms 'eastern Germany' and 'western Germany' refer to the same geographic territory subsequent to unification. In cases where a narrator refers to that territory during both pre-unification and post-unification times, the term 'eastern Germany' is used. This is not unproblematic, but it reflects very real issues of labelling discussed later in this paper.

[2] This chapter is part of a project entitled '(Inter)acting Identities in Dialect and Discourse: Migrant Western Germans in Eastern Germany', carried out by the authors and funded in 2003 by the Social Sciences and Humanities Research Council of Canada (File number: 410-2003-0378). We are also grateful for funding from the University of Alberta and the University of Waterloo.

Theoretical Framework and Background

Although most traditional work on narrative has examined literary genres, some scholars have recently argued that conversational narrative of
personal experience (Quasthoff, 1980) is the basic form of narrative from
which other forms of narrative are derived (Norrick, 2000; Ochs and Capps,
2001). In an analysis of narratives elicited by an interviewer's question
about a close encounter with death, Labov and Waletzky, 1967 and Labov,
1972 propose a general structure for a narrative of personal experience.
This structure includes an *abstract,* an *orientation,* a *complicating action,*
an *evaluation* of that action, a *resolution* of that action, and an optional
coda. This structure gives narratives a temporal and logical order, and
establishes coherence between a narrator's past and present experiences.
In order to capture the attention of the intended audience, narrators use
story prefaces, serving as spoken 'titles' which announce the narrators'
desire to tell a particular story and to hold the floor across a series of turns
(Norrick, 2000:108; Ochs and Capps, 2001:117). Story prefaces usually
make a case for the upcoming story as particularly interesting or important. Narratives can vary with respect to their *tellability,* that is, in the
extent to which they convey a sequence of reportable events and make a
point in a rhetorically effective manner (Ochs and Capps, 2001:33). The
degree of tellability may have to do not only with the quality of the story
or the quality of the telling, but also with the biographical background of
the narrator. Based on that background, co-participants may discredit
speakership.

We follow Labov (1972: 359-360) in defining narrative as "one
method of recapitulating past experience by matching a verbal sequence
of clauses to the sequence of events which (it is inferred) actually occurred". While clauses are ordered in temporal sequence to build a story
(ibid.), the conversational narratives examined for this chapter differ from
Labov's interview data in that participants influence the narrative's structure and the ways in which the narrators present their story. Since our
interest is in the intersection between narrative and identity, we will base
our analysis on the narrative structure as outlined by Labov, but also on
how other interactants (including the two researchers) influence the narration by participating in the conversation and by their simple presence.
In basing our analysis on a conversation analytic framework (Sacks, 1992;
Sacks, Schegloff and Jefferson, 1974), we draw particular attention to the
impact co-participants have in telling a story. Storytelling within a conversational context routinely involves questions, clarifications, challenges,

and speculations about the events of the narrative (Ochs and Capps, 2001:2-18). This can result in varying perspectives with respect to both the events of the narrative and the way these events are being represented. Through these different perspectives, narrators and listeners each take *moral stances* on the events described by focusing on an unexpected turn of events (ibid.:102).

Narrators position themselves when using *place formulations*, thus indexing familiarity with and empathy for different places. These place formulations include what we call *denotative place formulations*, which are cases of deictics in their strictest sense, and *connotative place formulations*, which are formulations evoking places based on mutual cultural knowledge. Both kinds of formulations belong to the kinds of deictics Haviland describes, considering that "[r]adiating from a deictic origo is a structured 'space' within whose surround deictics 'point', a 'space of relations'" (1996:280). Our use of the term positioning is more broadly based on Bakhtin's (1935/1981; 1953/1986) notion of voice and position, in that any utterance has the power to position speakers in particular ways. The positioning also depends on how the narrator and other participants perceive each others' identities. While identity is (co)constructed in the interaction (Antaki and Widdicombe, 1998; di Luzio and Auer, 1986), Bourdieu (1994), in his concept of *habitus*, points out that individual biographies, social perceptions about identity categories and current utterances are linked. Identity is also not merely constructed by researchers, but is a biographical accomplishment of an individual person (Ricker, 2000:9). Owing to their displacement of location, migrants are confronted with ascriptions of categories and labels by various people based on concepts already present in society which may or may not correspond to the ways migrants see themselves. Because categories may also be indexed by utterances with various contexts and perspectives, migrants' utterances may voice different, even conflicting categories simultaneously. Some of these categories are viewed within a given society as mutually exclusive (e.g. 'East German' and 'West German'), and migrants are consequently positioned as either one category or the other. Migrant identities are shaped in large part by the migrants' knowledge and experience of both their place of origin and their place of residence, and that knowledge and experience plays a role in the creation of narratives. In fact narration is the central method by which we "construct, interpret, and share experience" (Schiffrin, 1996:167). The need for positioning is sometimes forced through the narrative structure (as in the orientation).

In a narrative of personal experience, each utterance is also affected by two separate roles for the narrator: tied in one instance to the *storytelling performance,* which is the interactional context within which the speaker is telling his or her story, and in the other to the *story proper,*[3] or the series of events described by the story (Wortham 2001:13-19). Shifts between the story proper and the storytelling performance are one kind of what Haviland refers to as 'transpositions' (1996:271 ff.), which also include shifts of perspective and of cultural frames.[4] According to Haviland, transpositions "rely heavily on participants' knowledge – not only schematic socio-cultural knowledge, but also contingent facts of biography" (ibid.:272). For migrants, however, biographies are necessarily less contingent than they are for non-migrants because of the relocation. One of our aims is to reveal ways in which migrants deal with this discontingency on the linguistic level, a question that is also raised by Haviland in this volume. Our goal is to analyze the effects of narrative structure on positioning as well as the effects of positioning on narrative structure in migrants' narratives of personal experience.

Data and Analysis

The two narratives analyzed in this paper both occurred against the backdrop of a divided and then re-unified Germany. While widespread migration was the main reason for building the Berlin Wall in 1961 (Kritsch, 1985:11-15), migration ironically also led to its demise. In the summer and autumn of 1989, thousands of East Germans migrated to West Germany through the newly-opened borders in Hungary and Czechoslovakia. Under great pressure from the loss of so many young working people, the East German government made the decision on November 9th of that same year to allow free travel to the West. By October 3rd of 1990, the official unification of the two countries had been achieved, with East Germany formally becoming part of the Federal Republic of Germany (Glaeßner, 1992:38-51). Although supported by a majority of Germans, studies from the early 1990s indicate that the changes resulted in variable attitudes of Westerners toward Easterners and vice versa (Becker, Becker and Ruhland, 1992).

The two narratives are representative of some of the ways in which migrant identities are played out through stories. The experiences behind

---

[3] Haviland (1996:276) uses the terms 'narrated event' for the story proper and 'speech event' for the storytelling performance.
[4] See Haviland (1996:279) for a list of phenomena of transpositions that others have described under different terms.

these two narratives are strongly rooted in eastern German social life as experienced shortly after the migrants' relocation. In the first story, called 'Getting a Telephone', the migrant Walter presents his story about difficulties in getting a telephone installed after he moved into his first apartment. The second narrative, called 'Early Beginnings', is about the migrant Bernd's reasons for his migration and experiences in his first apartment. The narratives were both recorded in the migrants' own homes, with their partners and the two researchers present.[5]

First Narrative: 'Getting a Telephone'

The first narrative was recounted by Walter in the summer of 2000. Walter moved to eastern Germany in 1994 as a result of a job offer, and his partner Claudia is an eastern German whom he met after his migration. The other two conversation partners are the two researchers: GL, who is originally from East Germany but who has been living in North America for many years, and JD, who is an American but who briefly lived in East Germany before unification. The narrative is presented here in several segments for ease of reading and analysis. The first segment shows the beginning of the narrative: (GL and JD are the researchers. W=Walter, C=Claudia, B=Bernd, S=Silke)

'Getting a telephone': Segment 1[6]
1 W: das war schon ne (.) tolle wohnung
    that was a really (.) great apartment
2   aber (..) was ja wirklich kurios war (.) als ich damals hinkam
    but (..) what was really strange (.) when I arrived back then
3   (.) august (..) vierenneunzig? (..) da fragt ich so den (.)
    (.) august (..) ninety-four? (..) I asked the (.)

---

[5] While the narratives evolved within natural conversations, all participants were aware that the researchers were interested in migrant experiences, which may have had the effect of producing longer turns by migrants.

[6] Transcription conventions are as follows: German utterances are in normal type and English translations are directly beneath in italics. The transcript differs from usual orthographic spelling, e.g. capitalization in the transcript is used to mark loudness. Conversational overlap is indicated with square brackets. Pauses lasting a beat (.) or two (..) are indicated as shown; longer pauses are indicated in seconds. Laughter and parts deleted to save space are written in ((double brackets)), and =equals signs= are used to indicate a continuation between previous and following lines of talk. Some information has been changed in order to protect informants' identities.

4   meinen mitbewohner (.) das is heinz? (.) du sag mal wie siehts
         my roommate (.) that's heinz? (.) hey tell me how does it look

5   mit telefon aus? (.) aach telefon (.) das is (.) te- te-
         in terms of a telephone? (.) ohhh a telephone (.) that's (.) a

6   telefon is ne aktion (.) da hab ich jetzt n antrag (.)
         te- te- telephone is complicated (.) I put in an (.)

7   geschrieben (.) der war dann glaub ich n (.) n halbes jahr
         application (.) I think it had been (.) there for six months

8   schon da meint er (.) er hätte n bescheid gekriegt (.) in zwei
         already and he said (.) they told him (.) in two

9   jahrn würden wir telefon kriegen (..)   [da bin ich aus allen=
         years we would get a telephone (..) [I was completely=
                                                 [
10 GL: [puuhhhh
                                                 [*really*

11 W: =wolken gefallen (.) du sag mal (.) du spinnst ja wohl das
      =*flabbergasted (.) hey tell me (.) are you insane that*

12   kann ja wohl nich wahr sein
         can't be right

13 JD:das war nich zuhause? (.) das war im (.) büro?
       that wasn't at home? (.) that was at (.) the office?

14 C: [nee das war zuhause
       [*no that was at home*
       [
15 W: [nein nein (.) zuhause (.) zuhause
       [*no no (.) at home (.) at home*

16 GL:[mhm
      [*mhm*
      [
17 JD: [zuhause gehts noch (.) aber im büro das wär
       [*at home it's less of a problem (.) but at the office that*

18   schon schlimm
         would be pretty bad

19 GL:a-ha
      mhm

Walter begins his narrative in line 2 with what we call an *evaluative pref-ace,* in which he evaluates the upcoming story as 'kurios' (*strange*). He uses this preface to generate hearer interest, to indicate his attitude about the event related, and to signal to the hearers what kind of story to expect (e.g. Norrick, 2000:109). Later, the narrator uses two additional evaluative prefaces in lines 20 and 25, suggesting that he needs to re-establish the tellability of the story.

The narrator's migrant social identity emerges quite early, in the orientation following the preface, in which he situates the story in time and place (lines 2 and 3). In connecting to talk before the narrative begins (line 1), 'damals' (*back then*) in line 2 refers to the time when the narrator first moved to eastern Germany. The place to which he moved is indexed by the verb 'hinkam' (*arrived*), a combination of the motion verb 'kommen' (*to come*) and the directional adverb 'hin' (*toward*). The narrator does not specify the scope of the place, thereby leaving open whether he means the apartment, the town, or the community. Characteristic for motion verbs such as 'kommen' is that they denote a *trajector*, a moving object, and *landmarks*, points of reference for locating the trajector (Langacker, 1987:217). The trajector is the narrator who positions himself in relation to the places of departure and arrival as landmarks. Using 'kommen', the speaker positions himself at the place of arrival in East Germany, looking back to the place of departure. Using the adverb 'hin', however, the speaker indexes the opposite direction and positions himself at the place of departure in western Germany, looking toward the place of arrival. The use of this adverb-verb combination thus juxtaposes the story proper with the storytelling performance and is a kind of transposition in Haviland's sense. This juxtaposition may be triggered by the word 'damals' (*back then*), which takes the speaker back in time to his old location in West Germany. The combination of 'hin' with 'kommen' is pragmatically awkward, since the speaker cannot be in both places at the same time. Since place of arrival and place of departure for the speaker are in former eastern and western Germany respectively, the combination indexes his migrant identity as 'in between'.[7]

After the abstract, Walter begins telling the action of the story by re-enacting the conversation with his roommate. He first presents his question about getting a telephone as a direct quote in line 4. The way the question is formulated suggests that the narrator is not aware that it would take a

---

[7] The orientation towards place through motion verbs in combination with prepositions as indexes of an 'in between' identity has been discussed with similar data (see Liebscher, 1999; forthcoming).

long time to get a telephone hook-up. His roommate's response in line 6 is another direct quote in which the roommate formulates getting a phone as a difficult act. Walter then reports in indirect speech the answer they got from some third party (lines 8-9). Following the closure of this part of the story's action is Walter's first evaluation, in which he formulates his surprise that it takes two years to get a telephone hook-up (lines 9 and 11), and further re-enacts his answer to his roommate (lines 11-12). While repetition is a common element of narratives (Norrick, 2000:57-65), the fact that this repetition comes in the evaluation has the effect of conveying Walter's surprise and setting up co-participants to express similar reactions.

Based on the set-up of the story as something that was strange, surprise would in fact be the appropriate response here. Instead, JD asks a question (line 13) that looks at first like a request for clarification about the location of the event. It is, however, the beginning of a series of instances in which doubt is cast on the tellability of the story, and which we will call *evaluative digression*. The structure and intonation of JD's question is suggestive of the expected answer: since it wasn't that unusual to wait for a telephone connection for a private home in East Germany, this couldn't have been at home; it must have been at the office. With her question, JD starts the renegotiation of place as a focal point for the evaluation of Walter's story and, in fact, of Walter's knowledge of East Germany. The frame of reference or the 'space of relations' is not clear to JD. After she receives an answer from both Walter and his partner Claudia in lines 14-15, JD comments on the reason for her question as well as the tellability of the story in lines 16-17. By indicating that this situation should not be surprising to Walter, she casts doubt on the tellability of the story and suggests that he only regards it as surprising because of his insufficient knowledge about East Germany. By doing this, JD also presents herself as somebody with knowledge of life in East Germany. In contrast to JD, Claudia grants Walter implicit permission to tell this story by not attempting to interrupt him or to co-tell the story, despite the fact that she also lived in East Germany and has heard this story before (as demonstrated through her response to JD's question in line 14). There are two possible explanations for this: one, she may perceive Walter's social identity differently from JD, and two, she may be aware that the researchers are more interested in Walter's story than in her perspective on that story.

Walter does not recognize the centrality of place for his story in that he does not react to JD's comment or address the issue of tellability, but continues the story, introducing the next part with a second evaluative preface:

'Getting a telephone': Segment 2

```
20  W: und (..) ich mein der vorteil war ja (.)    [dass INNERhalb
        and (..) I mean the advantage was (.)      [that INSIDE
                                                   [
21  GL:                                            [hm
                                                   [hm
22  W: des gebäudes? (.) ein MÜNZtelefon (.) beziehungsweise (.)
        the building? (.) there was a PAY phone (.) actually (.) a
23      ein KARTENtelefon existierte so innovativ waren die da schon
        CARD pay phone that's how innovative they were already
24  ((LAUGHTER))
```

In contrast to the first preface, in which Walter evaluated the beginning of the story as 'kurios' (strange), he now formulates what is to come as a 'vorteil' (advantage) in line 20. Even though you had to wait for a telephone, at least there was a payphone nearby and, even better, a payphone where one could use a card instead of coins. It is possible that he perceived the fieldworkers' evaluative digression as a comment on his portraying eastern Germany as negative. Considering that one of the researchers (GL) is from eastern Germany, he may be accommodating to her, adding some positive fact about eastern Germany.

On the other hand, this section of the narrative cannot be seen as entirely positive and complimentary. His wording 'so innovativ waren die da schon' (that's how innovative they were already) in line 23 evokes laughter from all participants, suggesting that this formulation is understood and most likely intended as a kind of playful irony. The referent for the pronoun 'die' (they) is ambiguous, since Walter could be referring either to the specific group of people who had installed the pay phones, or to eastern Germans as a whole. He refers to this group using the demonstrative pronoun 'die', which positions himself outside this group of people with more distance than the personal pronoun 'sie', which would have an identical denotation. In so constructing an identity for himself other than 'die', he evokes the voice of a western German and contrasts himself with eastern Germans. This positioning, in conjunction with the use of the word 'innovativ' (innovative), adds to the irony because by western German standards finding a card pay phone in a building would not have been considered innovative in 1994. The adverb 'schon' (already) evokes the time before Walter's migration, contrasting the time of the story proper with pre-unification, East German times, and expressing surprise that they

had come so far by that point. Implicitly, Walter again suggests that he has
enough knowledge of East Germany to be able to make that comparison.

Rather than reacting to the laughter, Walter launches directly into the
next part of his story with a third evaluative preface:

'Getting a telephone': Segment 3

25 W: aber das problem war? (.) dass man da (.) nich angerufen werden
         but the problem was? (.) that you couldn't (.) receive calls
26   konnte (.)[zumal wenn dann war das ja ganz=
         there (.) [the only place you could was way down at the=
                    [
27 GL: [mhm
                   [*mhm*
28 W: =unten dann (..) direkt vor der turnhalle (..) und das
         =bottom (..) right in front of the gym (..) and
29   heisst (1.0) ich hab dann die initiative erstmal unternommen?
         so (1.0) I finally took the initiative?
30   (.)   [nachdem ich ne dresdnerin kennengelernt hatte (.) die=
         (.) [after I met a woman from dresden (.) who had=
              [
31 GL: [mhm
             [*mhm*
32 W: =ganz gut- ganz gute beziehungen zur telekom hatte (..)
         =really good- really good connections to the phone company (..)
33   [und d-
         [*and th-*
         [
34 JD: [aha?
         [*oh yeah?*
35 GL: aha
         uh-huh
36 W: und drei monate später hatten wir [telefon
         and three months later we had a [telephone
                                          [
37 JD: [da gings noch über
                                          [*you still had to have*
38   beziehungen
         connections
39 GL: ja ja
         yeah yeah
40 ((LAUGHTER))

41 W: das war wirklich so   [echt
      it was really that way [*really*
                             [
42 GL: [aha
                             [*uh-huh*

43 ((LAUGHTER))
44 GL: is ja wie im osten
       just like in the east
45 W: das [war ja auch osten
      it [*was the east*
          [
46 JD: [ja wir sind ja im osten
         [*well we are in the east*
47 W: das war ja noch der kluge osten (..) zumindest [für mich=
      it was still the wise old east (..) at least   [*for me=*
                                                       [
48 GL: [vierund-
                                                       [*ninety-*

49   [neunzig ja?
      [*four yeah?*
      [
50 W: =[als zuge- für mich- zumindest für mich als zugereister ja ja
      =[*as a m- for me- at least for me as a migrant oh yeah*
51 JD:vierundneunzig war ja nicht mehr DDR
      but ninety-four wasn't east germany anymore

By using a third evaluative preface in line 25, 'aber das problem war' (but the problem was), Walter evaluates the next part of the story as a further complicating action, hindering the outcome of the story. The word 'beziehungen' (*connections*) in line 32 evokes an East German context, connoting secrecy and insider knowledge. This positions the narrator as someone who experienced this East German context, and more specifically, someone who knows the tricks of East German society that only an insider would know. This positioning is noteworthy enough that both JD and GL index it through their comments of 'aha'. Walter does not react to these comments, but instead finishes this part of his narration with a coda in line 36.

The coda indicates that the narrator has finished his story, but a series of exchanges follow which serve to call into question Walter's representation of his position in the story. The result is a negotiation of positioning in which both Walter and the two fieldworkers take part. In lines 37-38, JD uses the first possible transition point to launch another evaluative digression by commenting on the word 'beziehungen', remarking that connections were still part of eastern German society as late as 1994. GL, in aligning herself with JD in line 39, presents herself as knowledgeable of eastern Germany. Walter does not join in the laughter in line 40, disaligning himself from GL and JD's. Instead, he reaffirms the truth and validity of his story in line 41, indicating that he perceives JD and GL as having misread his story. In line 44, GL initiates a repair, attempting to give further context to the situation by comparing (though not equating) the situation at the time of the story proper with the situation before unification. In conjunction with GL's formulation of 'im osten' (*in the east*) to index pre-unification East Germany, Walter's and JD's turns in lines 45-46 indicate that the same formulation (im osten) can be used to construct three different social spaces. Walter constructs eastern Germany in 1994 as a continuation from the pre-unification period without distinguishing between that period and 1994 in the way that GL does. Instead, he distinguishes between 1994 (the time of the story proper) and 2000 (the time of the storytelling performance). JD constructs eastern Germany as a continuation of East Germany, playfully commenting on GL's use of 'osten' as limited to pre-unification times.

In line 47, Walter again presents himself as someone with knowledge of pre-unification East Germany, in specifying directly that he views East Germany and eastern Germany in 1994 as similar enough to be equated. However, he also mitigates this positioning in lines 47-48 by representing his story as one told specifically by a 'zugereister' (*migrant*), rather than as either an eastern German with direct experience of pre-unification East Germany, or as a non-migrant western German possibly lacking knowledge and experience about eastern Germany. He evaluates eastern Germany in 1994 positively as 'der kluge osten' (*the wise old east*), which may be a reaction to a perception that GL and JD view 'beziehungen' (*connections*) as something negative. In the overlap in lines 48-49, GL asks for clarification whether Walter really regards eastern Germany in 1994 as the same as East Germany before 1990. JD aligns herself with GL in line 51 by pointing out that it was no longer East Germany in 1994.

What follows in lines 52-67 is Walter's presentation of other knowledge of eastern Germany at the time to position himself as someone who saw what eastern Germany used to look like and how it has changed:

'Getting a telephone': Segment 4

52 W: ja aber (..) die (.)   [infrastruktur
        yeah but (..) the (.) [*infrastructure*
                               [
53 JD: [da sah auch nichts mehr so viel nach DDR
                               [*nothing really looked like east germany*
54   aus (..)   vierundneun   [zig
        anymore either (..) ninety- [*four*
                                     [
55 W: [na jaaa (.) aber die soziale
                                [*I don't knooow(.) the social*
56   infrastruktur mitten in der city da gabs ja nur ganz wenige
        infrastructure downtown there were only a few
57   kneipen wo man hingehen konnte (.) da gabs das
        bars you could go to (.) there was the
58 GL: mhm
        mhm
59 W: das- das- äh bei (.) das haus von dem kabarett? (.) das
        the- the- uh over (.) the building the cabaret was in? (.) that
60   mittlerweile ja auch gar nich mehr existiert
        doesn't even exist anymore
((...))
61   mittlerweile ja eine kneipe neben der andern existiert [es gab
        in the meantime now there's one bar after another [*there*
                                                              [
62 GL: [ja
                                                              [*yeah*
63 W: den spittel? (.) aber den gabs ja schon zu
        was the spittel? (.) but that was already around when
64   DDR zeiten   [ne?
        [*it was east germany* [*right?*
        [[
65 GL:[ja   [ja ja
        [*yeah*   [*yeah yeah*
66 W: aber das war ja auch n restaurant (.) und keine kneipe in dem
        but that was a restaurant (.) and not a bar in the same
67   sinne
        sense

In this passage, Walter is less assertive in his knowledge, for example in
line 64 when he turns to GL in order to verify information about East

Germany by using the particle 'ne?' (*right?*), thus presenting someone
other than himself as the authority of knowledge. However, he does still
make reference to the 'spittel,' a restaurant which existed both before 1990
and at the time he arrived in 1994, demonstrating his unwillingness to
yield entirely his comparison between pre-unification East Germany and
the eastern Germany he experienced upon his migration.

Second Narrative: 'Early Beginnings'

The second narrative was recounted by Bernd in the summer of 2001. He
moved to eastern Germany for personal and professional reasons. His
partner Silke, also present during the narration, joined him in eastern Germany about a year later. The narrative consists of several parts following
a question asked by one of the researchers: "seid ihr berufswegen her-
gekommen einundneunzig?" (*did you come here in ninety-one for
professional reasons?*). Bernd is the first one to answer this question, possibly because he is the one who moved to eastern Germany before Silke
did. He gives some background information and then tells his story:

'Early beginnings': Segment 1

```
1   B:  das war so lustig weil so also meine freunde (.) da drüben also
        it was so funny because so well my friends (.) over there I
2       meine- ich hab ja seit neunzehnhundertVIERundsiebzig hab ich
        mean my- I said since nineteenseventyFOUR I said
3       gesagt also ich möchte gerne nach LEIPzig und alle freunde haben
        well I want to go to LEIPzig and all of my friends always
4       immer gesagt (.) naja (.) dann geh doch [aber klar ging=
        said (.) well (.) then go              [but of course it=
                                               [
5  GL:                                         [mhm
                                               [mhm
6  B:   =natürlich nicht         [(.) und als es dann ging sagten=
        =didn't just work like that[8]  [(.) and then when it did they=
                                   [
7  JD:                           [aha mhm
                                 [uh-huh mm-hm
```

---

[8] Migration between East and West Germany was possible, but difficult for political reasons before the border was opened in November 1989.

8 B: =die zuerst (.) na jetzt kannste ja rüber
      =said immediately (.) well now you can head over
9 ((LAUGHTER))
10 B: ich fühl mich auch sehr wohl
      And I am very happy

As Walter did in the narrative 'Getting a Telephone', Bernd introduces his story with an evaluative preface in line 1, 'das war ja so lustig' (*it was so funny*). This preface fulfills functions of the orientation by situating the story in the past through the use of 'war' (*was*). Bernd continues with the orientation by introducing some of the characters in the story: 'meine Freunde da drüben' (*my friends over there*). Similarly to the motion verb *gehen* in segment 1 of "Getting a telephone", by using the locative 'drüben' (*over there*), Bernd positions himself in the East as the current place of speaking (here), in contrast to the West (there), where his friends are at the current time but also where he himself was at the time of the story proper. This transposition between story proper and storytelling performance allows Bernd to evoke an East German voice for the current time, possibly expressing empathy with current eastern Germany because the locative 'drüben' had taken on the particular social meaning for East Germans to refer to West Germany throughout the 40 years of division.

By contrast, in line 2 Bernd clearly positions himself in the West by using 'nach leipzig' (*to leipzig*) when he refers back to the time before he moved. By quoting his friends directly in lines 3-4 and by using the motion verb 'gehen' (*to go*), he positions his friends in West Germany at the time, but not necessarily himself. In the continuation of quoting his friends from a time directly following the fall of the Wall in line 8, Bernd again positions his friends, but not himself, in West Germany, despite the fact that he was also there at that time. By using quoted speech rather than indirect quotes or simple reference, Bernd is only the animator, not the author (Goffman, 1974). The directional adverb 'rüber' (*over*) in this context evokes a West German voice by denoting the place of departure as West Germany and the place of arrival as East Germany.

Bernd ends this part of the 'Early Beginnings' story with an evaluation of his migration in line 10. He formulates his own feelings as positive and thus positions himself as emotionally close to eastern Germany. This corresponds with the way an East German rather than a West German perspective has emerged through Bernd's use of such terms as 'drüben' and 'rüber'.

JD then addresses both Bernd and Silke in her question about the apartment:

'Early beginnings': Segment 2

11 JD: habt ihr dann auch gleich diese WOHnung bekommen
     did you guys get this apartment right away then

12 B: ja ich hab ähm (.) das haus gekauft
    yeah I uh (.) bought the building the apartment is in

((...))

13 B: sanieren ging nicht (.) hatten wir kein geld für
    it couldn't be renovated (.) we didn't have any money for that

14 JD: [mhm
    [*mhm*
    [

15 B: [(.) so dass wir- am ersten so- winter hatte ich dann hier
    [*(.) so that we- during the first so- winter I had hired a*

16   einen studenten angestellt der HEIZte (.) wir hatten ja
    student who ran the HEATer (.) you know we had coal=

17   überall so   [(.) öfen (.) also unten im   [im im im im=
    stoves   [*(.) everywhere (.) down in the* [*the the the the=*
                [[

18 JD: [ach SO jaja   [ich kenn das noch
               [*OH of course*   [*I remember that*

19 B: =erdgeschoss (.) [und (.) dann wohnte ich schon im=
    =first floor (.)   [*and (.) back then I already lived on the=*
                 [

20 JD: [mhm
              [*mhm*

21 B: =ersten oG ((clears his throat)) und da hatten wir dann
    =first floor ((clears his throat)) and we had SEVENteen

22   SIEBzehn öfen insgesamt [(der/da) musste also morgens um fünf=
    stoves altogether   [*(he /one had to) get up at five in the=*
                         [

23 JD: [((LAUGHTER))

24 B: =aufstehen [da hab ich noch geschlafen damit es morgens um halb=
    =morning   [*when I was still asleep so that it would=*
           [

25 JD: [((LAUGHTER))

25 B: =acht oder so dann EInigermaßen warm war
    =be SOMEwhat warm at seven thirty or so

26 JD: SUper
    SUper

27 B: ((clears his throat)) naja (.) den NÄCHSten win [ter
    ((clears his throat)) so/well (.) the NEXT win [ter
                 [
28 JD: [das hast du also
                    [*so I guess you*
29   RICHtig miterlebt he
    were *REALLy a part of it all huh*
30 B: ja   [(1.0) ach sel- natürlich selber heizen das konnte ich ja=
    yeah [(1.0) well I coul- of course I couldn't run the heater=
          [
31 JD: [mhm
       [*mhm*
32 B: =nicht   [(probiert) aber das habe ich dann (gelassen)
    =myself [I tried but then I let it be
          [
33 JD: [hm
       [*hm*
34 B: [((LAUGHTER))
   [
35 JD:[mhm hm
   [*mhm huh*

Only Bernd answers JD's question, in line 12, possibly because he moved to the place first and Silke joined him later. Bernd's answer is also an opportunity for him to continue with his migration story. Bernd responds to JD's question in a portion about construction in the building that was omitted here and further starting in line 13 above, in telling a story about his first experiences there and the changes he and Silke have made. Here, Bernd switches between ‚wir' (we) and ‚ich' (I), thus alternately relating the experience as theirs and his own.

This part of the narrative begins in line 15 with an orientation in which Bernd gives essential information (who, what, when and where) for the new story about the coal stove. In the 'Getting a telephone' narrative, Walter portrays his experience as a cultural fact by saying 'so innovativ waren die da schon' (*that's how innovative they were already*), but Bernd formulates the fact that there were coal stoves in the building as simply his and Silke's personal experience rather than a cultural contrast, despite the fact that this was a widespread contrast between the two countries well into the nineties. He is able to disguise his migrant identity by not positioning himself as an outsider. A negotiation of that migrant identity takes place in the next few turns between JD and Bernd. It starts in line 23 when JD reacts with laughter to his formulation that there were seventeen stoves in the building, quite a large number considering that the apartment building only had three or four apartments.[9] Bernd continues with his narrative in overlap with the laughter. In this overlapping passage it is difficult to hear whether it was only the student helper who got up at five in the morning ('der', or *he*), or whether it was Bernd himself who did the heating ('da', or *one*). JD comments on that passage in giving a positive assessment: 'super' (*super*).

An assessment always makes a second assessment by the other person relevant (Pomerantz, 1984). Bernd's response in line 27 ('naja') could be interpreted as downgrading the first assessment (and translated as *well*), thus being a second assessment, or as continuing the narration (and translated as *so*). Bernd then continues with his narrative, but JD interrupts him in lines 28-29, giving a more specific reformulation of her first positive assessment. This refers back to heating the stoves, but the unspecified pronoun 'das' (*that*) is heteroglossic in that it also evokes the eastern German context. The thing that Bernd 'richtig miterlebt' (*was really a part of*) could therefore be either heating with coal stoves, or eastern Germany directly following unification. In response to this assessment, Bernd could present himself as knowledgeable about the East, as somebody who had experienced characteristics of East German culture first-hand. Instead, in lines 30-32, he responds to the assessment with a simple 'ja' (*yes*) and then downgrades the assessment by explaining that he did not usually heat the stove himself, though he may have tried (the recording is unclear).

After a long pause during which none of the other conversational participants chooses to speak, Bernd continues with the story of the renovation:

'Early beginnings': Segment 3
```
36 (3.0)
37 B:  =JA:: (.) und dann ham wir (.) äh (.) n jahr drauf GELD geLIEhen
        =OKAY:: (.) and then we got (.) uh (.) a year later a LOAN
38     von meinen eltern  [(.) gekricht sodass wir überhaupt erstmal ne=
       from my parents    [(.) so that we could put in a=
                          [
39 JD:                    [mhm
                          [mhm
```

---

[9] In East Germany, it was common to have a coal stove in each room in an apartment building.

40 B: =heizung einbauen konnten [auch schon mit warmwas-serversorgung=
      =some sort of heater with [a mechanism to heat the water too=
                                    [

41 JD: [mhm
                                   [*mhm*

42 B: =[aber davon reichte das geld dann nicht [(um in das) jetzt=
      =[but there wasn't enough money   [(to be able) to=
      [[

43 JD: [mhm   [mhm
      [*mhm*   [*mhm*

44 B: =bäder einzubauen (1.0) und das war dann erst (1.0) NOCH n jahr
      =build in bathrooms (1.0) and so it was (1.0) ANOTHER year

45   später die BÄder (.) doch da hatten wir auch nochmal geld
      later the BATHrooms (.) but then we got another loan

46   geliehen von meinen eltern die haben wir auf der EInen seite erst
      from my parents I think we built them on ONE of the sides first

47   glaub ich eingebaut auf der anderen seite noch gar nicht (.) ich
      on the other side not at all yet (.) I

48   glaub nur hier auf dieser seite
      think just here on this side

49 (2.0)

50 S: auf der anderen GAB (.) war es nicht nötig (.) da gabs EIN
      on the other there WAS (.) it wasn't necessary (.) there was ONE

51   bad (.) das haben wir dann erst jahre später saniert (..) und
      bathroom (.) we renovated it a few years later (..) and

52   unten drunter war die firma und die (..) andere seite HATte die
      underneath were the company offices and the (..) other side still

53   noch aber ganz ALte (1.0) also so in (.)   [ddr=
      HAD them but really OLD ones (1.0) I mean standard (.) [East=
                                           [

54 B: [ddr
                                          [*e. german*

55 S: =standard
      =german ones

56 JD: mhm mhm
      uh-huh uh-huh

57 S: genau und hier gabs keine (.) auf DER seite   [und da waren=
      right and here there weren't any (.) on THIS side [and there=
                                          [

58 JD: [mhm
                                        [*mhm*

59 S: =auch die toiletten außerhalb (.) also

        =*also the toilets were outside the apartment (.) so*
60 JD: ja
        yeah
61 B: und dann krichten wir aber (.) vierundneunzig krichten wir geld
        but then we got (.) in ninety-four we got money
62   von der bank (1.0) plötzlich
        from the bank (1.0) suddenly
63 JD: hm
        hm
64 B: und dann ham wir (.) ähm außen saniert neue fenster und [(.)=
        and then we (.) um renovated the outside new windows and [(.)=
                                                                  [
65 JD: [mhm
                                                                  [*mhm*
66 B: =dann konnten wir ordentlich geld reinschieben
        =*then we could really put money into it*

In lines 47-48, Bernd presents himself as being uncertain about some aspects of the story by using 'glaub ich' (*I think*) twice in the same turn, possibly triggering Silke's co-telling in lines 50-53. The information she volunteers fills the gaps in Bernd's narration about whether and why bathrooms were built in one side of the building only. Up until this point, Bernd has not referred to any of the things he is talking about as typical of East Germany, but both he and Silke do so for the first time in lines 53-54. His insertion of a label at this point is prompted by her pause, indicating a word search. He may therefore be providing a label that he himself would not tend to use, but providing her own term for her. She uses this label to specify 'ganz alte' (*really old ones*) and introduces this specification by 'also' (*I mean*), marking this specification as a reformulation. She evokes the East German standard in contrast to West German standards, and thus as different from where she is from. In providing the information in this turn, Silke gives the details that Bernd does not seem to remember. She does not, however, continue with the narration herself, but lets him continue. Bernd then finishes the story in lines 61-66 by telling the outcome of the difficulties renovating the building, namely that they ultimately got money from the bank and could finally renovate the rest of the building.

Summary

In this paper we have shown that not only the narrator, but also the conversation partners, play crucial roles in the construction of identities through narratives of personal experience. Not only do narrators orient toward the co-participants as an audience and select accordingly among possible choices of available linguistic material, but conversation partners also take part in negotiating the narrators' identities through talk. In situations of migration it is possible for conversation partners to challenge migrants' identities on the basis of their personal experience, but the ways in which migrants position themselves, i.e. index familiarity with the new place, may influence whether co-participants choose to do this. Within the same narrative, migrants may construct several different identities which may or may not correspond to the pre-determined labels and categories available to them in society, and which may or may not conflict with each other. Heteroglossia may emerge from migrants' utterances because migrant identities may relate to several of these categories simultaneously as a direct result of their displacement. This heteroglossia can obfuscate correspondence or lack of correspondence to societal categories, and this blurring of boundaries can be either a resource or a constraint for migrants. In the cases where it is a constraint, migrants may avoid heteroglossic voices that may otherwise emerge as a result of overlap of different time periods, places, and social positions by using resources such as quoted speech.

Within the structure of narrative, there are several junctures that are crucial for migrants' positioning. Story prefaces let conversation partners know how the narrator evaluates the story's content, and therefore what reactions they are expected to provide. Through their reactions, they then either meet or fail to meet those expectations, and in narratives about migration experiences, this can have the effect of affirming or disaffirming migrant identities. Orientations, by their very nature, are the point in the narrative where speakers fix elements of the story such as time and place, and for migrants these are often the first and most crucial ways moral stances are indexed even before the core content is conveyed. Anchored by these orientations, the migrants' change of place may then be reflected in pragmatically awkward uses of language in which multiple positionings are evoked simultaneously throughout the rest of the narrative. Since evaluations are a point in which it is possible to comment on the story proper from the perspective of current time, migrants telling their migration stories are required to present their perspectives on cultural artefacts which existed before the time of their migration. In the case of western Germans migrating to eastern Germany, these cultural artefacts are not only different from what migrants are used to, but they have also become devalued in a unified Germany in which the old West German culture has prevailed. The result is that positioning is not only relevant to their own biographies, but also carries weight with respect to various moral stances regarding social changes in eastern Germany. Since conversational narrative is one of the primary ways in which people construct their identities, migrant stories such as the ones presented here can provide us with further insights into the ways in which the social world is constructed and co-constructed through talk.

References

Antaki, C. and S. Widdicombe (eds.) (1998) *Identities in Talk*, London: Sage Publications.

Auer, P., B. Barden and B. Großkopf (1998) 'Subjective and Objective Parameters Determining Salience in Long-term Dialect Accommodation', *Journal of Sociolinguistics,* 2 (2):163-187

Barden, B. and B. Großkopf (1998) *'Sprachliche Akkommodation und soziale Integration. Sächsische Übersiedler und Übersiedlerinnen im rhein/moselfränkischen und alemannischen Sprachraum'* [Linguistic Accommodation and Social Integration. Saxon Migrants in the Rhine/Moselle-Franconian and Allemanic Language Regions], (PHONAI No. 43) Tübingen: Niemeyer.

Bakhtin, M. (1981) 'Discourse in The Novel', in M. Bakhtin, *The Dialogic Imagination* (pp. 259-422). Austin: University of Texas Press (Original work published 1935).

------ (1986) 'The Problem of Speech Genres', in C. Emerson and M. Holquist (eds.), *Speech Genres and Other Late Essays* (pp. 60-102), Austin: University of Texas Press (Original work published 1953).

Becker, U., H. Becker and W. Ruhland (1992) *Zwischen Angst und Aufbruch: das Lebensgefühl der Deutschen in Ost und West nach der Wiedervereinigung* [Between Fear and Uprising: Eastern and Western Germans' Attitudes toward Life after Unification], Düsseldorf, Vienna, New York, Moscow: ECON.

Bourdieu, P. (1994) *Language and Symbolic Power*, Cambridge, MA: Harvard University Press.

di Luzio, A. and J.C.P. Auer (1986) 'Identitätskonstruktion in der Migration: konversationsanalytische und linguistische Aspekte ethnischer Stereotypisierungen' [Identity Construction in Migration: Conversation Analytical and Linguistic Aspects of Ethnic Stereotypes], *Linguistische Berichte* 104:327-351.

Ganz, P. and F.-J. Kemper (2003) 'Ost-West-Wanderungen in Deutschland – Verlust von Humankapital für die neuen Länder?' [East-West-Migration in Germany – Loss of Human Capital for the New States?], *Geographische Rundschau,* 55 (Juni 2003) 6:16-18.

Glaeßner, G.-J. (1992) *The Unification Process in Germany: From Dictatorship to Democracy,* London: Pinter.

Goffman, E. (1974) *Frame Analysis*, New York: Harper & Row.

Grundmann, S. (1993) 'Migrationsbilanz der neuen Bundesländer unter besonderer Beachtung des Landes Thüringen', [Description of the Situation of Migration in the New Federal States with Particular Attention to the State of Thuringia], in K. Eckart and P. Sedlacek (eds.) *Thüringen. Räumliche Aspekte des wirtschaftlichen Strukturwandels,* Jena: Institut für

Geographie der Friedrich-Schiller-Universität, 1993 (*Jenaer Geographische Schriften* 3): 37-60.

Haviland, J.B. (1996) 'Projections, Transpositions, and Relativity', in J. Gumperz and S. Levinson (eds.) *Rethinking Linguistic Relativity* (pp. 271-323), Cambridge: Cambridge University Press.

Kritsch, H. (1985) *The German Democratic Republic*, Boulder, London: Westview.

Labov, W. (1972) 'The Transformation of Experience in Narrative Syntax', in W. Labov (ed.) *Language in the Inner City: Studies in the Black English Vernacular* (pp. 354-396), Philadelphia, PA: University of Pennsylvania Press.

------ and J. Waletzky (1967) 'Narrative Analysis: Oral Versions of Personal Experience', in J. Helm (ed.) *Essays on the Verbal and Visual Arts* (pp. 12-44), Seattle, University of Washington Press.

Langacker, R.W. (1987) *Foundations of Cognitive Grammar. Vol. I (Theoretical Perspectives)*, Stanford: Stanford University Press.

------ (1991) *Foundations of Cognitive Grammar. Vol. II (Prescriptive Application)* Stanford: Stanford University Press.

Liebscher, G. (forthcoming) 'Perspectives in Conflict: An Analysis of German-German Conversations', in J. ten Thije and Kristin Bührig (eds.) *Beyond Misunderstanding. The Linguistic Analysis of Intercultural Discourse*, Amsterdam: John Benjamins.

------ (1999) *Arriving at Identities: Voice and Positioning in German Talkshows between 1989 and 1994*, University of Texas at Austin: Unpublished dissertation.

Norrick, N.R. (2000) *Conversational Narrative: Storytelling in Everyday Talk*, Amsterdam, Philadelphia: John Benjamins.

Ochs, E. and L. Capps (2001) *Living Narrative: Creating Lives in Everyday Storytelling*, Cambridge, MA, London: Harvard University Press.

Pomerantz, A. (1984) 'Agreeing and Disagreeing with Assessments: Some Features of Preferred/Dispreferred Turn Shapes', in J. Maxwell Atkinson and J. Heritage (eds.) *Structures of Social Action: Studies in Conversation Analysis* (pp. 57-101), Cambridge: Cambridge University Press.

Quasthoff, U.M. (1980) *Erzählen in Gesprächen: Linguistische Untersuchungen zu Strukturen und Funktionen am Beispiel einer Kommunikationsform des Alltags* [Narrative in Conversation: Linguistic Studies on Structures and Functions using a Form of Everyday Communication as an Example], Tübingen: Narr.

Ricker, K. (2000) *Migration, Sprache, und Identität: Eine biographieanalytische Studie zu Migrationsprozessen von Französinnen in Deutschland* [Migration, Language, and Identity: A Biography-analytical Study of the Migration Processes of French Women in Germany], Donat Verlag: Bremen.

Sacks, H. (1992) *Lectures on Conversation* (edited by Gail Jefferson), Oxford: Basil Blackwell (Originally published 1964/1965).

------, E.A. Schegloff and G. Jefferson (1974) 'A Simplest Systematic for the Organization of Turn-taking in Conversation', *Language* 50:361-382.

Schiffrin, D. (1996) 'Narrative as Self-portrait: Sociolinguistic Constructions of Identity', *Language in Society* 25 (2):167-203.

Werz, N. (2001) 'Abwanderung aus den neuen Bundesländern von 1989 bis 2000' [Migration from the New Federal States from 1989 to 2000], *Aus Politik und Zeitgeschichte* (39-40):23-31.

Wortham, S. (2001) *Narratives in Action: A strategy for Research and Analysis,* Columbia, NY: Teachers College Press.

Section II

Displacement
and
Spatialization Practices

Displacement and Spatialization Practices

The chapters in this section address issues of space, place and mobility in narratives of dislocation: the choices made possible by the fragmentation or splitting of the deictic centre, the recontextualizations available in global flows and distribution of communicative orders, discursive accounts of trajectories through space and time, some at least apparently reversible, others irrevocable. The narratives analyzed here trace, in Haviland's memorable phrase, "the discursive tracks of migration and displacement". We examine through the deployment of globalized sociolinguistic repertoires, the grammaticalization of space and features of generic form, trajectories of both possibility and loss.

In the discourse of the migrant narrator, Mamal, analyzed in Haviland's chapter, fine calibrations of these deictic choices can either align him with the deictic centre of back home in San Cristobal or with his current space and time in Oregon. As Haviland points out, these deictic choices are optional rather than obligatory and hence can be used expressively. Mamal discursively constructs the ambivalences and uncertainties of migration processes by means of vivid shifts of deictic choice, through which at certain times he asserts his Zinacantec village and at others his new 'home' in Oregon as his deictic centre. We see how these orientations shift and change over time.

Haviland's chapter, describing how a tradition of migration becomes established in the community he is researching as an anthropologist, also unsettles the stereotypical relationship between the anthropologist and the research subject in which the mobile modern visits the stable traditional: here the stable 'timeless' community turns out not only to have a present of migration and displacement, but also a past history of it, as revealed in oral history narratives. Here both the anthropologist and the research subject are transnational individuals, engaged in transnational flows. Interestingly it seems that it is a combination of this social movement, including possibilities for regular travel back and forth, and of new means of communication (the cassette letter and the telephone) that creates these discursive possibilities that are becoming innovative foci for anthropological research into new transnational flows and movements.

The theme of transnational flows is picked up in the discourse fragment analyzed in Blommaert's paper, where space, indexed through speech varieties, is a central driver of the meaning construction, whether the prestige space of The University of Cape Town (UCT), the vernacular space of the townships, or the prestige global vernacular of Rasta slang.

Blommaert shows how such spaces are reinserted into the local discursive environment. The young woman calling from Khayelitsha momentarily blows away the delicately organized package of identity features that constitute Ras Pakaay's deejay persona and his own mobility, by calling him back through a codeswitch into Xhosa, to his original place in the townships. We are reminded that migration is not simply a question of transnational movements of people: people migrate within borders, shifting class positions, leaving other human beings behind. The chapter also makes the important point that not only styles but language varieties migrate, becoming resources for new kinds of identity work in new social conditions. Thus, speakers in discourse may not always collude with each other's identity work, but may challenge each other's position as the female caller in the fragment analyzed seems to be doing.

The narratives in McCormick's chapter, originally told as part of an oral history record, initiated during the Apartheid period, in post-Apartheid South Africa illustrate another possible function of storytelling: that of backing claims for restitution of lost land. The Protea narratives reconstruct the neighbourhood through its practices, its typical temporal cycles, in a way somewhat similar to how Haviland's Zinacantec migrant reconstructs deictically the here and now of his village of origin, from the remoteness of his diaspora. The Protea narratives are "before and after narratives", accounts that, according to McCormick, are "shot through with glimpses of life after removal". The author suggests that contrast is the most pervasive form of rhetorical organization, the contrast between the idyllic former life and brutal exclusion from it, and that "comparison is a stronger organizing principle than chronology". From another perspective, these narratives form part of an argument, and even potentially of a legal case. These recounts therefore provide a further example of the importance of the contextualization of narratives into larger speech events, a point underscored by Blommaert in his chapter.

The Protea narratives start from the nostalgia and pain produced by loss and dislocation, they graphically highlight the destructiveness of these forced removals, contrasting the predictable and familiar routines and spaces of the lost Protea life with the uncertainties and loss of agency and resources which forcible removal entailed. McCormick's focus on the Protea narratives, with their representation of legally enforced dislocations and relocations, provides a transition to the papers in Section III which discuss the strategies and categories through which institutions describe and impose identities on individuals or groups that are either physically or socially displaced, the complexities that derive from these

processes in the interpretation of identities constructed in narrative, and
the consequences of institutional pressure on narrative performance produced by migrants and displaced communities.

Dreams of Blood
Zinacantecs in Oregon

JOHN B. HAVILAND, *Mexico (CIESAS-Sureste) and US (Reed College)*

Dreams of Blood

A young Zinacantec man was telling me his dream. The date was June 26, 1988. His voice cracked with tension.

(1) Chep's dream of blood[1]

1   vo`one animal yan xal vayuk samel
As for me, I had an awful sleep last night.

2   syempre k'alal ta jvaychin yech chk li`e
Whenever I have this kind of dream,

3   syempre oy anima
someone always dies.

4   na`tik k'usi palta ta jnatik
Who knows what has gone amiss back home.

5   lek nan ti mi mu jchi`iltikuk o k'usi spase
It will be good if perhaps it is not one of our relatives who has suffered a misfortune.

6   k'alal oy k'usi ta jvaychin yech chk li`e
Whenever I dream something like this,

7   syempre chlok' anima
someone always ends up dead.

8   ijtzak jkot vakax
I was holding a cow.

9   ismil jkot vakax
They were slaughtering a cow.

10   tey is–
They were---

11   te ta kok yilel
It was there at my feet, it seemed.

12   isjis ti vakaxe
They were cutting the beef into strips.

13   te va`alon jk'eloj
I was standing there watching.

14   laj skotol li vakaxe
The whole cow was finished off.

---

[1] From Tape Z8812b, December 1988.

15   este
      Um,
16   k'alal ta jvaychin yech chk li`e
      whenever I dream like this,
17   o bu chkil bek'et
      if I see meat,
18   oy bu chkil ch'ich'el
      or if I see blood,
19   yu`un syempre chlok' anima
      someone ALWAYS dies.

Two days later this same man was dead, succumbing, as one says in Tzotzil, to *vovil-chvay* 'crazy sleeping' – a journey in which his *ch'ulel* 'soul' leaves behind his sleeping body and is then unable to return. In the lives of many Zinacantecs dreams carry messages, powerful visions, and often perils. In the case of my friend Chep, son of a *compadre* from the village of Nabenchauk in Zinacantán, in the highlands of Chiapas, México, the dream of blood was an omen of his own death. The dream was narrated to me far from Chiapas. It was told to me in my house in Portland, Oregon, a few blocks from Reed College. Two days later the dreamer's body awoke soulless on the floor of a rented apartment that was shared with some twenty other undocumented Mexican workers in Salem, Oregon, about 80 kilometres away.

My research in Zinacantán has centred on discourse, usually the face-to-face small talk of quotidian interaction. Charles Taylor cites language as the crucial "locus of disclosure" of the person, with an aphorism: "I become a person and remain one only as an interlocutor" (1985:276). To an ethnographer who spends the bulk of his time in conversation with acquaintances in bush, field, and village, this is congenial methodological ratification. As people's lives change, as their senses of self evolve and their worlds shift, they leave discursive tracks. I shall try to exhibit some of the footprints to be traced in recent, tentative, and largely pioneering Zinacantec treks north, across the border into the United States.

The Field Comes to Me
The First Footsteps in a Zinacantec Diaspora

Most of my anthropological career has been spent working with Mayan peasant corn farmers in south-eastern Mexico. For most of the past two decades, since I started teaching in Oregon, although I still go regularly 'to the field' in Chiapas, 'the field' has, of its own accord, come to me.

The received anthropological wisdom forty years ago was that Chiapas Indians were less peasants than Maya; that while Indians in other parts of Mexico had been robbed of their land, turned into peons and proletarians, Chiapas was a 'refuge region', where indigenous forms of social and cultural life had persisted since before the arrival of Cortéz.

But were Zinacantecs and their neighbours really 'taking refuge' from the rest of Mexico? Though they appeared quintessential corn farmers (no meal was complete without a tortilla, no divination possible without 13 grains of corn), what was one to make of autobiographical tales in which old men never touched a hoe, never grew a single *elote*, but instead hauled beer, salt, coffee, and cotton between their highland homes and the steamy lowlands? Although land and waterhole rituals, prayers to ancestors and the Earth Lord in caves soot-blackened from apparent centuries of witch offerings, bespoke a timeless occupancy of these mountains, how was one to understand the stories of my compadre Petul, whose grandfather talked about opening the land, clearing the forest, and selling house plots to landless relatives returned from the lowlands after being 'freed' from debt-servitude by Carranza's troops during the Mexican Revolution? What of Petul's father who boasted of capturing a mule in the ensuing counter-revolutionary battles in Chiapas? Despite appearances to the contrary, Zinacantecs had clearly been deeply engaged with non-Zinacantec worlds both before and after the Conquest.

Still, unlike other Mexican Indians it was only recently that Zinacantecs began to think about crossing *la linea* into the United States. Mixtecs of Oaxaca, for example, have for decades abandoned their arid home country for contract labour, picking cotton in Chiapas, tomatoes in Sinaloa and Baja California, and in recent years bringing in the strawberry, grape and apple harvests in California and the Pacific Northwest. And Oregon fields are routinely tended· by Indians and non-Indians alike from Yucatán, Guerrero, Oaxaca, and Michoacán, some of whom arrived as *braceros* in the 1950s, others who make the seasonal migration from year to year. As far as I know, no Zinacantecs attempted to join them until the late 1980s.

Still, the inhabitants of Nabenchauk were not immune to the changes that afflicted all Mexican peasants. The economic crises of the 1980s had various expressions, among them changes in the social organization of corn farming[2] and a proliferation of alternative forms of making a living,

---

[2] Among other things the government promoted dependence on chemical fertilizers, the costs of transport, and the resulting capitalization of all forms of agriculture, (see Collier (1990)).

including the cultivation and sale of flowers,[3] as well as other somewhat more sensitive commodities such as illegally cut timber, bootleg liquor, and marijuana. They also engaged in wage labour, especially in construction and government projects (at least in epochs when money was available to fund such projects), and above all in transport of goods and people. These alternative economic activities also grew out of the demographic profile of communities like Nabenchauk which experienced an explosion in the population of people from 15-30 years of age. At the same time important changes in the cost of corn production took place that were related to reliance on chemical fertilizers and relative increases in the cost of gasoline with concomitant rises in transport costs, without corresponding rises in the price of corn on the newly globalized market. Local social structure, coupled with these changes, determined the typical profile of a Zinacantec who in the 1980s found it necessary to *sa'abtel*, that is leave the village to 'look for work': a young man of 15-25, bachelor or newly married, without extensive highland property, sometimes with a few years of primary schooling, and often with urgent monetary needs or accumulated debts.

By the mid 1980s, the national economic crisis had eliminated nearly all sources of work on government funded public works projects, and intensive capitalization of agriculture had profoundly altered the social structure of the Indian communities of Chiapas. At this time, on the eve of the 1994 Zapatista rebellion that responded to the same factors writ large across the state, many young Zinacantecs were leaving for Tabasco, Veracruz, and Mexico City in search of work, usually as unskilled *peones* on construction sites. All that was missing was the next logical step in the migratory process – in a real sense, a *discursive* step: an idea, a conceptual presence, a body of information about the 'North' where one could go in search of work. To be sure, there already existed a few such discursive ghosts. There was talk about a man from the neighbouring hamlet of Nachij who had gone to live in some part of the United States – Texas, it was sometimes rumoured – who had sent fabulous quantities of *dólares* home to his parents. Word of mouth had it that there was an *enganchador* or labour contractor from Ocosingo who offered a salary of three dollars an hour (more than many were then earning for a day's work) for picking cotton, after a long trip in a pickup truck for which he would charge people 200,000 pesos (of the old variety – about $US300) to be 'delivered in Texas'. Several Chamulas, Tzotzil speakers from a neighbouring highland

---

[3] See Haviland (1993).

community, who had long travelled throughout Mexico and who could make a reasonable living selling handicrafts and clothing in the commercial district around Correo Mayor in Mexico City, had been bragging to their countrymen that they had 'dared to cross the line' to the North.

The first confirmed steps in a Zinacantec transnational diaspora were taken quite recently. A godchild of mine, the fabled *Chep Tojtik* 'Joe Pinetrees', left Nabenchauk in the late 1970s after abandoning two wives, spent a year in a Oaxacan jail reputedly for mistreating a third, and then was heard to have taken up with drug runners he had met in jail, moving first to Culiacán, and later, it was rumoured, to *Jaliwud*. The first ordinary Zinacantecs from Nabenchauk, in search of ordinary (though, they hoped, fabulously well-paid) jobs, as best I can tell ventured north of the border in June 1988 when my compadre Petul's son Chep and his cousin crossed at Tijuana and made their way to the strawberry fields of Oregon. Chep, the young man who had dreamed of blood, returned to the village almost immediately in a pine box. His surviving cousin remained in the United States while I accompanied the deceased's cadaver home for burial. That cousin – joined in 1994 by a nephew who entered the country illegally and then recently, in the first months of the new millennium, by his eldest son – lives still in Salem, Oregon.

Since then, the emigration of Tzotziles to the United States has mushroomed. In the introduction to a collection from 1995 of the testimonial accounts of three Chamulas then working in California, Jan Rus writes:

> Tan recientemente como en 1987 se empezaron a escuchar las primeras noticias de chamulas y zinacantecos que habían alcanzado por su propia cuenta los estados de Texas, California y Oregon. Aun en 1991 . . . el encontrar a tzotziles en los Estados Unidos era todavía una novedad. Pero ahora, apenas cuatro años más tarde, en las comunidades de los alrededores de San Cristóbal, parece que casi todos tienen algún amigo o familiar trabajando en "el norte"; en total, deben de ser ya miles. Tan es así que según las últimas noticias, ahora circulan nuevos coyotes en las colonias de San Cristóbal – los "polleros" – que ofrecen un "servicio completo" desde Chiapas a los Estados Unidos, con llegada garantizada, por sólo 500 dólares. (Rus and Guzmán López, 1996:2)[4]

---

[4] "As recently as 1987 one began to hear the first news of Chamulas and Zinacantecs who had managed through their own efforts to reach the states of Texas, California, and Oregon. Still in 1991 ... it was unusual to find Tzotzil speakers in

Rumours abound of Chamula traffickers in illegal workers from Chiapas and Central America – called *ok'il* 'coyote' in Tzotzil or, as Rus and Guzmán note, more commonly by the Mexican slang *pollero* 'chicken farmer' – with cellular telephones, and sometimes disguised as non-Indian *ladinos,* driving the Pan American highway with trailer trucks filled with desperate people in search of work, on the northern journey, and returning with TVs, stereos sets, gold chains, and thick bundles of dollars, hidden in their shoes and leather briefcases.

As is the case with other aspects of the black market economy which operates in a quasi-legal or declaredly illegal shadow, the undocumented emigration of Tzotziles and others to the USA, despite its undeniable existence, remains a poorly understood and understudied (indeed, barely studiable) phenomenon. There exist no reliable statistics about the migrants, their demographic characteristics, their jobs or salaries or working conditions, the amount of money they return to their communities, or about other social and political impacts of the migratory process. Nor is there even an adequate model of what sort of research or 'field investigation' might be up to the job of filling in these descriptive gaps, since such research would also have to exist in a similar kind of legal shadow.[5]

My aim in this short paper is not to try to give a more complete account of Tzotzil migration to the United States. Even the story of this first Zinacantec migration – how the cousin who stayed behind settled accounts with the family of the dead man (who blamed him for the death), how his relations with family and friends have changed, how his fortunes in the village have altered – although fascinating and analytically telling, is much too long and complex to present here. A related overarching theoretical theme – the reworking of notions of 'place' in such transnational contexts – is also more than I can deal with in this chapter.

Instead I will track a much smaller, discursive and grammatical residue

---

the United States. But now, only 4 years later, in the communities that surround San Cristóbal [de las Casas, Chiapas] it seems that almost everybody has a friend or relative working in 'the North'; all in all, there must now be thousands. This is so much the case that according to the latest news, there are new coyotes working in the poor neighbourhoods of San Cristóbal – the 'chicken raisers' – who offer 'full service' trips from Chiapas to the United States, with delivery guaranteed, for only US$500".

[5] When the two Tzotzil cousins from Nabenchauk were in Tijuana waiting to cross into the United States, I was uncomfortably aware of the legal ambiguities surrounding my own inquiries into the possibilities for finding *coyotes* who might help them. But that's another story.

of the parts of the process I have been able to understand with some precision and confidence. Over the last fifteen years there have sprung up new discourses linking the Zinacantec men in Oregon with their families and friends in Zinacantán. Cassette tapes, letters, phone calls, notes, photographs, videotapes, money orders, banknotes and other gifts are carried in both directions and serve as the medium for long distance conversations. Ironically it is often the ethnographer, free to cross the border in both directions and regularly shuttling between southern Chiapas village and northern Oregon city, who acts as middleman. I am also the Zinacantecs' most available interlocutor, answering distress calls and offering therapeutic talk all along the transnational Zinacantec chain. The most salient conversations, whether mediated or dyadic, and those on which I largely rely in this paper, are those between the expatriate Zinacantecs and parents, siblings, estranged wives, children, and friends *ta jnatik* 'in our [inclusive] home'. I will focus on a couple of tiny linguistic details in the disassembly and reassembly of Zinacantec 'identity', mostly drawn from the surviving cousin's communications with home.

The cousin is a fascinating and not altogether trustworthy man, as one could perhaps guess from his nicknames in the village: *Mamal* (a kind of clown active in Zinacantec New Year ritual, translated 'dude' by Laughlin, 1977), or sometimes *Troni* (short for *electrónico* 'electronic'). He has a reputation in the village for telling lies. Still, the content of the communications between Mamal and his town is intense, affectively charged, and of special interest to an ethnographer like me with an abiding fascination with 'gossip' as an anthropological resource (Haviland, 1977). At the same time, the details of his matrimonial circumstances, his fights with relatives about money and the responsibility for bringing up his five children back in the village, the family scandals (one of his sisters is an unwed mother, another made a bad marriage), his excuses and self-justifications, his angers are details perhaps too personal for treatment in this forum, and they would occupy too much space. Instead I shall concentrate on the complex dance of approach and avoidance, between 'here' and 'there', the endpoints [or end-'places'] in the chain of migration, through which Mamal gives constant signals of an ambivalence about where he belongs and where his loyalties lie in the world – probably an ambivalence to which migrants are all too susceptible.

The Language of Self and Place

It would be possible to study the transnational discourses between Oregon and Nabenchauk with respect to their content. What are they about?

What worries the interlocutors? How and in what contexts are different
positions and affective stances expressed? What about the 'dreams of
blood'? Dreams, indeed, appear with regularity as a theme in the communications between Mamal and home and in his conversations with me: a
symptom, no doubt, of the fragile and precarious state of a Zinacantec
soul which finds itself so far away from the protection of the ancestors
who occupy the mountains surrounding the village, and of the patron saint
jtotik santorenso, Our Father St. Lawrence.

(2) "I had the same dream as the deceased"[6]

207 ji animal ya:n x'elan xtal jvayich tajmek
     Yes, I had a terrible dream.
208 j; ijo
     Damn!
209 x; i ika'i ikil ya'el ti k'u cha'al este:
     I felt that I was seeing the same thing (as he did).
210 k'u cha'al liyalbon li anima k'alal mu to'ox chame
     *the same thing the deceased told me about when he was still
     alive.*
211 j; eso
212 x; i: ja'
     yes

           [
213 j;   a taj ali:
               Was it that...

           taj icham ya'el li vakaxe
           they were killing a cow?
                           [
215 x;   stot vakax
                           It was a bull.

(3) "I always dream with you all"[7]

963 mi ch'abal k'usi apasoji:k
     Has nothing happened to you all?
964 mi'n lekoxuk. akotolik porke
     Are all of you OK? because
965 oy ta jvay-
     I... have dreamed—

---

[6] Tape 89.22a20 telephone conversation between Mamal and the author.
[7] Tape 90.03b.

966 chajvaychinik tajmek. li imuy tal k'ak'ale
...have dreamed with you a lot these days

967 oy-

968 oy lek oy chopol li jvayich jujun k'ak'ale pero
And sometimes they are good dreams, and sometimes bad,
every day, but

969 muk' bu onox ta xkak' ta ko`on mi o k'usi chopol
I don't pay them much attention if they are bad

970 mi o k'usi palta pero
if there is some problem

971 ta jk'an chka`i mi-
But I want to know if—

972 k'usi

973 mu k'usi a-

974 mu k'usi: apasojik
-if nothing bad has happened to you all.

975 mi lekoxuk akotolik
if you are all well.

(4) *Mamal tells (his parents) about a dream that preceded a car*
crash (9631a)

328 vaychinemon chka`i
I think I had dreamed something.

329 mu jna` ch'ay xa onox xka`i k'usitik ta jvaychin
I'm not sure, I don't remember exactly what the dream was
about.

330 k'ex xa onox ti jvayiche
These days I am dreaming all the time.

331 k'ex xa onox oy vayiche
I always have dreams

332 k'ex onox chivaychin
I always dream..

333 ja` ti k'usi . laj .kilan ta jvayiche
Whatever I happen to see in my dreams—

334 komo mu onox bu chkich' ta muk'e pwes- bweno
Although I don't pay much attention, but- well..—

335 te ono nan k'usi chal timi`n chavich' ta muk' une
I guess it always is trying to say something if you pay atten-
tion to it

336 pwes ach'`ach' to`ox jvay- vaychinemon
Because I had just recently been dreaming

337 mu jna` k'usi ta jvaychin
Although I don't know what I dreamed.

The substantive theme that runs through the material I will present is the ambivalence suggested by these dreams, the contradictory mixture of closeness and distance, the complex dance between one place or one home and another, which is clearly expressed in the type of relationship Mamal, in emigrant's exile, has established with his town and his relatives there. The signals of Mamal's ambivalence about his Chiapas home come in many guises – perhaps most obviously the fact that he has returned to his village for a total of no more than about eight months in the fifteen years since he left. The visits he has made have been diffident as well as short. Approach and avoidance characterize his scant – now perhaps non-existent – money orders home to wife and children, his ways of referring both directly and obliquely to kinsmen, his apparent indifference to the affairs of his town, and even his choice of remote or proximate determiners.[8]

In particular in this chapter, I focus on Mamal's use of *deictic verbs*. Much recent work in linguistic anthropology has been dedicated to deixis, most notably in the Mayan context, the work of William Hanks on Yucatec (Hanks 1990;1996). *Deixis* is perhaps the most transparent nexus between language and the full context of speaking, equipped with interlocutors, bodies, socio-historical scenery, etc. Deictic categories at once penetrate and permeate both linguistic and contextual structures, making them potent conceptual and sociocultural mechanisms as deictic elements tend to be obligatory in speech. The methodological starting point of a study of 'migration' through a close attention to deictically anchored verbs is that, through these apparently small lexical symptoms, it is possible to diagnose attitudes and perspectives, in particular what I will call an ambivalent 'socio-centric' perspective on the part of this Tzotzil emigrant. Such an approach reaffirms the value of situated 'discourse' as an ethnographic resource, but it also implies rather minute attention to the details of linguistic structure.

Briefly, here are the formal details. The deictic centre, or 'HERE' is denoted by a proximal locative predicate *LI'*, which contrasts with the distal locative *TE* 'there'. Like most of its sister Mayan languages, Tzotzil additionally has four ubiquitous deictically marked verbs of motion: *tal* 'COME [marked]' vs. *bat* 'go [unmarked]', and *yul* 'ARRIVE HERE' vs.

---

[8] There is a basic contrast in Zinacantec Tzotzil between *li* 'the' (relatively close things), and *ti* 'the' (relatively distant things), as well as *taj* (truly remote things, beyond normal perceptual ranges).

k'ot 'arrive there'. These roots are frequent in Tzotzil conversation, sur-
facing as independent motion verbs, as auxiliaries, and as post-verbal
directional particles. Specifically, Tzotzil uses two directional particles,
themselves derived from verbs of motion, which can add to an otherwise
unspecified predicate a perspective indicating a deictically anchored vec-
tor. The directional *tal(el)*, derived from *tal*, indicates marked motion
towards the deictic centre, whereas *ech'el* (< *ech'* 'pass by') indicates
direction away from the deictic centre.

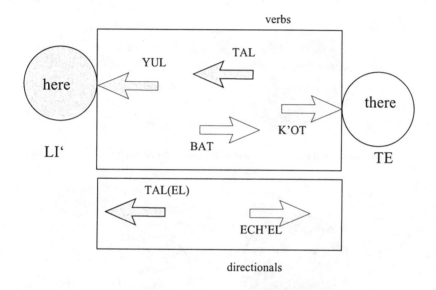

Figure 1: Tzotzil deictic verbs and directionals

When interlocutors share a deictic centre – a common 'here' – the perspective afforded by these paradigmatic alternates is straightforward and
insistent, though subject to characteristic transpositions (Haviland, 1996),
for example in quotation. In effect, a trajectory that *sets out towards the
deictic centre* (where the speaker is) is described with *tal*; a trajectory
setting out in any other direction requires *bat*. The 'arrival-verb' *yul* denotes a trajectory whose salient *endpoint is the deictic centre* ('here'); by
contrast, *k'ot* denotes arrival at some other unmarked locus. There is rarely
any choice in the matter (although the extent or scope of the deictic centre
– how much conceptual area it encompasses – may be contextually determined in familiar ways). The *perspective* for calculating 'here' and 'there'

is normally anchored in the immediate speech context. 'Here' is where the speaker is, though it is sometimes decoupled from the speaker onto the interlocutor. When I overtake you on the path, I will say *'la`* 'come along' and you will reply *'batik'* 'let's go'.[9]

The unmarked perspective is often adopted even in a more marked situation, for example in long-distance communications like those between Oregon and Chiapas, when the 'speaker' finds his or her self in one place and an interlocutor in another.

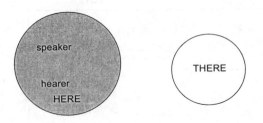

unmarked situation: speaker and hearer in the same place

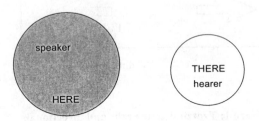

marked situation: speaker and hearer in diferent places

Figure 2

---

[9] One apparent exception may be observed in the following situation. You summon me, say, to a meal. If I mean to delay only a moment, I will say *"te chital* 'I'm coming'". If I do not intend to accompany you on the way, however, I must reply *"te chibat* 'I'm going'", thereby signalling that I expect to be there after you have left. Tzotzil conventions thus more resemble English than, say, Spanish where one virtually never abandons an egocentric perspective: *Tú vienes? Ahí voy.* And see below.

(5) "Return home, son!"

Mamal's father advises him to return home (1994)

203   mu xkaltik mi chepel tatak'ine
     We won't argue that you have piles of money.

204   pero solamente ya`el
     But only—-

205   ti bal nox ya`el ti . oy xaxanav o **tal** jtz'ujuke
     *—enough for you ta come walking back **this way** a little bit*

206   mas onox lek ya`el
     It would be better

207   timi chasut **talel** xun
     *if you return **in this direction**, Juan.*

208   mas lek ya`el
     It would be better

209   k'ano **tal** permiso k'u sjaliluk
     *Ask for permission (to come home **to here**) for some length of time.*

210   mas lek **tal** . k'opono lach'amaltake
     It would be better for you to **come** and speak properly to your children.

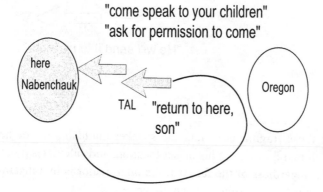

Figure 3

(6) "I'm going to send a paper" (Mamal offers to send a letter, and asks for a reply (1988)

2   pero mu jna` k'usi jalil **tey**
     *I don't know how long he [referring to the ethnographer] will be **there***

3   ta jtakbe **ech'el** jlik vun
     *I'll send a piece of paper [i.e., a letter] along with him **to there**.*

4   chich' **tal** li vune
        *And he will **bring** a paper [i.e., a reply] back with him*
5   ak'o stz'iba **tal** jlikuk
        *Have him write me a letter (and send it **here**).*
6   chich' **tal** li xun lavi tztzut **tal** ta orae
        *And Juan [the ethnographer] will **bring** it, since he is return-*
        *ing **here** soon.*
7   li xune, li` xa chistakbon **tal** ta mejikoe
        *Juan will send it on to me **here** from Mexico (City).*

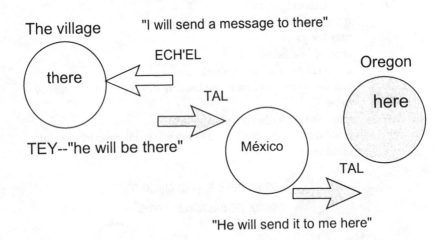

Figure 4

In all of these fragments of talk the speaker maintains his or her own deictic centre, representing his or her location, and calculates deictics accordingly, regardless of the fact that the interlocutor is in a distant place and may thus have a different perspective.

Mamal, talking by telephone to his relatives at home the day after the death of his cousin Chep, also adopts this unmarked, untransposed, interactively disjointed perspective – locating himself bleakly but firmly in Oregon.

*(7) "We got work **here** on arrival"*
        23   ali k'alal liyulotikotike
                *When we **arrived here**,*
        24   **yul** abtejkotikotik ta ora
                *We **arrived** and got jobs right away.*

Maintaining this separated perspective, he indirectly blames the jealousy of others in the village at home for what happened when he and his companion 'came' to the United States.

(8) "They're jealous because we came"

13 o sk'ak'alik yo`onik tajmek
  They are very jealous of us,
14 x`elan oy xi**tal**otikotik
  *because of the fact that we have **come**.*

And despite the urgings of his countrymen and a nagging moral certainty that he really *ought* to return with his cousin's body, he maintains his distance from home and expresses his intention to stay on in the north.

(9) "I'll steel my heart to stay here"

15 ta xkalbe ko`on ya`el ti **li**` chikome
  *I will steel my heart to stay **here**,*
16 pero yu`un yu`un yu`un —
  but then-
17 ja` ta xkak' o pwersa ya`el ti-
  I will make a serious effort
18 ta jsa` **ech'el** jtz'uj tak'in
  *to take a bit of money **(away from her** -i.e., back home).*

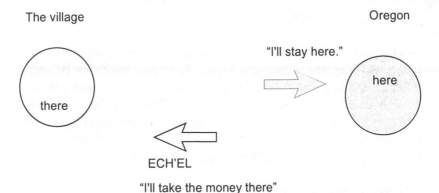

Figure 5

To return to Nabenchauk now would be to admit defeat and to expose himself to further financial ruin, since he had to borrow heavily to make the initial trip.

(10) "I would return there just as poor as when I left for here"
> 19   i xchi`uk k'usuk i solel timi xik'ot ya`ele
>   *and what's more, if I were only to **arrive (there)***
> 20   mismo onox yech chik'ot k'u cha`al lilok' **talel** =
>   *I would **arrive (there)** just the same as when I left **(for here)**.*
> 21   =i`i
>   *No.*
> 22   altik ya`el
>   *That would be no good.*

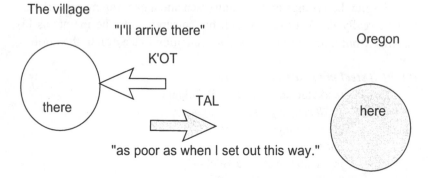

Figure 6

Transposition of Deictic Perspective
Expressive Conventions

Deictic perspectives must, of course, be shiftable or 'transposable' (see Haviland, 1991). The prototypical 'trigger' for such a shift is quoted speech, in which the values for those indices anchored in the speech situation must be recalculated from the perspective of the *quoted* or reported (putative) speech event. "John said, 'I'm hungry'", requires us to recalculate the referent of 'I' – the hungry one – as John. Such 'quoted' perspectives predictably surface in Mamal's communications with home.

(11) "If they ask you, 'When is he coming?'..."
> 1   mi oy stak' **tal** mantal
>   *"Has he sent any messages **here**?*
> 2   k'u ora **xtal**
>   *"¿When will he come?"*
> 3   mi oy yal **tal**
>   *"¿Has he told you **(here)***

4   k'u ora **chul,**
*"when he will arrive **here**?*

5   tzsut **tal**
*"when will he return **here**?"*

6   timi xayutike
suppose they ask you that ...

Conventional 'altero-centering'

When speaker and hearer do not share the same deictic perspective, deictically anchored verbs present a conceptual and interactive problem amenable to different sorts of solution. The familiar case is illustrated by the verbs *come* and *go* in English and, say, their Spanish 'equivalents' *venir* and *ir*. In a situation in which a person (the 'speaker') is inside a room, and someone else (the 'interlocutor') knocks on the door, the speaker in English is obliged to say 'I'm coming', thereby apparently adopting an *alterocentric* perspective, where the deictic centre to which he will 'come' is that of the knocker. In Mexican Spanish, by contrast, the speaker is obliged to say something like *ya voy*, literally, 'I'm going now', firmly anchored in his or her own deictic centre. The two languages completely

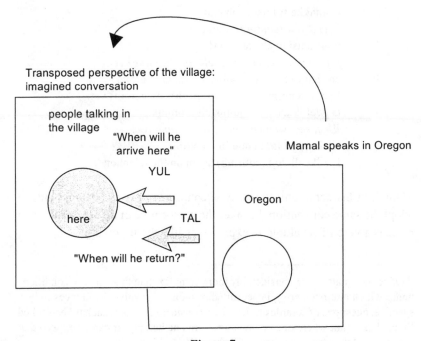

Figure 7

conventionalize the choice of anchoring but in opposite ways.[10]

It appears that in Zinacantec Tzotzil, in recent years when long distance communication – for example by letter or by telephone – has produced situations in which the deictic centres of speakers and hearers are geographically separated, one convention has developed in which a directional element attached to a verb of speaking reflects the *recipient's* perspective. Although the speaker, located in Chiapas in the following extract, refers with the deictic *li'* 'here' to his own location, the directional *tal* attached to the verbs of speakers represents a perspective in which the words will be 'coming' in the direction of the recipients, in this case in Oregon.

(12) "I send you a greeting" (t9715a1) LR -> XR

4	li'on ta jobel
	Here I am in San Cristóbal
6	li' ta sna li . jch'ul tot jorje
	Here I am in the house of my godfather George.
9	k'elavil . xun
	Look, Juan—
10	li' chakalbee
	Here I am telling you
11	chajtakbe **tal** jun chabanuk
	*I send you (**coming**) a greeting.*
345	muk' k'usi to chakalbe **tal**
	*I have nothing much to tell you (**coming**) yet.*
346	ch'abal to bu ta j- chajk'opon **tal** ta telefono
	I am not going to call you (**in this direction**) yet.
347	ta jk'eltik k'usi ora junuk ali . rominkoal
	We'll see whether one of these Sundays..
	chajk'opon **tal** ta telefono noxtok
	I will call you (**coming**) again on the telephone.

Mamal, in his communications by telephone or tape recording, tends to adopt the same convention: he takes the perspective of his *recipient* when he uses a verb of speaking, in expressions like the following:

---

[10] Of course, matters are considerably more complex than this, and the conditions under which alterocentering is permitted or required involve differences in perspective, questions of complex trajectories, considerations of what has been called 'home base' (not where one is now but where one belongs or can be expected to be) etc. See the classic studies of Fillmore (1966, 1975).

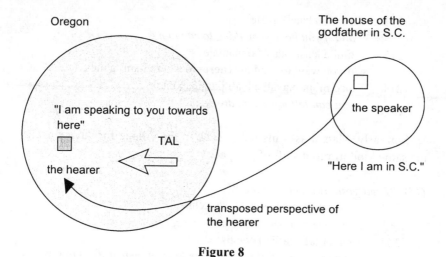

Figure 8

(13) Expressions conventionally altero-centered
chajtakbe tal "I send you"
chajk'opon talel "I speak to you"
chik'opoj talel "I am going to speak [with you]"
chakalbe tal "I am going to tell you [something]"
ta jtzak tal, ta jtz'iba tal, ta jpas tal grabar "I will inscribe, write, or
record [something for you]"

The implicit logic here is similar to that of English: there is an implied directionality inherent in the motion (of communication), where the end point or destination of the message resides with the recipient. As a result it is apparently the recipient's perspective that must be adopted to produce the correct directional element.

Of course, the same logic implies the possibility of a *change* of perspective. If I am talking about sending you a message, I adopt your perspective as the recipient of the message. But if on the other hand, you are going to send something to me, by the same logic the appropriate perspective on the action should be mine. Such shifts of perspective in directional elements occur in Tzotzil long-distance communication.

(14) Switching perspective in the use of the directional tal[11]
211   te cajk'opon **talel** ta telefono
          *I'm going to talk (**here**=to where you are) by telephone.*

---

[11] Telephone conversation, from tape t9715a1, LR talking to XR.

212   ati mi o k'usi cavale
      and if you have something to say to me...
213   timi o k'usi catak **tal** mantale
      if you want to send me (**here**=to where I am) a message
214   ak'o mi ja˙ xavalbe li ali jkumpa xune
      you can tell my compadre John.

Similarly, Mamal asks his father back in the village for advice using the same kind of rapid shift of perspective.

(15) "I tell you, and you tell me"[12]

343   k'usi nox tzotz tzotz ta jk'an chk-
      What is very very important for me...
344   chkal **tal** ava˙iik lavie ti-
      *is to tell you (**in this direction**=to where you are) so that you will know*
         ...

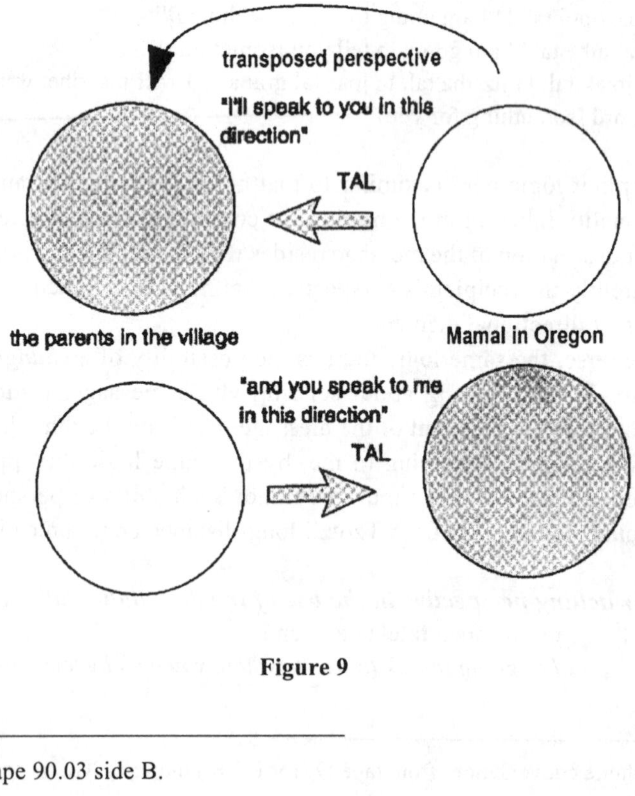

Figure 9

---

[12] From tape 90.03 side B.

347   timi chak avalbekon **tal** jay p'eluk ya`el mi-
        if you want you can tell me (**coming** = to where I am) a few
        words

348   mi: mi lek omi chopol
        (of advice) about whether (what I propose) is good or bad.

One way of understanding these apparent 'switches' of deictic perspective is to analyze the directionals attached to verbs of speaking (and perhaps to verbs of giving) as having lost their deictic force, that is, as being decoupled from the deictic centre of the speech event and re-semanticized with a different sort of perspective. Zinacantec Tzotzil exhibits a number of partially frozen or idiomatic expressions which contain verbs or directionals normally deictically anchored but whose meanings are partly conventionalized and emancipated from such anchoring.

(16) Frozen expressions with pseudo-deixis

imuy **tal** k'ak'al = the days are passing (lit., the day ascends **in this
        direction**)

ta**l**el **bat**el jjol = my thoughts are anarchic (lit., my head is **coming**
        and **going**)

ch**tal** vo` = it's going to rain (literally, the rain is **coming**)

ta j**yu**les ta jjol = it occurs to me that ...(lit., I make **arrive** [**here**] to
        my head)

chk'**ot** ta jchikin = I hear [rumours] (lit., they **arrive there** at my ears)

yu`un cha**bat** ta abtel, yu`un ja` to chasut **tal** ta xmal = if you go to
        work, you will only return **here** to your house late (here =
        your house, where you started from) [said from somewhere
        not 'home']

yak'oj **tal** kajvaltik = what Our Lord has given to **here**, that is, our
        destiny, our fortune

In these expressions the deictic centre of the speech act in which they occur is submerged, cancelled, or substituted by a more abstract, 'virtual' deictic centre.[13] This is, in other words, a conventionalized deictic transposition

---

[13] In Mam (England 1976) what may be analyzed historically as directionally anchored directional particles meaning 'toward here' or 'toward there' have taken on related but more abstract functions indicating, among other things, pronominal arguments to transitive verbs (a "to here" clitic marks a 1st person direct object, for example). Mam has thus carried further than modern Tzotzil a process of conventionalized abstraction from an original deictic perspective to a more grammatical function.

in which what begins as a deictically anchored perspective is harnessed
for other – here semi-grammatical – purposes.

Deictic Transposition in the Discourses of Emigration

There is another kind of deictic transposition in the communications between Oregon and the village back in Chiapas, which involves shifts in
and out of what I have been calling a 'sociocentric' perspective. There are
two notable features to such switching that give it special interest in the
discourses of emigration and dislocation. First, rather than being obligatory it seems to be optional and thus expressive; second, it is asymmetric,
involving changes in Mamal's perspective from his distant location in Oregon, and never appearing in communications to Mamal from his home
village – a tacit recognition of the fact that it is the emigrant who 'moves',
whereas his 'home' stays fixed. In his long-distance conversations between Oregon and Chiapas, Mamal can *choose between* perspectives,
between the physical 'here' of Oregon and the sociocentric 'here' of 'home',
a choice that enables considerable expressive play.

   Indeed, it is highly likely that Mamal will adopt the village of
Nabenchauk as his rhetorical deictic centre rather than the distant place
where he physically finds himself when he invokes images, people, and
activities bound up with his activities and obligations 'at home'. In the
following segment he asks his parents whether they have been to visit his
father-in-law (where his wife and children are living), knowing that the
father-in-law had been away from the village. His use of *yul* 'arrive here'
places him conceptually back home in the village.

(17) "Has my father-in-law arrived?"
>   47   li jni˙ mole mi i**yul** xa ...
>   *Has my father-in-law **arrived (here)**?*
>   48   mi muk' bu ay ak'opon
>   *Haven't you been to talk to him?*

Similarly, a central concern for the dead cousin on his arrival in Oregon,
and subsequently for the dead man's relatives at home, was the debt that
he had left behind in Nabenchauk. Mamal knew that as the lucky survivor
he would be expected to make good on his former companion's obligations and debts, and to this end he arranged to borrow money and have me
deliver it to the village. 'Ta xich' **tal**', he tells a distraught uncle, *'he'll
bring it'*. He continues with a description of my forthcoming movements
which is, from the point of view of normal Tzotzil conversation, deictically

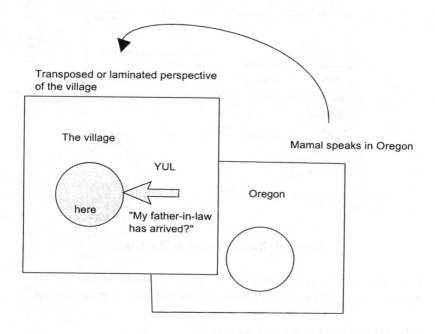

Figure 10: Has my father-in-law arrived?

bizarre, having transposed the perspective to the village while himself remaining physically distant from it.

(18) "I want to come, and he's coming tomorrow" (transposed
   version)

57   bweno vo`one kil ko`on xi**tal** pero k'usi
   *Well, as for me, I would like to **come**, but the thing is ...*

58   ta x- ta x**tal**
   *He's - he's **coming***

59   chlok' **tal** ok'ob
   *He's going to set out **(for here)** tomorrow.*

60   ta x(**y**)**ul** ta martex ta- ta mejiko ali
   *He'll **arrive (here)** to Mexico City on Tuesday,*

61   te la chvay jun ak'ubal ta- ta mejikoe
   and he says he'll sleep overnight in Mexico City.

62   ja` to ta yok'omal stzak **tal** jkot avyon li **chyul** =
   *Then on the next day he'll catch an airplane **in this direction***
   *and **arrive here**,*

63   =**tal**- **chyul**- ...
   *He'll **arrive to here**.*

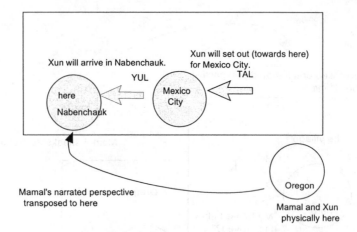

Figure 11: Xun is coming, he'll arrive.

Then, as he professes a *desire* to return to Nabenchauk, he places himself there deictically even as he reaffirms his intention *not* to make the trip.

(19) "How shall I come with no money?"

>   69   ak'o- kil ko`on **ta**likon lavi ya`el uke
>   *Suppose that I really wanted to **come** now, too.*
>   70   pero k'usi chi**tal** o
>   *But how could I **come**?*
>   71   ch'abal to tak'in
>   *I still have no money.*

Over the next few years, Mamal established a pattern in his talk about 'returning' to the village. He would set a date for making such a trip but then continue to postpone it. He would talk about his supposed trip as if he were already in the village, transposing his imagined perspective to that of his interlocutors at home who were expecting him.

(20) "I was going to come for the festival of the patron saint"[14]

>   44   chi**tal** ox ta mayo yu`un ta jk'an ox ja` ox .
>   *I was going to **come** in May, because I had wanted already*
>   45   li`on ta pwersa ta k'ine
>   *to be **here** for the fiesta.*
>   46   pero muk' bu li.**tal** ta k'ine
>   *But I didn't **come** for the fiesta.*

---

[14] From tape 90.03 side B.

47   solel i-
         only . . .
48   i:
49   ta jmala to ox jayibuk k'ak'al
         I was going to wait for just a few days
50   chilok' ox **tal** . tzlajeb xa (li eksamene?)
         Before setting out for here, after my exams [in English classes]
         were over.
51   tzlajeb xa ox li mayoe
         At the end of May.
52   tzlajebtik nan mayo chilok' ox **tal**
         It was going to be about the end of May when I set out for
         here.

On this occasion Mamal had hatched the plan to make the long trip from
Oregon to Chiapas with a small Toyota pickup truck, planning to leave
the vehicle behind in the village as a kind of payment to his father-in-law
for the several years he had by then invested in the care and feeding of
Mamal's five sons. Once again, in his deictic transposition, he adopts the
perspective of those in the village eagerly awaiting their new truck.

(21) "Perhaps I'll bring a truck"
163   ati chi**tal**e:
         If I come
164   bueno
         Well,
165   ta onox x:**yul** ku`un li karo a`a
         *I will surely be able to **bring** the truck, indeed.*
166   porke ak'o onox jtuk xi**tal**
         Because even if I come by myself
167   yu`nox ta x**yul** ta batz'i -
         Certainly I'll be able to get it here in...
168   ta jayib to tajmek k'ak'al
         in a few days [of driving]
169   pero ta ono nan x**yul**
         *but it will certainly **arrive here** sooner or later.*

By 1996 the transposed perspective in Mamal's discourse is firmly en-
trenched, perhaps even conventionalized, not only with the verb
'chajk'opon tal' 'I speak to you (in your direction, towards *here*)' but also
in all talk about trips and movements of others (in the following case, of
the ethnographer himself, as I was travelling to and from the village much
more regularly than was Mamal who only sent messages).

(22) *"Your compadre [i.e., the ethnographer] is travelling frequently"*[15]
    (96.31a)

21   ja' to chajk'oponik **tal** lavie
        *Today I am finally talking to you (in **this direction**)*
23   jk'anbe vokol j'ich' la.kumpareik xun
        This one time I asked a favour of your compadre John
24   x'elan ja' chy**ul**ilan onoxe
        *given that he is **arriving here** all the time..*

The option to adopt this alterocentric or sociocentric perspective, as I have remarked, affords Mamal a delicate expressivity. Moreover, the possibility of so switching to the deictic stance of the village from which he is patently absent makes it possible that the other possible perspective – that of his actual geographic location as speaker, which is normally unmarked and unremarkable, an automatic reflex of the speech situation – can suddenly itself acquire an intentional and contrastive communicative character. That is, if he customarily transposes himself discursively to the perspective of the village, occasionally NOT doing so allows Mamal to anchor himself consciously and expressively in faraway Oregon.

(23) *"I have come here forever, supposedly"*[16]

769   taj kajnile chi'uk nan . mas
        My wife, and perhaps others... ...
771   yu'no nan kapemik . nan
        perhaps they are angry with me
772   chi'uk nan stot sme' xkaltik porke
        and perhaps her parents, too, as we say, because
773   muk' k'usi
        nothing—
774   mu k'usi xka'i ta jmoj
        I have heard nothing from them at all
775   ali
        uh..
776   ti yu'un muk' bu ta j-
        perhaps because I haven't...-
777   mu xa bu ta jtakbe **ech'el** stak'in li jch'amaltake
        *lately I haven't sent them any money **(in that direction)** for
        my children*

---

[15] From tape 96.31 side A.
[16] From tape 90.03 side B.

778   na`tik
       who knows?
779   yu`un nan li**tal** o la
       *because people are saying that I have **come** forever.*

Here the normally unmarked perspective, that of the place where the speaker is, because of its contrast with the possible metaphoric re-centring of perspective on the village at home, begins to sound emphatically marked. 'I am HERE, and NOT there in the village'. Mamal distances himself, with his deictics, from both the village and the hearsay gossip of his in-laws.

He also displays constant ambivalence in his travel plans: while on the one hand reiterating his intention to return to the village, he nonetheless continues to mention the possibility that afterwards he will again travel to Oregon. Whenever he speaks of such a subsequent journey to the USA, he remains firmly anchored in his actual location abroad

(24) "I am going to come [to Oregon] one last time"

822   timi jta **ech'el** jpermiso li` toe
       *If I get permission (to **leave away from**) here...*
823   mu onox nan .
       Perhaps I won't
824   masuk jal chijok'tzaj ta na:
       stay very long at home
825   mu jna`
       I don't know
826   mu to stak' na`el
       There is no way to know yet
828   ti`n batz'i mase
       At the very longest
829   **te** no nan chibuk u oxibuk u k'u cha`al
       *I would stay **there** perhaps two or three months, whatever*
830   yu`nox kalojbetik ko`on ti chisut **tal** otro jtene
       *Because I have been thinking (lit., telling my heart) that I would return **here** one more time*
831   pero jten xa nox
       But just one more time
832   slajeb xa jten chi**tal**
       *That would be the last time I would **come***
833   timi`n tzk'an kajvaltike
       if God wills it
834   entonse
       So then

835   chisut **ech'el** u:n
        *I would return **to there***
836   i mu xa bu chisut **tal**
        *and afterwards I wouldn't return **here** again.*

Ambivalence
Switching Deictic Perspectives

More delicate still in this ambivalent two-step dance are the *deictic switches*
in which Mamal transposes himself discursively between the village and
the distant *Norte*, moving with sometimes dizzying speed from one stance
to another, almost as if he dares not anchor himself too firmly in one or
the other. When his cousin died he was in the terrible dilemma of knowing
that moral expectation in the village would have him accompany his deceased companion home, but at the same time feeling that he had to stay
on in the USA to earn some money after months of planning and expense.
For example, in his initial communications with home, he warned people
in the village that the dead man's cadaver, subjected by *gringo* law to the
horror of an autopsy, had been prepared 'here' for its 'coming home'. He
jumps from the firm anchoring of the 'here' of Oregon to the ambivalent
anchoring of the 'here' of the village to which the body will return.

(25) "The body is prepared" (1988)
108   mi tzk'el ya`el li krixchanotik much'u ch`atine =
        *If the people who wash (the body, i.e., at the Zinacantec fu-
        neral) look at him*
109   =pwes
        well,..
110   ali na`tik mi- mi lek van
        Who knows if they'll be pleased (by what they see)
111   mi chopol ya`el
        or if they'll be unhappy.
112   ali porke **li`to** che`e
        *Because **here**,*
113   tz'akiem xa ch**tal**
        *He will already have been prepared (and dressed) when he
        comes*

Acutely aware of the scandal that will be caused by the fact that he doesn't
return to the village himself with his former companion, Mamal pleads
with his father – who may expect certain hostility from the deceased's
immediate family – to attend the funeral. But he switches between the

verbs 'go' and 'come' in a tortured dance of ambivalence and uncertainty, metaphorically flying back and forth from distant exile to home.

(26) "Please go to the burial"

114   ali abulajanik un
       Well, please
115   **bat**anik me- **bat**anik me ta pwersa **ba** amukik un
       Go, go, you must go to bury him.
116   **bat**anik me **tal**anik me ta pwersa li chk
       Please go; please come, you must-
117   cha**tal** amukike li ali chepe
       -come and bury Chep.

Finally, in the same telephone conversation, he declares his intention *not* to return to the village, withdrawing even further from the suggestion that he 'come home' by recalling the crushing debts from which he fled to the United States in the first place.

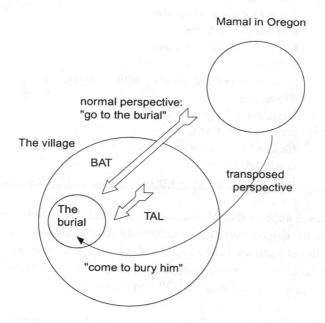

Figure 12

(27) "What shall I come to do?" (switching version)

118   ej i'i nan
       Eh, probably [I will] not [come home now].

119   pero k'usi **tal** jpas un
       But what will I come (i.e., back to the village) to do?

120   yech- yip onox il ta x**tal** jtik' jba noxtok
       I'll just come and get myself stuck in great debts

121   k'usi ta jch'amun **tal** jpasaje nan i
       First I borrow the money to come (i.e., to the north).

122   i luego oy to kiltikotik **te yo`e**
       And then I have debts there (i.e., in the village).

Most ambivalent of all, perhaps, is Mamal's relation with his immediate family: his children and 'their mother'. He is willing to have letters 'brought' to her, but he himself maintains his distance – his distinct origo – for her possible reply.

(28) "A letter for the mother of the kids, and her reply" (switching version)

78   albo ya`el li sme` li unetike
       Tell the mother of the children

79   te ta jtakbe to jlik vun
       I'm going to send her a letter.

80   te- te chich' **tal** li xune
       *John will bring it (**here**—i.e., to the village).*

81   ali xun une
       But as for John [the ethnographer],

82   muk' jal **tey** ta jnatik
       *He won't be **there** in our village for long.*

83   ta ssut **tal** ta ora.
       *He is returning right away (to **here**-i.e., to Oregon).*

Sometimes it appears that Mamal simply does not know how to locate himself in the deictic world the language enforces on his choice of verbs and directional particles. Is he aligned with his village or with his exile in a foreign land? Note, for example, how he speaks about the fabled truck that he has promised to – bring? take? – to the village.

(29) "I will take the truck (of which you have a photo) to here? there?"

187   oy **te** slok'ol nan chib oxib nan chka`i li
       ***There** you have a few photos, I think, perhaps two or three*

189   ali jk'ox pikop li-
       of the little pickup truck

190   li chkik' **ech'el** ta na timi`n yu`un ikich' **talel**
         *that I am going to **take (in that direction)**, if I manage to*
         ***bring it (in this direction)**.*

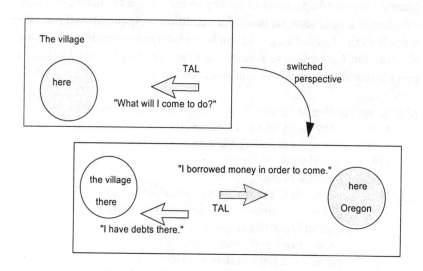

Figure 13: Switching perspectives

In a similar way, he appears to be confused about perspectives when he
thinks about the chance that the letters his parents will send him in response to his requests coincide with his own trip back to Mexico. In the
following fragment, for example, in lines 630-631 Mamal appears to jump
from his deictic centre in Oregon to that of his parents sending their letter
from the village, all within the same utterance.

(30) "Sending replies - but to where?"

626   timi`n muk' bu atakik **tal** ta ora
         *If you don't send me (the reply) to **here** right away.*
627   entonces
         then
628   yik'al nan . mas tz'akal to ch**yul** a-
         *perhaps it will **arrive here** to me afterwards*
629   ch**yul** li vune
         *the letter will **arrive here***
630   mas nan ba`yi chi**k'ot** . ta na vo`on timi yeche
         *But I will have already **arrived there** at home, if so.*
631   pero yan timi atak **ech'el** ta ora
         *On the other hand, if you send it **away** now.*

633   mas lek
        that would be better.

Mamal also sent large sums of money to the village to finance the construction of a new, separate house for his children. Again, Mamal presents
himself as firmly intending to return to the village to work himself on the
construction, but he does so always with a little deictic play that first brings
him close and then distances him from the village.

(31) "I am coming (or going?) to work on the new house"[17]

138   kil to`ox ko`on ya`el sutikon **tal**
        *Before I was feeling like returning to **here**.*
139   ta jk'el ya`el
        I wanted to see
140   timin ch**tal** . ch**bat** stam xa onox abtel **le**` ta na
        *If they were **coming**— **going** to start work **there** on the house.*
141   tzna taj kremotike
        on the house of the boys
142   yulem ox ta jjol mi ci**bat** van xici:
        *It had occurred to me—"Should I **go**?" I thought.*

Short Summary of Deictic Switches over a Decade of Exile

It is possible to quantify the changes in deictic perspective over the first
ten years of Mamal's emigration to Oregon during which he was in more
or less constant, if sporadic, communication with 'home'. If one looks
only at MARKED deictic forms (those specifically linked to the 'here and
now'), and eliminating what I have characterized as conventionalized non-
deictic uses (those associated with verbs of speaking, basically), we can
see a progression in the use of 'sociocentric' deictics that take the village
as the deictic origo as opposed to those in which 'here' is anchored in
Mamal's true geographic location far from the village. Compiling such
marked usages across the full collection of tape recorded telephone conversations and cassette-letters, the statistics are as follows.

    In more qualitative terms, we can analyze Mamal's communications
with his family as a progression of phases or stages. In the earliest exam-

---

[17] From tape 95.15 side A.

ples, from 1988, directly after his arrival in Oregon and the sudden death of his cousin, Mamal was highly ambivalent and uncertain of where he was in the world, or at least of how to represent his position vis-à-vis the village (see examples 25-27). His usage switched back and forth between anchoring his 'here' in the village and in his new surroundings in Oregon.

1988	1990	1994	1996
67%	100%	60%	91%

Table 1: proportion of sociocentric uses of deictically marked verbs and directionals

By 1990 he seemed, on the other hand, to have settled on a stance of closeness to home; his references to 'here' routinely project him as talking from the perspective of the village, as in the following extended passage which sustains a sociocentric perspective throughout.

(32) "I sent money with your compadre"[18]

86	ijtakbe **tal** jlik vun
	I sent a letter (to **here**).
87	chi`uk li- chi`uk lakumpa xune
	with your compadre John [the ethnographer].
88	i: ali tak'in k'u yepal avalojbon to`ox ti .
	and the amount of money that you had told me before
89	sk'oplal cha- chajtakbe **tal**
	*that I should send (to **here**)*
90	omi chkich' ox **tal** ti k'alal- k'al tin **tal**ikon ta =
	*or that I should **bring** you if I were to **come**.*
91	=mayoe
	in May
92	te ijtakbe **tal** li:- lakumpa xune
	*I have sent it along (to **here**) with your compadre John.*
93	te chayak'be
	And he will give it to you.

In 1994-95 Mamal seemed to have fallen into a patterned distance and indifference, in which he emphasized his separation from the village with a higher proportion of deixis centred on his faraway locale.

---

[18] From tape 90.03 side B.

(33) "I sent these words with the wife of your compadre"[19]

20   jay p'el nox k'usi chakalbeik tajmek
          I am going to say a few words to you

21   timin o k'usi . a yatel avo`onik chak'an chavalbeik **tale**
          And if any of you has any worries, and you want to tell them
          *to me (**here**)*

24   ijk'anbe **ech'el** vokol li yajnil li lakumpareik xun
          *I asked a favour of the wife of your compadre John (in **that***
          direction)

25   yu`un chk'ot yak'beik li sinta livi
          *and she will **arrive there** to give you this tape recording*

26   timin oy onox k'u ca`al . tak' **tal** avu`unike
          *and if you want to send something back to **here***

27   tak'bekon **tal**
          *send it to me (in **this direction**).*

Finally, after about a decade in the United States, with only a couple of short visits home, Mamal seems to have adopted again a kind of conventionalized 'closeness' in his deictic usage, talking about his planned and frequently postponed visits to the village as if he were empathetically already there. Indeed, his final remark in this last illustrative segment (34) is a perfect, apparently self-contradictory, expression of his ambivalence about home versus exile – the village versus the adopted world of a foreign land. "(Were it not for the latest of my excuses for NOT returning home) I should be here now", says Mamal in line 90.

(34) "I would be here [in the village] were it not for ..."[20]

82   ti k'u cha`al kalojbeik- lakalbeik komel ava`iik
          As I told you (when I left there)

83   ti k'alal ti li**tale**
          *when I **came***

84   ta ox tzk'an chisut **tal** lavi jabile
          *I had wanted to return **here** again during this year*

85   ti manchuk li x`elan k'usi jpase
          if it were not for what happened to me [a back injury at work]

86   i: ti manchuk i x`elan ijpase
          And if it weren't for what happened to me

87   li**tal** ox yech
          *I would have **come** as planned*

---

[19] From tape 95.15 side A.
[20] From tape 96.31 side A.

88 **lital** ox ta . jtob xchi`uk vaxakib li. li novyembre
I was going to come on the 28th of November
90 **li**`on xa yechuke
*I should be **here** now..*

Postscript

The mechanics of deictic centring may seem a most trivial expression of the negotiation of 'place'. Nonetheless, just as Mamal's movements – both physical and rhetorical – between Chiapas and Oregon are complex, so too his verbs are a sensitive index to his attitudes. We are familiar with the dual face of other indexical signs – T vs. V pronouns, for example, and other markers of deference and social distance and their opposites – both presupposing certain aspects of social context to mark pre-existing relationships and attitudes, and also creatively producing those relationships by, in use, altering and producing contexts. The once novel circumstances of the Zinacantec emigrant, suddenly unimaginably removed from home but at the same time intimately linked to the village, forced Mamal to adapt even the ordinarily most highly presupposing deictic indexes – those having to do with spatial proximity – to the changed communicative circumstances of remoteness and separation. Spatial deixis became a creative vehicle for discursive shifts in virtual location and alliance.

In his later interactions with home, Mamal established somewhat more firmly his distance and indifference: he brought a truck back to Nabenchauk and abandoned it there, but now it is 'his father-in-law's business'. He had a house built in the village for his children (but not for 'their mother'). His sister back home lived through a scandal, but 'what's it to me?' Little by little the telephone calls, the letters and hand-delivered cassettes, and even the money orders began to dry up, and no longer pass through the ethnographer's hands. Mamal was joined in Oregon by another cousin, then most recently by his eldest son, and now other Zinacantecs have begun to make the long and dangerous trek north. People in the village no longer ask after their lost village mates, or do so only rarely, as though the contradiction of being at once 'here' and 'there' is less remarkable, less interesting, less problematic, and perhaps less important than it was when Mamal left with his deceased, dreaming cousin. The next chapters of the history of this Indian emigration must await another telling, as I have here tried only to show that not only bodies and lives are dislocated in the process, but also the indexical devices of grammar itself.

References

Collier, G.A. (1990) 'Seeking Food and Seeking Money: Changing Productive Relations in a Highland Mexican Community', Discussion paper 10, United Nations Research Institute for Social Development, Geneva.

England, N.C. (1976) 'Mam Directionals and Verb Semantics', in M. McClaren (ed.) *Mayan Linguistics* (pp. 202-211), UCLA, American Indian Studies Center.

Fillmore, C. (1966) 'Deictic Categories in the Semantics of Come', *Foundations of Language* 2:219-227.

------ (1975) 'Santa Cruz Lectures on Deixis', Bloomington: Indiana Univ. Linguistics Club.

Hanks, W.F. (1984) 'The Evidential Core of Deixis in Yucatec Maya', in J. Drogo, V. Mishra and D. Testen (eds.) *CLS 20: Papers from the Twentieth Regional Meeting of the Chicago Linguistics Society*:154-72.

------ (1990) *Referential Practice,* Chicago: University of Chicago Press.

------ (1996) 'Language Form and Communicative Practice', in J. Gumperz and S. C. Levinson (eds.) *Rethinking Linguistic Relativity* (pp. 232-270), Cambridge: Cambridge University Press.

Haviland, J.B. (1977) *Gossip, Reputation and Knowledge in Zinacantan,* Chicago: University of Chicago Press.

------ (1990) 'The Grammaticalization of Space (and Time) in Tzotzil', Working Paper Number 2, Cognitive Anthropology Research Group at the Max Planck Institute for Psycholinguistics, Nijmegen, The Netherlands.

------ (1991) 'Projections, Transpositions, and Relativity', Paper prepared for Wenner-Gren conference on Rethinking Linguistic Relativity, Ocho Rios, May 3-11, 1991, Working Paper: Cognitive Anthropology Research Group, Nijmegen.

----- (1993) 'The syntax of Tzotzil Auxiliaries and Directionals: The grammaticalization of "motion"', *Proceedings of the Nineteenth Annual* Meeting of the Berkeley Linguistics Society: Special Session on *Syntactic Issues in Native American Languages:* 35-49.

------ (1996) 'Projections, Transpositions, and Relativity', in J.J. Gumperz and S.C. Levinson (eds.) *Rethinking Linguistic Relativity* (pp. 271-323), Cambridge: Cambridge University Press.

Laughlin, R.M. (1977) *Of Cabbages and Kings: Tales from Zinacantan,* Washington D.C.: Smithsonian Institution.

Mateo-Toledo, B. (2004) 'Directional Markers in Q'anjob'al (Maya): Their Syntax and Interaction with Aspectual Information', Qualifying paper, Dept. of Linguistics, University of Texas at Austin.

Rus, J. and S. Guzmán López (1996) *Jchi'iltak ta Slumal Kalifornia,* San Cristobal de las Chiapas: INAREMAC

Taylor, C. (1985) 'The Person', in M. Carrithers, S. Collins and S. Lukes (eds.) *The Category of the Person* (pp. 257-281), Cambridge: Cambridge University Press.

In and Out of Class, Codes and Control
Globalization, Discourse and Mobility

JAN BLOMMAERT, *Ghent University, Belgium*

Introduction

This paper intends to address a theoretical issue, that of the connections between speech resources and place, and consequently between speech resources and mobility. Mobility is here to be understood as the potential to make specific speech resources function more or less adequately across different spaces, physical ones as well as social ones (and the two usually coincide). While addressing the main issue, I also hope to demonstrate some other points. First, I hope to show, through the use of a particular kind of data (South African radio DJ talk), how narrative coheres with other speech genres and can indeed often hardly be extracted from wider complex speech events including, in this particular case, conversation and role-play. I intend to show how the analysis of narrative – seen here as a particular mode of formal structuring in talk – with a focus on its embedding in larger speech events and modes of talk can have some analytic purchase.

Second, I hope to show how the deployment of particular resources can be thematically organized – Goffman's 'frames' come to mind here as a valuable metaphor (Goffman, 1974). People organize speech by means of intricate correlations between speech forms – linguistic and communicative resources – and speech topics, themes or domains, and there is suggestive evidence that this phenomenon of speech topics narrowly connected to the deployment of specific resources could be the most tangible and empirically demonstrable level of identity-in-action (see Maryns and Blommaert, 2001; Maryns, this volume; Blommaert, 2004:chapter 8). At this level of situated individual identity articulations, we see complexes of thematically organized patterns of speech, displaying delicate subjective orientations towards the topic and the relational frame dominating the communicative event. People construct their identities through orientations to topics and interlocutors, and small shifts in topic development generate shifts in the orientation towards interlocutors, and are expressed in shifts in speech style or genre. Identities, therefore, come in *packages* of delicately organized, shifting orientations towards particular topics and interlocutors. People speak differently, formally as well as in terms of voice – what sort of individual speaks – depending on whether they speak about love or about business and depending on who they talk to about these topics.

The overarching concern here, as in other papers in this volume, is to come to terms with the theoretical challenges offered by globalization phenomena to discourse theory (see also Chouliaraki and Fairclough, 1999). It is obvious that the introduction of the world as a context for the use of language (the logical consequence of globalization) compels us to face a number of difficult, sometimes embarrassing theoretical issues. One such issue is the impact of 'global' formats and resources on 'local' speech economies and the effects this has on locally valid patterns of function, value-attribution and distribution of resources (Blommaert, 2005), in itself an ingredient of a wider complex of phenomena that relate to the problematic, more muddled production of 'locality' in the context of globalization (Appadurai, 1996). I believe we need to see language in globalization as a general, global system marked by inequalities that operate at various levels. Immanuel Wallerstein's world systems analysis is an important source of inspiration for this (Wallerstein, 1983, 2000, 2001). Wallerstein argues, amongst other things, for the fundamental interconnectedness of phenomena operating in different places in the world, in which developments in one part have effects on developments in other parts. He also argues for the existence of 'core' regions and 'peripheries' in the world, with systemic forms of inequalities governing traffic across them. Thus English from the 'core' – British or US. accents – will be seen to be 'better' than English from the 'peripheries' – African, Indian or other varieties. Belgians will spend enormous efforts acquiring an American accent in English; no Belgian will make any effort to acquire a Nigerian or a Pakistani variety of English. And the variety of English that buys one a ticket into the middle class in Nairobi may be a variety that generates stigma in London or New York. The value of resources is dependent on where the resource 'comes from', and this is not an accidental but a systemic feature.

This is a sociolinguistic problem, but it has an obvious impact on our capacity to analyze chunks of discourse and narrative, and the more we think about globalization the more we will need to look for a closer connection between sociolinguistic insights and discourse or narrative analysis. I will argue below that one of the effects is difference in mobility. Some resources, when introduced, seem to offer a different semiotic potential than others. The introduction of vernacular varieties of English as widespread lingua francae in Africa for instance, has resulted in an increased mobility for those who have access to these varieties, while it has also reduced the mobility of those who do not have access to them. Endogenous African languages, now perhaps more than before, 'fix' people in particular places, while access to varieties of English offers enormous potential for moving across physical spaces as well as across social spaces, by imbuing specific identities attributed to the use of English (Blommaert, 2003). We are perhaps facing a new dimension of the old Bernsteinian connection between class, codes and control here (Bernstein, 1971; see also Bourdieu, 1991 and Hymes, 1996), one in which such locally operating relations are defined, determined or modulated by transnational developments leading to a reordering of repertoires and their internal structure, and thus reshaping the patterns through which particular codes come to index status and prestige.

The empirical key to understanding these phenomena, as suggested above, is indexicality. Indexicality covers non-referential aspects of meaning, connecting linguistic forms to contextual attributes such as social position, status, frames or universes of meaning (Silverstein, 1977, 1985, 1992; Ochs, 1990, 1992). An utterance such as "this theme is the *basso continuo* of this study" invokes referential and contextual worlds that have to do with academic genres and identities, knowledgeability in classical music, hence intellectual and cultural elite identities, all articulated through particular indexical links between the utterances and contextual worlds (e.g. the recognition of the term *basso continuo* as derived from the world of classical music). Indexicalities are eminently social and cultural, and they are stratified. The utterance above suggests elite identities because of stratified associations between elements in the utterance and (perceptions of) elites in society. This connection between indexicalities and social structure or cultural conventions is what makes them 'ideological' (Woolard and Schieffelin, 1994; see also Kroskrity, 2000). Whenever we communicate, we orient to such a stratified complex of indexicalities, distinguishing between 'good' and 'bad' possible resources, and packaging our utterance in a complex of social and cultural attributions.

This paper will look into the way in which globalized resources affect a local semiotic economy and offer specific identity opportunities, convertible into and articulated through particular discursive moves. The paper will differ perhaps in two ways from the other papers in this book: (a) it will address 'placing' rather than 'dislocation', in the sense that I shall focus on the ways in which translocal resources become localized and are being made locally meaningful; this in turn allows for indexicalities of localization and movement – where one is from, where one has moved into, and so on; (b) as noted earlier, I shall use 'atypical' data: the data are mass-mediated interactional data in which micro-narratives are embedded as part of a general characterized by intensive shifting between speech styles and genres. To these data I now turn.

The World System in Action

The data I shall investigate are a fragment from a radio show on UCT Radio, the radio station operated from the University of Cape Town, South Africa. The show is a Reggae programme, deejayed by a young man who calls himself Ras Pakaay. It is a call-in show and listeners can request particular songs. The show was broadcast on Sunday afternoons, and this recording was made in December 2000.

We are facing a rather typical globalization product here: a mass-media format in which one of the transnational globalized art forms *par excellence*, Reggae music, originating in the Caribbean, is staged in Cape Town, the Southern tip of Africa. In Appadurai's terminology, the data instantiate the new global mediascapes that provide "large and complex repertoires of images, narratives, and ethnoscapes to their viewers through-out the world" (Appadurai, 1996:35). The audience is a mixed one, composed of both black and white South Africans from the Cape Town region, most of them rather young. And the show is done in English, though, as we shall see this is far from a simple proposition.

I will focus in my discussion on the issue of *identity as semiotic po-tential*. We shall see how globalization offers tremendous discursive opportunities for the deejay and his listeners, and how the deejay can move across various thematic spaces by means of a variety of discursive shifts that also indicate shifts in identity. The discursive shifts involve shifts in topic, genre (i.e. recognizable complexes of stylistic features), orientation (or 'stance', see Biber and Finegan, 1989) and voice (i.e. the particular position or role from which one speaks). The participants (and in particu-lar Ras Pakaay) talk as different individuals through such shifts, and what happens (or can happen) in one genre or on one topic depends on the relative contrasts with what happened (or can happen) in other parts or on other topics. Note that all these shifts occur *simultaneously*, and that dis-tinctions between topic, genre, stance and voice will fade as we delve deeper into the analysis of the data.

Let us have a look at the transcript first. There are four parts in the fragment. The fragment begins with Ras Pakaay commenting on the song he just played (part 1). Next, he engages in anecdote telling, which will be rendered in the transcript by an ethnopoetic organization of the lines (part 2). After that he enters into a telephone conversation with a female listener (part 3). A conflict occurs, and Ras Pakaay terminates the phone conver-sation (part 4).

Ras Pakaay uses at least four identifiable linguistic varieties in the fragment: 'Standard English', 'Black English', 'Township English' and

'Rasta Slang'. I use scare quotes for these varieties, because they have to be seen and understood in terms of local repertoires, accents and potential for realization. Thus, the 'Standard English' utterances bear a marked South-African black accent, and the 'Black English' varieties (imitations of hip-hop North American black accents) also sound eminently South-African. When Ras Pakaay shifts into Rasta Slang, we hear an attempt towards producing Jamaican Creole accents, blended with some 'typical' Rasta lexemes. In the transcript, I will use Roman for the 'Standard English' fragments, italics for the 'Black English' parts, and bold to indicate 'Rasta Slang'. There is a one-word shift into 'Township English', which I mark in Courier. I will also provide glosses in phonetic script for heavily marked utterances.

{music}

Part 1
 R. definite he is.
 I'm a noossssssmoke [smo:k]
 No chronic to bother no one [no kronik. tu bo:də nowa ʃ]..
 but=I man [maɲ]. ..

 Yes: my brethren.
 you must {laughin voice} <u>ha= ( ) with a smoke [smoᵃk] you know=</u>
 I had a smoke [smo:k]
 <u>I tell you my brethren</u> {end laughin voice}.
{style shift}
 While it =am. time is=has goneh twelve minutes pas the hour of five o'clock
 on UCT radio wonderful point five fm studio .

Part 2
{style shift}
 <u>I just had a brethren right</u> **now [no:ʷ].**
 <u>he's actually calling</u> **all the way [o:l dᵊ we:ᵃ]** *from* (Heideveld [hiᵃ:dᵊ feld])
 I say
   yo Ras Pakaai gone to heave'.
   *Bush *Band
 an=I say
   <u>my brethren I do have</u> **Budj Band**
 and I say ↓yo.
   Why do wanna come live on air
 I said allright allright allright

and then az' I was preparing to pu' the man [man] 'pon line.
the man [maɲ] got *cut [kot] off with Ras Pakaai.

but then on that very same **note [noªt]**
beautiful listeners of this=e show
we have. a caller on the line {technical sound}
..

Part 3
cottin edge hoi

F.   hello?

R.   hello yo live on air [ɛ:]

F.   OK

R.   yea who'm I speaking to everythin is all right thanks and how 'bout you?

F.   yeah I'm fine

R.   yeah. an=

F.   *(=   vilukazi)*

R.   hehehe *vilukazi mlan*GINI. everythin is all right. I know you're calling from **all the way [o:l dǝ we:ª]** .what am calling now **all the way [o' :l dᵉ we:ª]** from **Khayelitsha [koyᵉlisha]** is that right

F.   yeah

R.   allright..how may I help you

F.   yeah OK I would like to uhm if you just wanted(ed) to play mh. this song for *me please

R.   What song you'd like me to play for you

F .   [= by Luciano

R.   by? Luciano

F.   [=yeah

R.   well. I don know what's happenin' with Luciano today.. Ehm what a song you'd like me to play for you

F.   =Kiss me again=ja

R.   **Kiss me again olmos' I gat Jah.** I'm definitely gonna play that song for you my sisterene allright?. And who'd you like me to play the song for

F.   for ↑my*se:lf

R.   for yourself?.   Oh really. hahahahha an you=

F.   yeah   =what you *laughin
                                          {laughing voice} at me (about)?

R.   ehhr?

Part 4

F.   why you laughing at me?

R.   no I'm not laughin'

my sisterene otherwise [a:dɑwais] I thaught you would ehm actually want to play the song.. or want me to play the song for
somebody else or:. for some people **dem** seen?

F.   =just for myself

R.   =just for yourself.. so you just sitting at home?

F.   yeah

R.   =listenin' to reggae music. with Ras Pakaai on UCT radio

F.   yeah

R.   ([kom tru yu]) my sisterene sha me do dat (   ) all right?

F.   okay

R.   yeah give thanks [tʃanks]

F.   (   )

R.   {laughing} thanks for callin my sisterene all right?. and=e keep
dem things under control [kᵉntroⁿl]. I don know

{jingle}

Let us take a closer look at what happens in this fragment. The first thing
we notice is the connection between shifts in linguistic varieties and specific parts in the fragment. The connection appears to be mainly thematic.
Whenever Ras Pakaay talks about the world of Reggae – song lyrics, Rasta
values and atmosphere – he shifts into Rasta Slang. We see this in part 1
when he recaps the theme of the song he just played; in referring to the
place where the listeners' calls are made from (Heideveld and Khayelitsha,
both Townships in Cape Town) in parts 2 and 3; the song title the female
caller has requested in part 3, and of course towards the end of part 4. The
anecdote he tells in part 2 is predominantly in Black English, though some
lexical shifts into Rasta Slang occur ("Budj band"), and the telephone
conversation with the girl as well as the announcements of the time and
the station are predominantly in Standard English.

These are relatively general correspondences which should not ob-
scure the finer shifts occurring in several parts. *Part 1* starts in Standard
English, then a shift occurs into Rasta Slang when Ras Pakaay quotes
from the song lyrics. A third shift occurs immediately afterwards: the song
just played was about smoking marihuana, and Ras Pakaay confesses to
his listeners that he too has had 'a smoke'. He produces this confession in
Black English and with a giggling voice and a dragging intonation, suggesting a slightly intoxicated state of mind. But then a fourth shift occurs:
Ras Pakaay shifts into Standard English again, and produces a formulaic,
rapidly spoken statement on the time, identifying his radio station.

Part 2 starts with a style shift. Ras Pakaay shifts back into Black English mixed with markedly Rasta Slang lexemes, slows down the pace of
his speech, and starts placing strong sentence stress on certain words,

using creaky voice. He tells an anecdote of a man who called him during the previous song with a request. When Ras Pakaay asked him to come live on air, the line was cut off. We see shifts into Rasta Slang in 'right now' and in 'all the way from Heideveld', as well as in the reference to the Reggae group requested by the caller ("Bush Band"). A final, small shift occurs towards the end, in 'that very same note', after which Ras Pakaay engages in another activity: announcing a caller on the line. This announcement is made in Standard English.

Parts 3 and 4 are the most complex parts. In *part 3* Ras Pakaay welcomes the caller in Black English ('yo live on air') but then shifts into Standard English. The caller mentions her name and Ras Pakaay repeats it. He continues in Standard English but shifts shortly afterwards into Rasta Slang, when he mentions the place where the caller is from. The utterance here is identical to the one he produced earlier in part 2: "all the way down from [place]". The conversation goes on from there in Standard English. The girl requests a song title, which Ras Pakaay reiterates in Rasta Slang ('kiss me again olmos' I gat Jah'). He then asks who the song is for, and the girl answers that it is a song she wants to have played for herself. There is surprise in her voice when she gives her answer: a strong stress on the second syllable of 'myself', and a lengthened, dragging vowel in the second syllable: "my*se:lf". Ras Pakaay starts laughing, and this is where a small conflict emerges: the girl giggles and asks him "what you *laughin at me (about)?" reverting the question-answer pattern established during the conversation.

Part 4 is the conflict-and-repair sequence prefaced towards the end of part 3. Ras Pakaay did not catch the girl's question and the girl reiterates it, in a flat and serious intonation. The sequence, thus far, is in Standard English. Ras Pakaay responds in a very serious, flat and declarative intonation, and he responds at length. Two small shifts occur: a one-word shift ('otherwise') into Township English – a markedly different accent from the Standard English one thus far used by Ras Pakaay, and a one-word shift into Rasta Slang in 'dem'. The girl reacts, and there is a brief, friendly exchange between Ras Pakaay and the girl in Standard English. He then mentions "listenin' to Reggae music on UCT radio", and this triggers both a style shift and a code shift into Rasta Slang. Ras Pakaay shifts gear, speaks faster and in an excited voice, and produces Slang phrases such as "kom tru yu", "give thanks" and "keep dem things under control".

There is dense stylization going on in this fragment, and if we introduce space into the analysis, we may get a clearer picture of that. The finer correspondences between shifts and discourse functions can be related to an iconic pattern of spatial and identity features. Several such spaces and identities are at play here:

1. There is, first, an identity of *Reggae deejay* at play, connected to a transnational, globalized cultural space, that of Reggae and Rastafarianism. Ras Pakaay iconicizes this space and identity through shifts into Rasta Slang. This variety connects his discourse to the globalized genres. The same goes for Black English. The use of a particular intonation contour, some lexemes such as 'yo' and some grammatical patterns ('why do wanna come live on air') connect his speech to transnational 'Gangsta English' and hip-hop culture. He speaks *in* South Africa, but not *from* South Africa. He uses the voice of an international black youth culture. But this voice is also a *masculine* voice: the talk produced in these varieties is distinctly 'tough' and 'virile', with references to illegal behaviour (smoking mari-huana). So space, identity, linguistic variety and style come in one package here.

2. Another space is *UCT radio*, the radio station of the University of Cape Town. This is the space of mass-media appealing to an (in principle) undifferentiated audience-at-a-distance. Furthermore, and here we delve into the micro-geography of the Cape Town area, it is not just any radio station but UCT Radio. UCT is an affluent university predominantly populated by upper middle-class white students. Its campus is on the slopes of Table Mountain on an estate donated by Cecil Rhodes, overlooking the 'Cape Flats' plain with the Townships of Heideveld and Khayelitsha. Ras Pakaay is probably a student at UCT, and his being black makes him a member of a privileged minority of black students who obtained a place at this prestigious university. Here, we also enter the realm of the history of class stratification in South Africa: the identity articulated here is a *class identity* and Standard English iconicizes this class identity. As with everywhere in the peripheries of the world, Standard English is a rare commodity in South Africa, tightly controlled both by patterns of race stratification and by patterns of access that often have to do with education trajectories. Standard English marks this elite space, and Ras Pakaay systematically uses it whenever he refers to UCT radio. He also uses it as his 'default' code in the interaction with the girl. The style he uses in this variety is 'neutrally' conversational: it is a friendly yet non-egalitarian (elite) code.

3. A third space is again connected to the micro-geography of the Cape Town area. The girl is from Khayelitsha, a black, poor Township in

the Cape Flats where Xhosa-speakers predominate. This is a third space: that of *the black Townships*. The girl triggers the identity categorizations here by spontaneously giving her (ethnically marked) name to Ras Pakaay. She metaphorically drags Ras Pakaay out of his elite UCT space as well as out of the (equally exclusive) transnational Reggae space, and drags him into the Township which, in all likelihood, is his space of origin. This micro-movement (a micro-dislocation, one could say) has class dimensions: the girl ascriptively identifies Ras Pakaay as a *black South African man from the Townships*, thus denying the asymmetries previously established by Ras Pakaay's use of elite and exclusive codes, Standard and Black English and Rasta Slang. Another probable aspect of this is *gender*: Ras Pakaay finds himself in a male-female conflict (the girl challenges his presupposition that it is an unexpected thing that a girl requests a song 'for herself'), which needs to be repaired by reverting to 'original', 'authentic' codes. Ras Pakaay obviously gets drawn into this: in trying to repair the conflict with the girl, he briefly lapses into Township English ('otherwise'). Ras Pakaay is twice made to speak 'from within the Township', once when he responds to the girl's name, another time when he shifts into Township English in order to repair the conflict. But interestingly, in order to get out of the conflict (and out of the Township, in a micro-relocation), he shifts into the asymmetrical codes again, Standard English and Rasta Slang. He moves back into the privileged, safe spaces over which he has full control: that of his elite university and that of the globalized Reggae world.

The delicate shifts, mobilizing complex multilingualism as well as a range of generic and stylistic resources, appear to be governed by orientations to space. These spaces organize the particular indexical order that steers the deployment of elements from the multilingual repertoires. We see orientations to transnational centres as well as to social spaces within South Africa, all in one fragment. Thus, all kinds of scales are interlocked here: some utterances orient to large-scale, globalized complexes and forms of mobility therein, while others orient towards small-scale, local complexes and evoke micro-mobility across these complexes (e.g. from the Townships to UCT). We also see stratification: the transnational and national elite codes clearly afford better opportunities for Ras Pakaay to conduct his preferred business, and the space of strict linguistic, ethnic and class 'origins' is dispreferred. In short, we see the hierarchies of the world system simultaneously at work in this one small fragment, including distinctions between centres – transnational Reggae culture and local elite membership – and peripheries – the black Township.

This stratification is an effect of both local South African (even Cape Town) dynamics as well as transnational ones, and of slow processes (the spread of transnational cultural genres such as Reggae, and the commercialization of such genres in a worldwide media industry) as well as of faster ones (e.g. the presence of a black Township boy at UCT, which is an effect of the disappearance of Apartheid). These developments result in semiotic potential for Ras Pakaay: a potential to produce fine-grained distinctions in identities organized in a repertoire, and to deploy them strategically in interaction. The identities produced here defy simple categorization: we are facing delicate shifts that include cultural, class, gender and ethnic aspects occurring in a variety of combinations. Ras Pakaay speaks in a very masculine, dominating voice whenever he speaks Black English and Rasta Slang; this outspoken masculinity disappears as soon as he shifts into Standard English, but he still remains a member of an elite class; this elite identity vanishes as soon as he engages in the conversation with the girl, who proves to be a member of his geographical, ethnic and social 'group-of-origin'. We are confronted with packages of identity features occurring in a variety of permutations, and all indexed by big and small discursive shifts. These shifts, it should be stressed, are not merely forms of code-switching. The shifting from one linguistic variety into another is part of a bigger package which includes shifts in the space from which one speaks, identity shifts and style shifts.

In theoretical terms, what we have encountered here can be summarized as stylization (in the sense of Rampton, 1999 – the deployment of a wide variety of stylistic resources creating both meaning and subjectivity), but within a *polycentric and stratified system* which defines both the repertoires of speakers and the indexical validity of moves in discourse (see Blommaert, 2005; Blommaert, Collins and Slembrouck, 2004a, 2004b). The material mobilized in this stylization process is astonishing in scope and variety. This is in accordance with Rampton's emphasis on the 'unpredictable mobility' of linguistic resources in view of identity effects. At the same time, these resources display *different* effects, depending on their connections with particular – ordered – indexicalities. That the transnational and local elite codes carry more weight than the strictly local ones should be no surprise, even if for instance Rasta Slang would have little purchase in social life outside the niche of Rasta subcultures, and even if all of this has to be seen as tied to local, South African value-scales. There is structure and stratification in this mobility.

A second theoretical implication is that 'identity' becomes a matter of details. Large categories such as 'male' versus 'female', 'black' versus 'white', 'upper class' versus 'lower class' and so on only tell part of the story. What occurs in discursive work are delicately organized packages of identity features indexed in talk, with rather intensive shifting between such packages, which are infinitely small in the eyes of the analyst but may be very important to the participants in the interaction. The performance of identity is not a matter of articulating *one* identity, but of the mobilization of a whole *repertoire* of identity features converted into complex and subtle moment-to-moment speaking positions.

Discussion

Let us now return to the general argument. One of the effects of globalization in the field of language is the reordering of local repertoires due to the influx of translocal, often transnational semiotic resources such as English, Rasta Slang and Reggae music. Such resources do not enter an empty space. They enter an already existing sociolinguistic system (Hymes, 1996) filled with codes and indexicalities, forms of normativity, established and recognizable genres and styles. Thus what happens is not the creation of something completely new (as is often suggested in literature on Linguistic Human Rights, where the influx of English is seen as the import of alien value-systems that remain intact) but the reorganization of existing 'orders of indexicality' – stratified patterns of social meanings often called 'norms' or 'rules', to which people orient when communicating – (Blommaert, 2003, 2005), in which – to summarize a complex process – English, Rasta Slang and so on become *local* resources, embedded in local patterns of value-attributions and potential for identity-construction and sense-making. This explains why what can pass as 'good' (standard) English in Nairobi may not be seen as such in London or New York: the variety of English is 'good' *in Nairobi*, and it offers its users opportunities for semiotic work *there*, within the locally valid economies of signs and meanings. Thus, Ras Pakaay could pass as an expert user of Rasta slang, even if he would by no means qualify as an expert speaker of Jamaican Creole, and even if his utterances display a marked African accent. The Rasta Slang he produces is recognizable *as Rasta Slang,* carrying the full package of attributions given to it and thus as marking an identity of Reggae expert *in Cape Town*, and that is what counts.

To some extent, this process implies the dislocation of globalized resources such as English, Rasta Slang and so forth. These resources are 'taken out' of their (perceived) original indexical frames, normative forms and so on, and get inserted into local economies and orders of indexicality. Thus, it involves the reallocation of value, or the localization of function, of semiotic resources often seen as 'superior', monolithic and stable. This imagery definitely applies to many widespread views on English in the world, but also for particular modes of language production such as literacy, to which we also often ascribe a particular, presumably stable set of functions and indexicalities. It is the reverse of processes more often observed and commented upon, in which 'inferior' resources – minority languages, substandard codes, grassroots literacy – meet orders of indexicality based on the sociolinguistics of 'superior' resources such as European languages and fully developed literacy (see, for example Hymes, 1996; Gumperz, 1982; Street, 1995).

Both processes operate simultaneously and they provide the basic sociolinguistic layer from which people engage in discourse activities. They converge in particular, globalized speech genres such as the African asylum seeker's narrative produced for Belgian asylum officials (Maryns, this volume; Blommaert, 2001), where 'localized' varieties of English, French or other lingua francae are being used to translocally produce meanings. This is where we see that *mobility* is the issue, rather than the features of particular codes: the asylum seeker's problem – the fact that he appears to control 'inferior' resources – stems from the transfer of his particular variety of English or French to Belgium – a move in space, not in linguistic variety. His French may be perfectly adequate in Kinshasa or Kigali, but it does not work in Brussels. The resource that offers tremendous potential in one place proves to be a clumsy, even endangering instrument elsewhere. Consequently, this is where we see that we need a broader framework to talk about discourse nowadays, one that includes space and mobility as central analytic tools.

This may lead us towards infinitely more refined images of what people do with language and what language does to people. As seen in the previous section, the import of transnational resources and their insertion into existing sociolinguistic systems results in tremendously complex forms of shifting across repertoires, and it results in highly intricate moves in discourse in which shifts across language varieties correspond to shifts in genre, speaking position, stance, style and identity. I have tried to illustrate this complexity as well as its purchase for analysis and theoretical reflection through the choice of data in which several genres co-occurred. It is the connection between the deployment of resources in conversation, announcing or other genres on the one hand, and narrative on the other, that shows us the particular indexical value of the resources deployed in either one of these genres. Storytelling usually co-exists with several other genres in a speaker's repertoire, and understanding the particular codes of storytelling may benefit much from a look at the *modus operandi* of resources in other genres. It is a point made by Dell Hymes many years ago: what we may need is a description of sociolinguistic systems under-pinning descriptions of specific speech activities that develop within them. The interesting thing is that various aspects of such a system often co-occur in our data. The remarkable thing is how often we overlook them.

Acknowledgements

Parts of this paper are based on chapter 8 of Blommaert (2005), a book I was able to write during my tenure as a visiting professor at the Depart-ment of Anthropology, University of Chicago in the winter of 2003. I am grateful to Michael Silverstein, Jim Collins, Ben Rampton, Elif Yalabik, Dell Hymes and Chris Bulcaen for comments on the draft and for stimu-lating discussions on the main lines of the argument developed here. I am also grateful to Anna De Fina and Mike Baynham for being vigorous yet compassionate editors.

References

Appadurai, A. (1996) *Modernity at Large: Cultural Dimensions of Globalization*, Minneapolis: University of Minnesota Press.

Bernstein, B. (1971) *Class, Codes and Control, Vol. 1: Theoretical Studies Towards a Sociology of Language*, London: Routledge.

Biber, D. and E. Finegan (1989) 'Styles of Stance in English: Lexical and Grammatical Marking of Evidentitality and Affect', *Text* 9/1:93-124 (special issue on *The Pragmatics of Affect*, edited by Elinor Ochs).

Blommaert, J. (2001) 'Investigating Narrative Inequality: African Asylum Seekers' Stories in Belgium', *Discourse & Society* 12/4:413-449.

------ (2003) 'Situating Language Rights: English and Swahili, in Tanzania Revisited' Paper, *Annual Meeting of the AAAL* , Arlington VA, March 2003 (also on http://africana.UGent.be)

------ (2005) *Discourse: A Critical Introduction*, Cambridge: Cambridge University Press.

------, J. Collins, and S. Slembrouck (2004a) 'Spaces of Multi-lingualism', *Working Papers in Language, Power and Identity 18* (http://bank.ugent.be/lpi/)

------ (2004) 'Polycentricity and Interactional Regimes in "Global Neighborhoods"', *Working Papers in Language, Power and Identity 19* (http://bank.ugent.be/lpi/)

Bourdieu, P. (1991) *Language and Symbolic Power*, Cambridge: Polity Press.

Chouliaraki, L. and N. Fairclough (1999) *Discourse in Late Modernity: Rethinking Critical Discourse Analysis*, Edinburgh: Edinburgh University Press.

Goffman, E. (1974) *Frame Analysis: An Essay on the Organization of Experience*, Boston: Northeastern University Press.

Gumperz, J. (1982) *Discourse Strategies*, Cambridge: Cambridge University Press.

Hymes, D. (1996) *Ethnography, Linguistics, Narrative Inequality: Toward an Understanding of Voice*, London: Taylor & Francis.

Kroskrity, P. (ed.) (2000) *Regimes of Language*, Santa Fe: SAR Press.

Maryns, K. and J. Blommaert (2001) 'Stylistic and Thematic Shifting as a Narrative Resource: Assessing Asylum Seekers' Repertoires', *Multilingua* 20/1:61-84.

Ochs, E. (1990) 'Indexicality and Socialization', in J. Stigler, R. Schweder and G. Herdt (eds.) *Cultural Psychology* (pp. 287-308), Cambridge: Cambridge University Press.

------ (1992) 'Indexing Gender', in A. Duranti and C. Goodwin (eds.) *Rethinking Context* (pp. 335-358), Cambridge: Cambridge University Press.

Rampton, B. (1999) 'Deutsch in Inner London and the Animation of an Instructed Foreign Language', *Journal of Sociolinguistics* 3:480-504.

Silverstein, M. (1977) 'Cultural Prerequisites to Grammatical Analysis' in M. Saville-Troike (ed.) *Linguistics and Anthropology (GURT 1977)* (pp.

139:151), Washington DC: Georgetown University Press.

------ (1985) 'Language and the Culture of Gender: At the Intersection of Structure, Usage, and Ideology', in E. Mertz and R. Parmentier (eds.) *Semiotic Mediation* (pp. 219-259), New York: Academic Press.

------ (1992) 'The Indeterminacy of Contextualization: When is Enough Enough?', in P. Auer and A. Di Luzio (eds.) *The Contextualization of Language* (pp. 55-76), Amsterdam: John Benjamins.

Street, B. (1995) *Social Literacies*, London: Longman.

Wallerstein, I. (1983) *Historical Capitalism*, London: Verso.

------ (2000) *The Essential Wallerstein*, New York: The New Press.

------ (2001) *Unthinking Social Science* (second edition), Philadelphia: Temple University Press.

Woolard, K. and B. Schieffelin (1994) 'Language Ideology', *Annual Review of Anthropology* 23:55-82.

Working with Webs

Narrative Constructions of Forced Removal and Relocation

KAY McCORMICK, *University of Cape Town, South Africa*

> "... as a general rule we don't just live lines, moving inexorably through one thing after another, we live spirals of remembrance and return, repetition and reconfiguration, under the spell of ... mythopoeic desire". (Freeman 1998:47)

This chapter explores ways in which such lines and spirals are inscribed in a set of narratives dealing with people's lives before and after forced removal from Protea, a neighbourhood in Cape Town, South Africa. Intersections of lines and spirals create a web that, I argue, is evident in the Protea stories at two levels: structure and content. Their web-like structure is congruent with the tellers' construction of the kind of life they value, namely one in which the individual is sustained in a web of familiar and inextricably interrelated social, temporal and spatial practices.

The narratives are autobiographical and, as is always the case with such texts, they are shaped in part by the historical context and the circumstances of their elicitation. I attempt to show the relationships between context, the narrators' concerns, and the structure of the stories.

I start by giving background to the Protea narratives, to the historical period to which they refer, and to the context of their elicitation. I then describe the way in which I worked on them. Thereafter I give a brief account of the theories of time, neighbourhood and narrative upon which I draw in my analysis of the Protea stories. The analysis focuses first on structure and then on representations of life before, during and after the forced removal.

Background to the Protea Narratives

Historical context

During the Apartheid era in South Africa (1948-1994) millions of people were forcibly uprooted from places where they had lived for decades and moved to unfamiliar sites. Typically, they were given no choice about where and among whom they would be relocated. Under the Population Registration Act of 1950 all residents were classified as belonging to what was called a 'race group'. The Group Areas Act, passed in the same year, was then implemented to determine where the duly classified could live and own property. Group Areas designations were not guided by considerations of which 'race group' was already in the majority in an area.[1] Overwhelmingly, the pattern was that blacks[2] were moved out of areas considered desirable by whites. When established communities were moved they were seldom re-housed together, with the result that individuals and families were torn not only from homes and physical neighbourhoods, but also from the social fabric of their communities.

Protea was a small, long-established settlement in an extraordinarily beautiful site between Kirstenbosch Botanical Gardens and Bishopscourt, an upmarket residential area in the Cape Peninsula. It was a working-class pocket in a middle-class area. By the 1960s, many families had been there for three or more generations, working locally as stonemasons, builders, gardeners, flower-sellers and domestic workers as well as in various capacities at the nearby university, the botanical gardens, and the Anglican diocesan estate (from which Bishopscourt derives its name). In 1957 Protea and the surrounding area were declared a 'white group area'. Since the residents of Protea had been classified 'coloured' they were not allowed to continue living there, although there had been no history of bad relations between them and their white neighbours. Between 1964 and 1969 the entire community of approximately 120 households lost their homes, whether they were home-owners or tenants. They were moved from the semi-rural environment of fertile small-holdings and cottages with gardens to unfamiliar, built-up areas on the Cape Flats, where they were unable to sustain their former way of life. Although only about 20 kilometres separated Protea from the new locations, they were radically different social and physical environments. A few families were able to re-settle as a group, but the majority were scattered among strangers. Not only were they without their anchoring and supportive social network, but they also found themselves in places which did not enable them to produce food to supplement what was bought. Their new homes had either no gardens or only small patches of infertile, sandy soil that was able to provide little or nothing in the way of fruit, vegetables, medicinal and other

---

[1] For example, when Cape Town's District Six was declared a white group area in 1966, almost all of its approximately 60 000 inhabitants were people who had been classified 'coloured' under the Population Registration Act.

[2] The terminology of racial categorization changed over time. Here I use the term 'blacks' to include people formerly classified as 'Native', 'Coloured', or 'Asiatic' under the original Population Registration Act.

herbs. Nor did municipal rules allow for the keeping of livestock which, in Protea, had provided eggs, milk and meat. The difference in quality and possibilities of life between their old and new homes was enormous.

Like the residents of Protea, the majority of people who were unwillingly relocated had little socio-economic power and no vote. For this reason, their views on the removals were largely ignored by the government ministries charged with implementing the Group Areas Act. Where people tried to resist being moved, physical force was used. Occasionally the voices of people who were being relocated reached the wider public through inclusion in media coverage. Some were later incorporated into documentary films, poems, plays and fiction about the removals.[3] In the 1970s university-based Oral History projects[4] started interviewing members of dispossessed communities, collecting and archiving their stories so that they would be available for researchers and members of the public. In the post-Apartheid era the work of collecting these stories has continued but the institutional contexts and purposes have diversified. Now, for example, the national government is also involved through its Department of Land Affairs.[5]

---

[3] The following are a few examples. Two films on forced removal from District Six, *Dear Grandfather your Right Foot is Missing*, directed by Yunus Ahmed (1984), and *Last Supper at Horstley Street*, directed by Lindy Wilson (1986) use the stories and voices of former residents. William Kentridge and Angus Gibson's documentary film (1987) on forced removal from Sophiatown does the same. Poets who have written about life in District Six include Adam Small, Abdullah Ibrahim (the musician formerly known as Dollar Brand), S.V. Petersen, and Achmat Dangor. Melvin Whitebooi's play *Dit sal die blêrrie dag wees* ('That'll be the Bloody Day') deals with a family's response to their receipt of an order evicting them from District Six. *District Six, the Musical* by David Kramer and Taliep Petersen (2003) depicts life in the area before the forced removals and the grief occasioned by them. Achmat Dangor's story, *Waiting for Leila* (1981), is set in District Six in the period following the start of the demolition.

[4] These projects include: the University of the Witwatersrand's South African History Archive (www.wits.ac.za/saha); the University of the Western Cape's oral archive in the Mayibuye Centre (www.mayibuye.org); the University of Natal's 'Sinomlando project' (www.hs.unp.ac.za/theology/sinomlando); the University of Cape Town's Centre for Popular Memory (www.popularmemory.org).

[5] In 1994 the country's first democratically elected government established the legal and procedural means to facilitate restitution for loss of homes and land. Thousands of the people who applied for restitution had no documentary proof of their former occupation or ownership of property. In such cases employees of the Department of Land Affairs were told to elicit claimants' stories about when and

Context of elicitation

In order to understand any narrative it is necessary to know how it was elicited (Martin and Plum, 1997:307). Both content and narrative structure are influenced by the immediate context of elicitation (Schegloff, 1997; De Fina, 2003). Moreover, since tellers are influenced in their recreation of memories by the present context (Norrick, 2000:2) and by their sense of the future (Brockmeier, 2000), it is important to be aware of the situation in which stories are told and also, if possible, of the future which the tellers imagine for themselves and for their stories. A brief account follows of why and how the Protea narratives were elicited,[6] with a consideration of possible effects of the context of elicitation on the narratives.

In 1995 a group of former residents of Protea established a committee (known as PROVAC) to assist with claims to the Department of Land Affairs for financial recompense and land restitution. Five years later, in consultation with PROVAC, the District Six Museum, which focuses on forced removals, decided to mount an exhibition about Protea and its people before and after the removals.[7] The involvement of former residents was seen by the organisers as a crucial feature in the mounting of the exhibition, and it was assiduously sought through various networks. People were asked whether they would like to be involved through telling their stories, donating or lending photographs or video footage. A letter from the Museum told the interviewees that the material collected would be archived and made readily available for them, their descendants or any other interested people to see or hear. They would thus have known that

---

for how long they had lived in the place to which they now laid claim, and about their removal and relocation. Their stories are then checked against other available information in order to establish the validity of the restitution claims.

[6] Interviews with 26 people were studied. I wish to thank the people who so vividly told their stories, the interviewers from the District Six Museum for their skilful and sensitive role in the construction of these narratives, the transcribers for their careful work, and the District Six Museum and PROVAC committee for allowing me to use the Protea collection.

[7] The exhibition, which ran from October 2002 to April 2004, presented personal accounts and visual images of family and community life in Protea. They were contextualized against the background of information about the history of the area, and in relation to a chronology of actions and laws (dating from 1660) which have affected settlement in the area. There was a big mural map, constructed collectively from memory by former residents. On it the location of all institutions was indicated, as were the sites of the homes of all families who could be traced.

their stories could reach people who knew them and the community, as well as people whose knowledge of Protea was fragmentary or non-existent. By the time the stories were told to interviewers from the Museum, it was known that return to Protea was no longer an impossible dream. This was overtly taken into account by some interviewees who speculated about whether the kind of life they had known and were describing could be recreated in Protea by those who returned. I think it likely that a sense of public purpose and audience influenced many of the narrators who weighted the communal more heavily than the individual in what they selected to describe about Protea. By contrast, their accounts of the process of removal and of their lives in the new neighbourhoods focus on their own individual experiences.

Narratives elicited in the context of an interview are dialogic, not only in the Bakhtinian sense in which all utterances are dialogic in that the speaker bears in mind an audience's needs and responses (Bakhtin, 1986), but also in a more overt sense: they are shaped in part by questions that the interviewer asks, by comments that he or she makes, and also by the explanation given about the reason(s) for doing the interviews and inviting narratives within them. Tightly structured interviews may influence tellers into following a predetermined thematic or chronological route. Loosely structured interviews, on the other hand, take on more of the qualities of conversation, and as Ochs and Capps (2001) demonstrate, conversational narrative is overtly jointly constructed. During the course of the story, narrative paths, digressions and returns may be prompted by the main teller or by conversational partners: "Co-narrators wander over the temporal map, focusing on the past then relating it to the present and future and then returning to another piece of the past" (Ochs, 1997:191). None of the Protea interviews was tightly constructed, and several are like conversations.

Three people, experienced in the methods of oral history, were responsible for doing the interviews with former residents. Most of the 26 interviews were audio-recorded in interviewees' current homes, and some were done in workplaces. A few were video-recorded on the site where Protea had been. In some cases two people, friends or relatives, were interviewed together. English, Afrikaans and the local code-switching vernacular were used but most of the material is in English. The following topics were covered, but the order was not prescribed: basic biographical information (for example about birth-dates, how many generations of the family had lived in Protea), memories of childhood, features of the area and of life there, removals, experience of relocation and land claims. The loose and informal interview format and the interviewing style were intended to encourage interviewees to take the lead in moving from topic to topic, to choose how much and what kind of detail to offer, and not to feel they had to talk about topics that, for whatever reason, they did not wish to discuss. It is apparent from the occasional switching off of the tape recorder that there were things which people would say only off the record. Some interviews were characterized by frequent turn-changing, with the respondent giving rather short answers to questions, while in many others the interviewer asked very few questions because the interviewee gave expansive answers and moved on to cover other material at length. In looking at structural patterns, I concentrated on the latter group.

All of the interviews were transcribed by people with previous experience of transcribing for the Museum's archive. They punctuated the text for ease of reading, using conventions commonly applied in printed text. Pauses are not indicated. False starts and repairs are evident in some but not all transcripts, as is the case with indications of non-verbal aspects of the interview such as tears, laughter, and the getting and showing of photographs or other memorabilia. In some instances, the transcriber used non-standard orthography in an attempt to capture characteristic dialect features. I obtained permission to use these transcripts and my analysis is based on them, not on the original audio or video recordings.

Analytic procedures

I regarded each interview as a jointly constructed narrative in the sense that interviewer and interviewee co-operated to construct an account of individual and community experience of life before, during and after a significant event. The narratives thus produced are autobiographical, though they are not 'life stories' as defined in Linde (1993). They do not meet her criterion of "having as their primary evaluation a point about the speaker, not a general point about the way the world is" (ibid.:21). The narrators appear to be more concerned with describing and evaluating the way of life in the Protea community and explaining the nature and effects of its destruction than they are with making a point about themselves as individuals. Since my interest is in narrative construction of community and its loss, my analysis seeks to identify common features of content and structure.

From reading other sets of interviews about dispossession (held in Cape Town University's Centre for Popular Memory Archives), I had a sense of the topics that commonly come up. After reading through the transcripts several times, I categorized the topics and sub-topics that were mentioned in each interview. I noted those which appeared frequently and those which had been mentioned in other local dispossession narratives that I was familiar with[8] but which did not appear in the Protea narratives, for example language or economic differences within the dispossessed community. Thereafter I gave close attention to linguistic and discourse features of the construction of the topics and the relationships among them, focusing on the handling of time, the constructions of temporal, spatial and social relationships in Protea and the new locations, and constructions of identity.

Experience of time, place, people and self

Although I recognize the force of arguments that time, life and narrative are intricately linked (Ricoeur, 1980; Freeman, 1998; Freeman and Brockmeier, 2001), I wish to treat them separately for the moment before commenting on the narrative theory upon which I have drawn in the analyses of the Protea stories.

As I read and re-read these stories, I was struck by how strong a presence temporal cycles had in structuring the accounts of life in Protea and how, in turn, these accounts of experienced time were tied to the affordances of that particular place and community, and contrasted with those of their subsequent homes. In my attempt to understand the web of temporal, spatial and social relationships as represented in these narratives, I drew on Ricoeur's theory of time and Mayol's account of the nature of neighbourhood (Mayol, 1998). Aspects of these two theories which were particularly important in my approach to the Protea narratives are described very briefly

---

[8] In addition to the narratives in the CPM's collection of interviews, I am referring to stories told by participants in my research on District Six (which culminated in a book: McCormick, 2002), to narratives used in articles on communities removed from Windermere (Field, 2001), *Tramway Road* (Paulse, 2001), *District Six* (Swanson and Harries, 2001), *Simons Town* (Thomas, 2001), *Lower Claremont* (Swanson, 2001). I refer also to published memoirs by people who had been moved from District Six: *William Street District Six* (1988) by Hettie Adams and Hermione Suttner, *Birds on a Ledge* (1992) by Andrina Dashwood Forbes, Linda Fortune's *The House in Tyne Street: Childhood Memories of District Six* (1996), Nomvuyo Ngcelwane's *Sala Kahle District Six* (1998) Noor Ebrahim's autobiography, *Noor's Story: My Life in District Six* (1999), and to narratives in *Piecing Together the Past,* edited by Anne Schuster (2000), which is a published anthology of writings from a workshop on memory and narrative held at the District Six Museum in 2000.

below. Examples of their resonance with the narratives will appear later, in the analyses of the stories.

Drawing on Heidegger, Ricoeur suggests that at one level of temporal organization, 'within-time-ness', our sense of time is determined by our preoccupation with "the things of our concern. ... *das Vorhandene* ('subsisting things which our concern counts on') and *das Zuhandene* ('utensils offered to our manipulation')" (1980:172). Engagement with these things and utensils is individual, but it is also situated more publicly: "because there is *a time to do* this, a right time and a wrong time... we can reckon *with* time" (ibid.:173). I take this to mean a communally established sense of appropriateness, related to what he refers to later as 'heritage' (ibid.:188). Later in the essay he talks of the function of repetition in extending time conceived of as time stretching between birth and death (ibid.:182). Repetition involves a sense of extension into the past and into the future and for Ricoeur, also an extension beyond the individual into the communal (ibid.:188-189). In the Protea narratives the experience of days and years before the removal is presented in terms of what there was to be done at various times of the day and seasons of the year, and a great deal of attention is paid to repetitions of various kinds which created an enduring sense of stability that extended beyond the individual's life-time. Glimpses, perhaps, of Heidegger's "plural unity of future, past and present" (ibid.:171).

In Mayol's account of the individual's relation to neighbourhood, repetition of the practices which construct and express stable community relationships is regarded as important. This gave me a way of understanding why the sense of loss would be strong and pervasive in daily life for a long time, and why forced loss of neighbourhood would so deeply affect people's sense of identity.

In *The Practice of Everyday Life* Mayol (1998:7-14) gives an elegant and illuminating account of how a sense of neighbourhood and of belonging to one are constructed through everyday practices. In brief, he argues that neighbourhood is "the sum of all trajectories" (ibid.:11) that start from the home, on foot. It is a transitional space between inside and outside, private and public; a social space in which people manifest "a social 'commitment'; ... an art of coexisting with partners (neighbours and shopkeepers) who are linked ... by the concrete, but essential, fact of proximity and repetition" (ibid.:8). Neighbourhood practices are governed by propriety of dress, behaviour and speech. Respect for the local norms of propriety enables people to be in good enough standing to access symbolic benefits. The neighbourhood "is a known area of social space in which, to a greater or lesser degree, [the resident] knows himself or

herself to be recognized" (ibid.:9). Walking is crucial in the gradual process of inscribing oneself in a neighbourhood, and it is done not only with
a particular purpose in mind but also for pleasure, giving occasion for
greeting and the casual chatting which Mayol claims is essential in the
maintenance of neighbourhood. His account suggests that space, time and
social relationships are experienced in terms of one another, and that individual identity is enacted in the 'space' constructed by these relationships.
By implication, then, spatial dislocation would disrupt experience of time,
social relationships, and self. The Protea narratives bear this out thematically and structurally, as is evident in the extracts quoted later.

Accepting the commonly made distinction between the chronological
sequence of real or fictive events that 'provide' material for a narrative,
and their (often non-chronological) configuration in the narrative itself,
the first thing to be noted about autobiographical narratives is that their
temporal organization is seldom strictly chronological. They are not simple 'recounts' of all remembered events in sequence, but endeavour "to
discern patterns, constellations of meaning" (Freeman, 1997:173). Autobiographical narrators select what to include from what is remembered,
being guided by what now seems salient or significant though it might not
have at the time of occurrence (Freeman and Brockmeier, 2001:82). They
seldom present it in linear order "for the act of interpretation, via memory,
brings with it a mode of time that is rather more like a circle or spiral,
embodying a dialectical movement from present to past and past to present,
at once. This movement is in turn conditioned by the future as well" (Freeman, 1998:43). This kind of ordering is readily apparent in the Protea
narratives. Brockmeier (2000) argues that the temporal order(s) chosen
for a narrative are influenced by what one might call the teller's 'world
view' or desire. In some but not all of the narratives, in the sections dealing with life before the forced removal, the narrator's desire for a vanished
way of life constructs a kind of golden age,[9] not quite mythical, but
having something of the quality that Freeman associates with 'mythical
time'. By contrast, life in the new places is construed as changeable and
threatening, reflecting qualities of 'historic time': "… in place of eternal
recurrence and essential sameness there is change and difference; in place
of certainty there is uncertainty and accident; in place of perpetual reap-
pearance there is disappearance and death, the sense of an ending final
and irrevocable" (Freeman, 1998:34).

---

[9] Soudien (2001) discusses the functions of narrative constructions of this kind in
the lives of people who had been removed from District Six.

Autobiographical stories that deal with a single radical dislocation (as distinct from a series of such events) could be seen as having the following components: a description of life before the disruptive event, an account of the stages of the event and a description of what happened after the event, all three components being infused with indications of their meaning for the teller. These components correspond with the elements of personal narratives identified in Labov and Waletsky (1967), namely orientation, complicating action, resolution, and evaluation. In their model, orientation was not an essential component of personal narrative. Recently, Baynham has argued that in some kinds of narrative, orientation is the key structural element. Writing about narratives of migration and settlement, he argues that "Orientation/disorientation/reorientation in space and time, far from being a simple contextual backdrop *is* the story" (2003:251). In this regard, narratives of forced dislocation and relocation seem to me to constitute a sub-set of the narratives with which Baynham was concerned.

Structure of Protea narratives

Brockmeier and Carbaugh speak of "the meandering, discursive web of narrative in which all our knowledge ... is entangled" (2001:3). This metaphor of the web of narrative seems particularly apt in relation to the Protea stories. These narrators can be seen to be working with webs on two levels: firstly, in the way they sequence and link components and episodes of their stories, secondly and relatedly, in the images they construct of the web-like qualities of neighbourhood life in Protea.

Although, in general, narrators tell the story of their removal from Protea after they have described their life there, chronology is not a strong structural principle: accounts of life in Protea are shot through with glimpses of life after removal. The two most prominent structural devices are the weblike linkages, and the pervasive use of contrast.

As I have indicated above, the construction of time as cyclical is a striking feature of the orientations to life in Protea. By contrast, cycles are strikingly absent in accounts of life in the new places. Instances of linear constructions of time are found in some brief, summary-like accounts of individual lives or events, or in stories of traditions handed down from generation to generation. The temporal webs of orientation to life in Protea can be conceptualized as temporal cycles (natural and cultural) intersected by lines (life-spans or traditions reaching into the past, projections reaching into the future). The intersections function as nodes, allowing for a

change of narrative direction or focus. Narrative focus shifts among relationships that are primarily social (kinship, friendship networks), those
that are primarily spatial (the network of intersecting routes and topo-
graphical features), and those which are primarily temporal (connections
between time periods). I imagine the filaments of the web as triangular in
cross section, their sides being the temporal, spatial and social facets of
both life and narrative.

   The following extract is the most compact of the examples of characteristic web-like structure of reminiscences about life in Protea, which at
the same time give passing reference to the contrasts with life in the new
places. It is an example of autobiographical narrative which is "not so
much about time, but about *times*" (Brockmeier, 2000:58). I have translated it from Ms Ackerman's original Afrikaans. It is the translated version
that I analyze. Because the phrasing is mine rather than hers, I do not
analyze it in detail, but comment on broader features of the structure of
the extract as an illustration of a typical sequence used by narrators in
constructing the experience of time and times in physical and social spaces.
The transcript of the original is followed by the translation. (The transcriber's orthographic rendering of some accent features accounts for
non-standard spelling.)

   Maar die lekkerste part was toe die buste daar begin ry daar bo. Al
   die mense wat daar gebly het, het met die bus gery en als hulle trug
   kom dan is die maantjies vol groceries. Ja, daar was een gewees,
   Tewelle, sy gehad cream doughnuts (laughs)… en dit was **so** lekker
   gewees. Ons het party keer ons vriende en ons susters en broers, dan
   gaan ons Kaap toe Sondag aande dan loop ons bietjie rond. Dan
   gaan ons perare toe, dan koop ons milkshakes, ginger beer… dan
   loop ons rond in the Kaap… dan loop ons rond in die Kaap, dan kom
   ons weer met die bus huis toe… die bus mense het ons goed geken,
   almal was baie bekend met die driver en die conductor. In die aande
   ook, as 'n mens uit gaan sal jy nie die eene sien nie, maar hy kom
   sommer en sê 'Naand!' … en niemand het geworry met niemand nie,
   jy kon sommer Claremont toe geloep het en niemand het vir jou
   gemolesteer nie.
   Ek is te bang om nou te stap in die rondte, is baie snaaks vir my om
   nou in the Township te bly… ons het baie vryheid gehad daar. As
   daar bruilof is, is dit nie nodig dat jy genooi is nie, jy moet net kom,
   kom eet en drink en 'be merry' met almal… mense het lekker daar
   onder die akker bome gehou…
   Saterdag middag dan speel die manse rugby, dan sit die mense almal
   in die pad… van die pad bo tot onder, hulle kyk hoe speel die jongers.

In Bishops Court was daar ook 'n cricket court, in my Pa se tyd het
hulle cricket daar gespeel.

Dit was lekker, net jammer die mense moet geuit het. My oupa het
altyd gesê 'Kinders! Nou is dinge lekker maar in twintag jaar se
tyd, sal ek nie meer daar wees hie – en dan sal daar groot verandering wees.'

En die verandering het gekom… daardie jare was hy al lank
oorlede…ons het die lyk op gedra, soos die Slamse mense gedra die
kis het, al die mense agterna…toe gaan ons op by die begrafplaas by
die kerk. (Christina Ackerman)

1. But the best part was when there began to be buses up there.
2. Everyone who lived there used to travel by bus, and when they came home then the baskets would be full of groceries.
3. Yes, there was someone, Tewelle, she had cream doughnuts (laughs).
4. And it was so nice.
5. Sometimes our friends and our sisters and brothers – we would go to Town on Sunday evenings, and we would walk around a bit.
6. Then we'd go to the Parade, then we'd buy milkshakes, ginger beer.
7. Then we'd walk around in Town, then we'd walk around in Town.
8. Then we'd come home again by bus.
9. The bus people knew us well.
10. All of us were well known to the bus driver and the conductor.
11. In the evenings, too, if you went out, you might not see someone, but he'd just come up and say "'Evening!"
12. And no one worried with anyone – you could walk to Claremont, and no-one would molest you.
13. Now I'm too scared to walk about in the neighbourhood.
14. It's very odd for me to live now in the Township.
15. We had a lot of freedom there [meaning in Protea].
16. If there was a wedding, it wasn't necessary to be invited, you just had to arrive, come and eat and drink and be merry with everyone.
17. People used to have wonderful times there under the oak trees.
18. Saturday afternoon, then the men played rugby.
19. Then everyone sat in the road, in the road from the top to the bottom, and they watched how the youngsters played.
20. In Bishopscourt there was also a cricket pitch.
21. In my father's time they played cricket there.
22. It was wonderful, just a pity the people had to be removed.
23. My grandpa always said "Children, now things are good, but in twenty years' time – I won't be here any more – and there will be a big change".

24. And the change did come.
25. At the time he had been dead for a long time already.
26. We carried his body, in the way the Muslim people carry the coffin, all the people behind.
27. We went up to the cemetery at the church.
     (Christina Ackerman)

Within what is only part of one conversational turn, the narrative links spatial and social aspects of weekly routines and special days, different generations of Protea people, the national political context and forced removal and relocation. Although foregrounding the past, the account is punctuated by references to the present, as it deals with the social, the spatial, and the temporal. While one facet of the web's three-sided filament is uppermost, the other two are there, ready to emerge when appropriate.

The first section (sentences 1-10) is framed by 'the bus', starting with the introduction of the bus service and its routes, and finishing with a comment on being well known to the bus driver and conductor. In between, there is talk of routines: weekly shopping expeditions and Sunday strolling in Town, all of which are facilitated by the bus. The temporal (weekly cycles, sequenced actions), spatial (bus routes, Town), and social (friends, family, bus staff) dimensions are inseparable.

The link between the topic of the bus and the next topic, walking in safety, is an instance of Mayol's notion of 'being recognized': passengers were known by the bus staff, residents are recognized and greeted by passers by. This section (sentences 11-14) shows very clearly that constructions of the past are framed by the present. Commenting on the past in Protea, the two negative statements "no-one worried with you", "no-one would molest you" invoke a present which is different. This form of evaluation, the use of the negative to evoke its opposite, is one of the evaluative strategies identified by Labov (1972:380-387). It is very common in the Protea narratives. Much of the sense of how people experienced the relocation is encoded in brief phrases, frequently in negative mode, which evoke 'what is not' in one place or the other.

The idea of freedom provides the link to the next section (sentences 15-22): *freedom from* fear leads to talk of *freedom to* participate in other families' festivities (social), to sit in the road (spatial), to play cricket at Bishopscourt (social – also in class terms). Playing cricket at Bishopscourt happened in a previous generation – by implication, it did not happen in the narrator's time (temporal reference). Her general comment (sentence 16) picks up the notion of change, which the following section develops.

In the fourth section (sentences 23-25), the narrator evokes the national political context through quoting her grandfather's prediction, and its fulfilment. Temporal structuring is very layered here. In the narrative present, Ms Ackerman tells of her grandfather who, in the past (because of his implied reading of a past that was further back), predicted the future. And that prediction came to pass: that imagined future came to be 'the present', but only after he had been dead a long time. His death is the topic of the last section of the extract.

In the last section, the focus moves back to the social and spatial. The grandfather's funeral is contextualized as being similar to that of Muslims. (Since Muslim funerals in Cape Town are the only ones that still happen in this way, this is offered as a reference point for a contemporary listener). Just as for weddings (previously mentioned) everybody participates in the funeral of a resident and the burial happens within walking distance of the home. Most of the Protea narratives comment on one or more of the major life events (births and christenings, weddings, death and funerals) happening *in* the neighbourhood and being appropriately marked by everyone. Since it is remarked upon, the implication is that this is no longer the pattern, that these life events have been 'displaced' to hospitals, halls and funeral parlours.

In these narratives, constructions of life before the removal are infused with constructions of life after the removal, and vice versa. It is only the stages of the forced removal itself that are presented chronologically. My reading of numerous accounts of traumatic forced removals and resettlements suggests that in such narratives, comparison is a stronger organizing principle than chronology. The comparisons may be implied, oblique or direct. They always have an evaluative function. (Contrast and comparison are identified in Labov (1972) as among the evaluative devices used by narrators.) In the Protea texts, the comparisons are set up on the basis of three key oppositions that are significant to the narrators. They are the presence in Protea versus the absence in the new locations of predictability and safety, familiarity and recognition, and of power and agency. These factors are interrelated, as one is constantly reminded through the structure of the narratives, and the details of the descriptions.

Given the trauma of the disruption of stable life patterns caused by the forced removal from Protea, high value is ascribed to predictability. In the narratives it is foregrounded in the description of life before the removal. This is achieved, for example, through frequent reference to recurrent natural and cultural cycles, iterative verb forms ('used to...'), and modals and adverbials combined in phrases like 'could always ...', and adverbs such as 'usually'or 'often'. Closely related to predictability is safety. Two meanings of 'safety' are relevant here. Firstly, there is the sense of existential safety that comes from being able to assume that one's world is a predictable place. Secondly, safety is construed as the absence of threat of injury or death. Safety of the first kind and its loss are usually represented indirectly, through what is said about the predictability and the unpredictability of life before and life after the removals. Concern for safety of the second kind is the subject of frequent and overt comment. It is related to the second set of factors, familiarity and recognition: knowing one's way around a place, recognizing people and knowing the norms of behaviour.

Familiarity with the landscape and its resources is constructed mainly through the level of fine detail in descriptions of habitual trajectories and their purposes. Also important is the spatial orientation offered to the listener through references to how routes and landmarks relate to one another. Familiarity is a concept applied not only to the spatial but also to the social, to being aware of (or familiar with) what is considered right, what is allowed and what is necessary. Propriety of behaviour, dress and speech is alluded to chiefly in references to 'the elders' and how they taught and monitored the young: recognition is linked with this. In the context of a neighbourhood, recognition means both "knowing who and what someone is and how they fit into whatever matrix is relevant", and also "according due respect for status or achievement" (my definitions). In the narratives, recognition of the first kind is talked about overtly and in detail, with regard to Protea. We hear who is related to whom, where they live, where they work. In accounts of the new neighbourhoods, that kind of recognition is conspicuous by its absence – there are no descriptions of named people and their connections. It is also noted in negative statements, such as Charles Wilson's "we didn't know the people, who come from where". Recognition in the sense of 'due respect' is explicitly mentioned in many narratives of Protea, and people talk about how proud they were of the achievements of other members of the community. In accounts of people adapting after relocation, this form of recognition is presented as important. There is explicit description of former Protea residents gaining the respect of the new neighbourhood because of knowledge that they have and share. Recognition of this kind is an acknowledgement of the person's power.

Power and agency are constructed in various ways. The narratives make it very clear that power and agency are domain-specific. The form of power and agency that manifests in ability to choose and to act – particularly to 'act on' someone or something – does not automatically transfer from one domain to another. In the case of the Protea narratives, people shown as powerful within their neighbourhood and work-skills domain are represented as disempowered when confronted with the forces of the law and its agents. The contrast between experience of power and of disempowerment is encoded lexically (people name their feelings), and also syntactically through the way they represent agency and processes.

Living Within and Without a Neighbourhood Web

The extracts given below give glimpses of the ways in which the residents of Protea describe a way of life sustained by a long established web of ties among familiar people, created through repeated practices appropriate to different natural and social cycles, enacted in a space that was familiar by day and by night and in all its seasonal affordances. It is clear from the extracts that narrators conceptualize some of the key contrasts between Protea and the places of relocation in relation to the hallmarks of neighbourhood identified by Mayol (1998).

One of these hallmarks is the centrality of walking. It was evident in the extract quoted from Ms Ackerman's narrative, and it features in all the other Protea stories as well. Walking was the normal way of getting to work, school, shops and other local resources, making routes so familiar that they could be easily traversed in the dark (something that was necessary, since there were no street-lights in Protea). By contrast, spatial disorientation was one of the experiences commonly alluded to in accounts of the first few days and weeks of life in the new places. Walking in Protea is described as sociable, and largely pleasurable. In many of the new locations it was experienced as dangerous, causing people to walk as little as possible and to be wary of people encountered on the way. This avoidance would obviously have affected their ability to make the new neighbourhood their own, to become familiar with it and recognized within it. The contrasts are sometimes explicitly drawn, and sometimes indirectly expressed through a range of linguistic and discourse choices such as foregrounding, repetition and the use of negatives:

[In Protea] This road is dark, there's no lights, I can whistle and I know the people there. I know the whistle and I will whistle back. That was a long road but you know everybody there. (Charles Wilson)

Ja, hoeveel mense was dood, van onse removals? (…) Ons was scatter hier, ons was scatter daar, jy kon nie eers by hulle kom nie. Waar gaan jy kom? Hulle skiet jou dood voor jy weet waar jy moet die mense kom. Dit was so deurmekaar! *Die* plek was daar nooit die besigheid. Maar daar maak mense ander mense dood. (Frances van Gusling)

Yes, how many people died of our removals! (…) We were scattered here, we were scattered there. You couldn't even get to people. How would you get there? They would shoot you dead before you would know where to find your people. It was so confusing. [In] *this* place [Protea] there was never that kind of thing. But there people killed other people. (Frances van Gusling, translated)

The scale of Protea was such that residents were within walking distance of one another and of river, mountain and shop. It was also within walking distance of the main places of employment in adjacent areas. Children walked to school, adults walked to work, and everyone walked to the shop. The narratives show vividly that the network of spatial trajectories was also experienced as social, and safe:

Early in the morning with the frost still on the grass, bare feet and you cross two rivers, sent on an errand and nobody interfered with you. We were very safe. (Eileen Nomdu)

[In the early evening] this street was humming with children! I can remember going to the shop with my wheel. You take a big wheel of a bicycle. You push the spokes out, you take a wire, curl it round, and you push the wheel … and you see the guys coming down with their wheels, up and down, going to the shop. … As a young boy you kind of hang around here [the shop]. Because the girls must come to the shop, you see, the girls must come. You meet them here. Their mothers will send them to the shop. (John Valentine)

Destinations outside the neighbourhood (some shops, places of work or entertainment) would have been reached by a limited number of routes because of the geography of the area. Since private cars were a rarity, if residents could not walk to destinations beyond the neighbourhood, they used buses and often travelled together. Bus rides frequently feature as examples of sociable occasions. In a few new locations people felt safe enough on public transport to get to know their neighbours through sharing public transport with them. But in other areas this was not a possibility:

> Now you stay in Manenberg, get a train ... end of the month, knife on your heart with the people standing around you, 'Take your wages out of your pockets'. (Geoff van Gusling)

Mayol talks about the importance of knowing oneself to be recognized (1998:9). These narratives bear this out. Many accounts stress how well residents knew one another in Protea. They knew their neighbours' histories, who was related to whom, their strengths, their weaknesses. The contrast when people first arrived in the new places was that they were 'recognized' only as strangers, as not belonging. Sometimes that recognition was benign, sometimes not:

> One day I came home from work – told another chap 'I want to show you where I stay', and I ride the whole place – I don't know where I stay. Then the lady shouted at me 'You moved in last night. You stay behind me.' (Felix de la Cruz)

> I was with a girl and we were standing and they hit us with a panga. ... seeing him with a girl, they don't like because he intrude on their area. (Charles Wilson)

One of the prime differences between life before and after removal was that in Protea, but not in the new locations, the homes and domestic life were intimately bound up with the natural environment rather than just the built environment. Thus, the stories are rich in accounts of leisure time spent walking or sitting about outside in public space. People made music, told stories. In contrast, in the new places these habits could not find equivalent expression:

> [In Protea] You have a galley outside ... you make a fire in there. And you just sit around this ... and you tell these spook stories ... it was very exciting because the big guys used to tell you those stories and you go home and you can't sleep that night! (John Valentine)

> Where we used to stay in Kirstenbosch we could have walked where we wanted to, and up there [Manenberg], there was no actual facility where we could go to anywhere nearby or anything. (Victor Josephus)

Describing Protea's built environment, people stress the individuality of structures, and a sense of their history, of a long engagement between people and place, of the use of local natural resources such as the stones. By contrast, in the mass housing on the Cape Flats, there was none of that. Alexander September's image of a field of tents in his new environment captures the wholly different relationship between buildings and land, and the resulting sense of impermanence and lack of individuality. There is no urge to belong to such an environment – Mr September saw himself as 'camping' there.

> It tooks me a very long time to get right down here. Because every time when I look through the window I think I am camping – and see all the tents, you know, tops of the houses.
> Int. There were tents?
> No, no – I mean it looks like tents, you know, here from upstairs. And it tooks me about three, four years to come right with this place. (Alexander September)

Because of the nature of household economy in Protea, and because of the essential natural resources available within or near the village, residents encountered one another frequently as they went about their daily and weekly routines. There was no electricity and few homes had running water, so every day there would be people – particularly children – walking to the spring for water and the mountain for wood. Weekly washing was done at the river. One of the few features that people anticipated eagerly about life in the new places was that there would be electricity and running water in their homes. But then they found the burden of having to pay for water, heating and lighting very difficult.

Representations of Protea are of a bountiful natural environment, with access to free food and medicinal plants. Adults and children were involved with the growing and gathering of food and natural remedies, not just with the buying of products from shops. They were thus very aware of seasonal changes, with their associated harvests, joys and hardships:

> Oh, the river, that's where we started our summer days... we learned to swim there. (Alexander September)

> [In winter] I always had to walk bare feet. And it was icy cold, and it was freezing and I used to walk numb to school in the morning. (Ivy Pillay)

> There was pigs and hens and all ... we lived off our place because

there was vegetables and fruit … If you need something immediately they just cut it or they went and get something off the place and that was our meal for the evening. (Lydia Veldsman)

Sunday mornings in the mountains – meat you get up in the mountain – you eat anything you catch. … You get two pheasants, you've got food for the night. (Geoff von Gusling)

If you hadn't got money, it's easy for you to go and make some acorns for the pigs … pay you ten cents a tin full and if you had ten cents you can go to the bioscope, ja, in the Sixties, when the Beatles was, A Hard Day's Night, that film – we had to make plans for that. (Charles Wilson)

Kirstenbosch people were so good at recognizing herbs, they used to go and collect herbs in the mountain and sell them at the Grand Parade. … And castor olie every month, boegoe, and a lot of herbs, my mother used to concoct. She got it from the old people, it didn't taste nice at all but we had to drink it. And so did all the children of Kirstenbosch because the place was mad on herbs! (Abdullah Hoosain)

According to the narratives, generations of Protea residents had developed and passed on an intimate knowledge of the natural resources in their neighbourhood and surrounding areas. Against the background of hardship caused by lack of money in Protea, people represent themselves not as victims of poverty but as people who knew how to use their environment productively and sustainably. A striking feature of stories about life in Protea is the strong sense of agency. As is evident from many of the extracts quoted above, residents are constructed as agents, doing things successfully within the sphere of everyday life because they knew the hows and the wheres. (In encounters with bureaucracy, they do not construct themselves as agents. This is discussed below.) A point made by several of the interviewees was that several old people had died shortly before or shortly after the move. They attribute these deaths to the move, particularly to the loss of freedom and independence, to disengagement and loss of ability to be an important contributor in the daily life of family and neighbourhood:

My uncle, when he came to Manenberg, he was sitting there at that flats, and that's where he died, because he was looking up to the mountain and thinking, "This beautiful place where I've planted and all the greeneries and all that. I can't do nothing down here". And that's how they faded away. And even the other people as well, that was just

sitting and doing nothing! You know, they're hear- heart-broken. And
that's how they died actually, with a broken heart. (Cecil McLean)

By contrast, descriptions of Protea abound in references to the important
role of old people even when they were no longer breadwinners. Protea's
old people are represented as active, assertive, essential figures in maintaining – literally – the life and health of residents, and also the propriety
of the social fabric:

> Old people didn't take any nonsense … If you stepped out of line,
> they were entitled to give you a hiding … if you then went home to
> tell your parents that such an aunt or uncle[10] gave you a hiding along
> the road, you can rest assured that you'll get another hiding. That is
> how we were brought up. (Frank van Gusling)

Implicit in many stories of trying to adapt in the new neighbourhood is the
sense of loss of competence, or at least a lack of scope for showing one's
competencies, even if there was no call for their use. None of the new
neighbours would have known that individuals or families had these hidden skills, whereas in Protea everyone knew who was good at what, even
if they no longer exercised those skills. There, people took pride in being
able to say who the builders, fixers, midwives, musicians, story-tellers,
correctors of the young were. Midwives and healers were members of the
community, known and respected by the people they had brought into the
world and attended in sickness:

> I remember Mrs Idas who lived at No. 1 Kirstenbosch Drive … she
> was like the nurse of the community, but not just the medical nurse,
> but spiritually. … And if anyone was sick, the families would come
> from near or far in the area. We knew when adults went in there look-
> ing very sombre that somebody must be very sick or somebody might
> have passed away. And then Mrs Idas would be fetched. She would
> wash the body, direct how it must be laid out. When a baby is born
> and there's difficulty, and the Nurse du Preez or whoever the midwife
> is was not there yet, Mrs Idas would be called in. She would comfort
> the person, and she just knew the homes, the way they do it in their
> homes. Yes, she was a very respected lady. (Ann Ntebe)

---

[10] 'Aunt' and 'uncle' were frequently used as terms of respect for adults whether
or not they were relatives.

Children learned to recognize traces of previous generations, to know who had built what, who had made artefacts still in use:

> They used to tell us quite a bit about the old days and that's how we knew about who built what, and in the Gardens, who built what wall, the stone walls that was built in the Gardens, all that stone cottages that was built, it was built all by our forefathers, that was built. (Wilfred Smith)

In the accounts of those who did adapt to their new area and came to feel at home and integrated into the community, among the factors that are foregrounded are the ability to be proactive, to provide service, knowledge and skills that are valued in the neighbourhood. Teaching people how to garden and healing with natural remedies are two of the competencies that are mentioned. Other factors that are noted as having helped people to settle are the maintenance of routines at home, and – very important – being able to become involved in a local parish.

It was not only once they were in the new neighbourhoods that people began to feel diminished and unrecognized, literally and metaphorically. For many, the sense of who they were was profoundly shaken by the treatment they received in the processes surrounding the removals. This is seldom said directly, but it emerges in the way they describe what happened. Choice of words and repetitions suggest a shocked realization of how they must have been regarded by those who thought it appropriate to treat them so badly[11]. Phrases commonly used refer to being 'thrown out', 'kicked out', 'pushed around'. The residents are represented as 'not having', 'not being able', 'not knowing what was going to **happen to us**', not initiating action but being on the receiving end of other people's actions. In the following extract I have put in **bold** features that are typical of the way agency is constructed with regard to the removals.

> **We didn't have** the choice – **we never had** the choice to say "I want to go to Manenberg" or "I want to go to Steenberg". .... **They sent us** all down to the rent office in Grassy Park, and **there they give us** a key for this flat and so on, and **here we are**. ... **They tell us we had to stay where we are going to stay**. (Alexander September)

---

[11] Bruner talks of how "Self-making is powerfully affected not only by your own interpretations of yourself, but by the interpretations others offer of your version" (2001:34).

Some stories show anger protecting people from internalising these stunting identities as victims. These narrators express anger at having been naïve enough to trust in the basic humanity of those who had power. Others show how thoroughly disabling the experience of being disregarded has been with respect to the maintenance of self-esteem and trust. One of the most poignant expressions of that was given by Cecil McLean in explaining why some people were not going to try to lodge a claim for land restitution: "they've got that frightedness in their souls".

Conclusion

In the Protea narratives, the webs of commitment that linked people with one another are represented as being shaped by the affordances of place and time, what it was possible to do in particular locations at particular times. People's experience of time and social relationships is infused with their sense of neighbourhood, as is their sense of their own identity. The stories show that being compelled to uproot from a familiar place is extremely disruptive even if the place to which one is relocated is only a short distance away in the same city, and even if the people among whom one is placed speak the same languages. Such a move disrupts not only daily routines, but also the sense of personal identity that is created in part through these routines. In a word, sudden forced loss of neighbourhood is profoundly 'disorienting'.

In all cases most of the interview is devoted to an account of life before the forced removal. As I indicated earlier, the context and purpose of the interviews may well have had some influence on the choice of focus. However, it is also clear when one examines structural features of the narratives that Protea has an importance in people's lives that the places to which they were removed do not have. In the accounts of life before and after the forced removal, the pervasiveness of comparison and the difference in temporal ordering establish life in Protea as the reference point for a desirable life (its considerable hardships notwithstanding). Repetition with its links between past and possible future is present in various forms in these narratives: in representations of temporal cycles, habitual spatial trajectories, and familiar community norms and practices. This repetition holds the time-place-life of Protea present. As Soudien says about memories of other loved places from which people were removed, "in remembering [them]…, people remember possibility, they remember what it is they can be. This memory for them is a powerful allegory, a myth of how life, even in poverty, can provide for them the support of community, the ability to be that which they desire" (2001:104).

References

Adams, H. and H. Suttner (1988) *William Street District Six,* Diep River: Chameleon Press.

Ahmed, Y. (1984) *Dear Grandfather, Your Right Foot is Missing* (Film), Distribution in South Africa by Ahmed Productions, Cape Town; distribution elsewhere by Seawell Films, Paris.

Bakhtin, M. M. (1986) 'The Problem of Speech Genres', in C. Emerson and M. Holquist (eds.) *Speech Genres and Other Late Essays* (pp. 60-102), Tr. Vern W. McGee, Austin: University of Texas Press.

Baynham, M. (2003) 'Narratives in Space and Time: Beyond "backdrop" Accounts of Narrative Orientation', *Narrative Inquiry* 13(2):347-366.

Brockmeier, J. (2000) 'Autobiographical Time', *Narrative Inquiry* 10(1):51-73.

Brockmeier, J. and D. Carbaugh (2001) 'Introduction', in *Narrative and Identity: Studies in Autobiography, Self and Culture* (pp. 1-22). Amsterdam and Philadelphia: John Benjamins.

Bruner, J. (2001) 'Self-making and World-making', in J. Brockmeier and D. Carbaugh (eds.) *Narrative and Identity: Studies in Autobiography, Self and Culture* (pp. 25-37), Amsterdam and Philadelphia: John Benjamins.

Dangor, A. (1981) *Waiting for Leila,* Johannesburg: Ravan Press.

Dashwood-Forbes, A. (1992) *Birds on a Ledge,* Cape Town: Buchu Books.

De Fina, A. (2003) 'Crossing Borders: Time, Space, and Disorientation in Narrative', *Narrative Inquiry* 13(2):1-25.

Ebrahim, N. (1999) *Noor's Story: My Life in District Six,* Cape Town: The District Six Museum Foundation.

Field, S. (2001) 'Squatters, Slumyards and Removals', in S. Field (ed.). *Lost Communities, Living Memories: Remembering Forced Removals in Cape Town* (pp. 27-43), Cape Town: David Philip.

Fortune, L. (1996) *The House in Tyne Street: Childhood Memories of District Six,* Cape Town: Kwela Books.

Freeman, M. (1997) 'Why Narrative? Hermeneutics, Historical Understanding, and the Significance of Stories', *Journal of Narrative and Life History* 7(1-4):169-176.

------ (1998) 'Mythical Time, Historical Time, and the Narrative Fabric of the Self', *Narrative Inquiry* 8(1):27-50.

------ and J. Brockmeier (2001) 'Narrative Integrity: Autobiographical Identity and the Meaning of the "good life"', in J. Brockmeier and D. Carbaugh (eds.) *Narrative and Identity: Studies in Autobiography, Self and Culture* (pp. 75-99), Amsterdam and Philadelphia: John Benjamins.

Kentridge, W. and A. Gibson (1987) Sophiatown (Film), Free Film-makers, for BBC Channel 4.

Kramer, D. and T. Petersen (2003) *District Six, The Musical,* Cape Town: Musicmakers cc.

Labov, W. (1972) 'The Transformation of Experience in Narrative Syntax', in W. Labov (ed.) *Language in the Inner City: Studies in the Black English Vernacular* (pp. 354-396), Philadelphia: University of Pennsylvania Press.

------ and J. Waletsky (1967) 'Narrative Analysis: Oral Versions of Personal Experience', in J. Helm (ed.) *Essays on the Verbal and Visual Arts: Proceedings of the 1966 Spring Meeting of the American Ethnological Society* (pp. 12-44), Seattle: University of Washington Press.

Linde, C. (1993) *Life Stories: The Creation of Coherence,* New York and Oxford: Oxford University Press.

Martin, J. R. and G. A. Plum (1997) 'Construing Experience: Some Story Genres', *Journal of Narrative and Life History* 7(1-4):299-308.

Mayol, P. (1998) 'The Neighbourhood', in M. de Certeau, L. Giard and P. Mayol, *The Practice of Everyday Life* (pp. 7-14), edited by L. Giard and translated by T. Tomasik, Minneapolis and London: University of Minnesota Press.

McCormick, K. (2002) *Language in Cape Town's District Six*, Oxford: Oxford University Press.

Ngcelwane, N. (1998) *District Six: An African Woman's Perspective,* Cape Town: Kwela Books.

Norrick, N. (2000) *Conversational Narrative: Storytelling in Everyday Talk*, Amsterdam: John Benjamins.

Ochs, E. (1997) 'Narrative', in T. A. van Dijk (ed.) *Discourse as Structure and Process* (pp. 185-207), Thousand Oaks, CA: Sage.

------ and L. Capps (2001) *Living Narrative: Creating Lives in Everyday Storytelling*, Cambridge, Mass., and London: Harvard University Press.

Paulse, M, (2001) '"Everyone had their Differences but there was Always Comradeship": Tramway Road, Sea Point, 1920s to 1961' in S. Field (ed.) *Lost Communities, Living Memories: Remembering Forced Removals in Cape Town* (pp. 44-61), Cape Town: David Philip.

Ricoeur, P. (1980) 'Narrative Time', *Critical Inquiry,* Autumn 1980:169-190.

Schegloff, E. (1997) '"Narrative Analysis" Thirty Years Later', *Journal of Narrative and Life History* 7(1-4):97-106.

Schuster, A. (ed.) (2000) *Piecing Together the Past,* Cape Town: The District Six Museum Foundation.

Soudien, C. (2001) 'Holding on to the Past: Working with the "Myths" of District Six', in C. Rassool and S. Prosalendis, *Recalling Community in Cape Town: Creating and Curating the District Six Museum* (pp. 97-105), Cape Town: The District Six Museum.

Swanson, F. (2001) '"Mense van die Vlak": Community and Forced Removals in Lower Claremont', in S. Field (ed.) *Lost Communities, Living Memories: Remembering Forced Removals in Cape Town* (pp. 100-116), Cape Town: David Philip.

------ and J. Harries (2001) '"Ja, so was District Six! But it was a Beautiful

Place": Oral Histories, Memory and Identity', in S. Field (ed.) *Lost Communities, Living Memories: Remembering Forced Removals in Cape Town* (pp. 62-80), Cape Town: David Philip.

Thomas, A. (2001) '"It Changed Everybody's Lives": The Simons Town Group Areas Removals', in S. Field (ed.) *Lost Communities, Living Memories: Remembering Forced Removals in Cape Town* (pp. 81-99), Cape Town: David Philip.

Whitebooi, M. *Dit sal die blêrrie dag wees* [That'll be the Bloody Day], Unpublished play.

Wilson, L. (1986) *Last Supper at Horstley Street* (Film), Distributed by Lindy Wilson, Cape Town.

Section III

Institutional Placement
and Displacement

Institutional Placement and Displacement

In this section we group together three chapters that deal with narratives told as part of institutional procedures in contexts where, as Jacquemet puts it, stories, instead of being told casually to friends, are retold to strangers in situations "in which the techniques, tactics and devices of authority, legitimacy and dominance operate". Two of the chapters (Maryns and Jacquemet) are concerned with claims for asylum, the third (Barsky) is concerned with the homeless and procedures for claiming benefits. In all of the chapters the authors show how institutional discursive practices work against the contextualization of a narrative producing, progressively, effects of misunderstanding, communicative entropy, anger and silencing. Barsky concludes by making a claim for fictional narrative as a way of telling the untellable story.

Maryns analyzes the role of narratives told in the interviews in the Belgian asylum procedure, suggesting that since only a minority of applicants can provide documentation, experiential narrative "is basically the only tool for explaining and supporting the application". Working with a hypothesis that the importance of discursive contextualization work increases in relation to the degree of distance between interactional participants, she goes on to examine the discursive processes at work in these interviews. She identifies a range of issues, including conflicting genre expectations in the interview, especially in relation to norms and standards of evidence and legally established categories. Expectations that the asylum seekers' narratives will be organized along principles of temporal order, precision, detail, coherence and consistency, echo established conceptions about the canonical narrative, ignoring or devaluing for example the importance of spatial orientation in these narratives of the displaced, so vividly demonstrated in other contributions to this book.

This analysis demonstrates how the asylum seekers' narratives can routinely be found wanting in the face of the interviewer's sustained probing to elicit confirming detail to substantiate a claim. The normative constraints of the interview context and the expectations of the interviewers work against the contextualization that would allow interlocutors to make sense of the stories as they are told. Maryns' analysis shows from a number of perspectives how these processes have ample potential for putting asylum seekers at a disadvantage and for allowing authorities to discard their claims.

Jacquemet's chapter provides another angle on the re-telling of stories in institutional settings. The techniques, tactics and devices used in those social environments are overwhelmingly discursive and we find in the chapter many echoes of Maryns' treatment of issues of contextualization in the Belgian asylum seeker interviews. In particular, Jacquemet describes the consequence of a decision to disallow narrative evidence in the Kosovan asylum seeking procedure, in favour of the collection of circumstantial evidence in the shape of place names and cultural insider knowledge. The asylum seekers in Kosovo attempt to transform the decontextualized request to recite place names into a narrative format (reminiscent of a similar process described by Maranhao [1993] in anthropological fieldwork interviews). In taking the narrative turn, they unwittingly transgress the distinctive norms of these interview speech events and in fact lessen their credibility.

In Maryns' and Jacquemet's chapters, we see how narratives could be *other-censored*, either by explicit policy or through systematic misreading of contextualization cues. Based on his interviews with street people Barsky shows how a story can be *self-censored*: not told because the narrator fears it will get him into more trouble. Greg from Alberta echoes the danger demonstrated in the Kosovan interviews of failing to provide the right amount and type of detail in the appeal interview: "He couldn't get the things he needed. Like the last day of school, the last day of his job, the name of his boss, all the little things that you cannot seem to get". Welfare recipients, homeless people and asylum seekers are all outsiders to the administrative/discursive procedures that decide their fates. This, according to Barsky, often results in stories that are left untold, for fear of the consequences.

Fictional texts, in contrast, provide a space for telling the untellable story, through the special kind of permission to speak, which constitutes fiction. The hero of Fajardo's story, summarized by Barsky, reluctant to return home to Chile even for his mother's funeral, echoes Mamal with his dilemma as described by Haviland. The saturated texts of fictional narrative provide a way of giving voice to the subjectivity and pain of dislocation/re-location processes: "In the case of Fajardo, writing becomes a way of expressing what cannot be expressed to persons around him". Barsky concludes his chapter by exploring, not altogether optimistically, the potential of outsider law to permit the telling of these stories.

Reference

Maranhao, T. (1993) 'Recollections of Fieldwork Conversations, or Authorial Difficulties in Anthropological Writing', in J. Hill and J. Irvine (eds.) *Responsibility and Evidence in Oral Discourse* (pp.260-288), Cambridge: Cambridge University Press.

Displacement in Asylum Seekers' Narratives

KATRIJN MARYNS, *Ghent University, Belgium*

Introduction

Over the last few years, many democratic regimes in Europe have gone through a continuously changing societal mobility and diversification.[1] The differentiation between people and the crossing of socio-cultural boundaries cause our societies to push out traditional political, social and ideological frontiers. It is important, however, to take into account that such large population movements are not new to our contemporary political world. Even the distinction in legal status between autochtonous inhabitants and refugees goes back to Roman times (Kristeva, 1991), so it would be erroneous to consider displacement "an anomaly in the life of an otherwise whole, stable, sedentary society" (Malkki, 1995a:508). Still, these days in many European countries the asylum seekers issue forms one of the main problems in national politics. One of the consequences of this large-scale movement of people is that institutional systems have to deal with increasing floods of refugees and displaced persons, which considerably complicates the processing of administrative bureaucratic cases. A case in point is the Belgian asylum procedure. The functioning of the asylum application procedure clearly reflects degrees in societal maturity with regard to changing mobilities.

Sociolinguistic discussions reflect upon this continuously changing societal mobility. New linguistic ideologies are proposed that leave static conceptions of linguistic behaviour behind and move towards a more mobile approach to human interaction. It is in this context that I want to situate my research. What is striking in the asylum seekers' data is the fact that the speakers are displaced. This explains why the concept of 'mobility' is a pivotal one in my analysis: the discourse is analyzed from the perspective of *interactional 'transferability'* of resources to new contexts

---

[1] Research for this paper was made possible by a personal research grant from the FWO. I would like to thank Jan Blommaert, Anna De Fina and Chris Bulcaen for their comments and suggestions. I am very grateful to the people working at the Immigration Office, the Commissioner General's Office for Refugees and Displaced Persons and the Permanent Commission for Appeal for their co-operation and I owe the greatest debt to the asylum seekers who allowed me to examine their applications.

of use. I will argue that this approach serves as a theoretical perspective on any kind of dialogic semiotic behaviour: mobility of repertoires is in fact an issue in any form of human communication, as soon as there is a transmission of some kind between two or more individuals. But of course, there are gradations of semiotic mobility and the hypothesis is that the more boundaries participants in interaction need to cross, the greater the differences in how discursive forms, functions and the relations between them are being contextualized, and hence the more discursive efforts will be required to make individual contextualization work explicit in interaction. My research attempts to show how these dynamics are disrupted in institutional practices. Analysis illustrates how the Belgian asylum procedure, a procedure in which different boundaries are transgressed simultaneously, offers little space for contextualization. Instead, there is a tendency towards an imposition of institutional contextualizations which often entails a devaluation of the social-discursive potential of the asylum seeker. These dynamics do not take the socio-cultural and therefore inherently variable character of the produced text-context relations into account, so these relations tend to lose their mobility in the transfer.

This paper explores the impact of dislocation on narrative production and interpretation in the eligibility determination interview. On the basis of narrative data taken from procedural interviews with a group of young female African asylum seekers, it is my intention to show: (a) how the interaction between the African asylum seeker and the public official can be characterized by an enormous gap in accessibility to contexts of discourse; (b) how the asylum seeker is offered very little space for contextualizing and negotiating meaning and (c) how institutional contextualizations are imposed upon the asylum seeker's utterances with considerable implications for identity attribution. The chapter is organized in the following way: in the next section I focus on displacement and mobility in asylum seekers' narratives and discuss some of the main features of the data; I then offer a data-based discussion of the impact displacement has on three different though closely related dimensions of information exchange in institutional encounters viz. language ideology, institutional pragmatics and professional vision. Finally, I briefly recapitulate the issues discussed.

Mobility

Social behaviour is eminently semiotic: no matter what people want to get across in the social world, it will always involve the interpretation of indexical links between semiotic signs, means or modes and attributed meanings, functions or values. Communication is a dialogic practice that is defined by the participants' availability of means and their assessments of means-meaning indexicalities. And both aspects of this semiotic process are matters of contextualization. Meaning creation at any point in interaction involves the contextualization of forms, i.e. forms derive their meaning from the ways in which they relate to the entire network of contexts participants have access to. Contextualization is a matter of accessibility to contexts of semiotic activity. Every individual disposes of contextualization potential. This covers everything one can potentially draw from to attribute meaning to form. Context and contextualization are used as very broad concepts here ranging from the macro to the micro; from large economies of social, economic, political, cultural, etc. value attribution, linguistic and sociolinguistic systems, to interpersonal relations, accessibility to discursive strategies and mere contingency factors.

As all people are different, so are the contexts of discourse they have access to, their contextualization potential. It also follows logically that the interpretation of indexical relationships between forms and functions in a particular speech activity varies between individuals. In this respect, mobility of form-function indexicalities, i.e. the transferability of intended meanings or functions across contextualization spaces, is an issue in any form of human communication. For no two individuals belong to exactly the same social networks, share exactly the same experiences and can draw from exactly the same discursive repertoires. The social variability characterizing interlocutors and their contextualization potential implies that the contextualization of messages and hence their assessment of what may or may not become meaningful in interaction, will always be subject to potential variation between language users: forms may be attributed new functions or meanings and they may get contextualized differently as they are interpreted by different individuals. In short, communication is probably most obviously social in its dialogic dimension and therefore meaning creation is an intrinsically variable process.

This however does not imply that communication is by definition a problematic practice. Interlocutors often, remarkably, cope with the complexity inherent in speech activities. Yet pretextual sharing, interactional negotiation and control over meaning construction cannot be taken for granted in communication. There are gradations of semiotic mobility that need to be addressed. These gradations can be seen in the context of frequently discussed tensions between structural and creative forces in communication. Communication is social interaction and therefore an intrinsically creative practice, but at the same time it implies the input of individuals with ultimately unique contextual networks and constraints on contextualization potential. And it is this co-occurrence of social creativity and individual constraints that turns the process of contextualization into a very complex one to grasp. According to Gumperz:

> We can never be certain of the ultimate meaning of any message, but by looking at systematic patterns in the relationship of perception of surface cues to interpretation, we can gather strong evidence for the social basis of contextualization conventions and for the signalling of communicative goals. (1982:170)

In other words, although lots of things can potentially affect conversational understanding, there is always a systemic dimension to contextualization. I propose to use the notion of contextualization in terms of a complex interplay between systematically constrained aspects of context – accessibility to socially organized contextualizing spaces – and interactionally creative dimensions of contextualization – directions for contextualization and metapragmatic framing.

The hypothesis is that as difference increases between individuals, the more important discursive contextualization work will be. It is the relation between individual contextualizing spaces that qualifies the need for interactional contextualization and negotiation: the more boundaries participants have to cross, the more interactional efforts will be required to understand each other, to achieve semiotic mobility. And that's only logical. However, in some domains of social organization, variability is simply ignored and, paradoxically enough, it often concerns institutional practices in which all sorts of boundaries (social, generic, sociolinguistic) are transgressed simultaneously. Pragmatic and sociolinguistic work on institutional discourse concentrates on the discrepancies underlying information exchange between clients and bureaucrats in discursive gatekeeping processes (Agar, 1985; Drew and Heritage, 1992; Sarangi and Slembrouck, 1996). This work focuses on the entextualization, i.e. the de-and recontextualization of the produced discourse in the direction of standard criteria that are often not accessible to the people concerned, an asymmetry that is to a large extent discursively realized (Silverstein and Urban, 1996; Urban, 1996). Institutional entextualization processes entail a remodelling and remapping of the produced form-function indexicalities, all of which causes these relations to lose their initial functionality in the transfer.

The bureaucratic treatment of asylum seekers' cases shares many of the features described in the work on institutional discourse. What makes this domain of investigation so particular, however, is the fact that speakers are displaced in the literal geographic or spatial sense of the term. The interaction between officials and applicants in the asylum procedure doesn't merely involve the crossing of social, generic and stylistic boundaries, but also implies a movement across geographic spaces, all of which intensifies the mechanisms observed in other institutional practices.

Mobility and Displacement in Asylum Seekers' Narratives

The Belgian asylum procedure, like many other bureaucratic procedures, is an interview-based procedure in which, given the fact that only a minority of applicants are able to submit official documents, experiential narration is basically the only tool for explaining and supporting the application. As the main input in the legislative procedure is language-based, each case can be approached as a textuality complex in which the narrative of displacement occupies a central place. Direct interaction between applicants and officials forms the input of long and complicated textual trajectories across different stages of investigation.

My research aims to describe and analyze how meaning is produced and attributed in the asylum procedure. On the basis of a corpus comprising thirty-nine administrative files collected at the different authorities for determining refugee status – and for each file I witnessed and recorded at least one of the interviews between a public official and the asylum seeker concerned – I investigate different stages in the procedural sense-making process by focussing on how the interaction between applicants and public officials proceeds, how this interaction becomes the discursive input of long and complicated text trajectories and how the outcome of this procedural processing affects the decision-making process. A great deal of what happens in the interaction between applicants and public authorities can be related to the displacement of individuals and the re- and decontextualizations of their discourse. The nature and the impact of displacement in the asylum procedure are many-fold. In the first place, asylum seekers are physically displaced, and this is the main subject of their narration. Yet, physical displacement not only defines the subject of the information exchange, it also qualifies the way in which meanings are produced and interpreted. In the interaction between the applicants and the asylum authorities all sorts of social, geographic, generic and linguistic boundaries need to be crossed. The distance between the participants in the interaction involves an enormous diversity in contextualizing spaces that covers many aspects of communication: different expectations about the actual purpose of discursive activities, different code perceptions, differential accessibility to linguistic, pragmatic and sociolinguistic resources, different interpretations of interactional strategies, etc. It is this differential access to contexts, resources and epistemic domains that turns the assessment of meaning and functionality into a highly variable and problematic process. Utterances may be attributed new functions or meanings; they may get contextualized or interpreted differently as they move across contextualization spaces. Therefore, interactional contextualization work and metapragmatic framing in asylum interviews turn out to be crucial for making intended meanings explicit. The asylum procedure, however, offers very little space for interactional negotiation. Although the contextualization and negotiation of what they want to convey is indispensable for the applicants in order to make themselves understood, it is not picked up as such by the officials. In some cases it is immediately suppressed and disqualified as irrelevant and gets re-oriented towards institutional sense-making criteria. As their utterances become institutionally entextualized, they are attributed meanings that are far beyond and often totally at odds with the intentions of the asylum seeker. It is in this entextualization process that a third dimension of displacement can be observed: the discourse produced becomes subject to de-and recontextualizations as it moves from one stage in the procedure to the next. In short, instead of being negotiated in interaction, meanings are unilaterally imposed by the asylum authorities and become subject to institutional entextualizations that are far beyond the asylum seeker's control. The displacement of asylum seekers indirectly qualifies the functionality of the whole set of semiotic means and discursive contexts they can draw from in order to make themselves understood.

It is my aim to clarify and illustrate these textual dynamics on the basis of three data cases. The data is taken from a set of interviews conducted at the Immigration Office and concerns a group of young African girls who have chosen to do their interview in English. I have selected these fragments because their narratives apparently display some striking similarities in both narrative structure and linguistic resources: they consist of short and vague narratives that are told in a 'broken' variety of English.[2] On the basis of the data analysis I want to show: (a) how the interaction between the African asylum seeker and the public official can be characterized by differential accessibility to contexts of discourse; (b) how the asylum seeker is offered very little space for contextualizing and negotiating

---

[2] Fieldwork has been conducted at the Belgian asylum authorities in Brussels over a period of 10 months (October 2000- July 2001).

meaning and (c) how institutional contextualizations are imposed upon the asylum seeker's utterances with considerable implications for identity attribution. These dynamics will be explored from three perspectives that are central to the practice of information exchange in institutional encounters, viz. language ideology, institutional pragmatics and professional vision. The first data case relates to language ideological issues. It illustrates the effects of displacement on code variation and code perception and shows how the possibility for interactional contextualization work is precluded from the very start due to the non-sharedness of linguistic resources. The second case illustrates how displacement gives rise to differential accessibility to narrative ordering principles: what for the asylum seeker serves as important contextualization work for structuring the narrated events is not picked up as such by the official. The asylum seeker is interrupted and her contextualization work loses its function in the entextualization process. The third case investigates the impact of displacement on event perspective and addresses differential accessibility to experiential versus professional contexts of discourse: what serve as important epistemic and affective contexts for the asylum seeker becomes subject to professional vision. Before I turn to the first data case, however, I want to emphasize that the phenomena observed do not equally apply to all cases of procedural information exchange: both asylum seekers and applicants are individuals with different backgrounds, expectations, knowledge and lots of things – often contingency factors – can potentially affect the communication. But still, although to a great extent these variable factors qualify the interaction, I believe that some specific tendencies can be observed in the interaction between applicants and officials and I will now turn to their analysis.

Displaced textuality resources and deterritorialised language perceptions

Significant work in various disciplines focussing on language and society has shown that diversity and variation between and within languages has to be dealt with if we want to understand what language is all about. It is taken for granted now in sociolinguistics that instead of being conceptualized as abstract and homogeneous categories, languages need to be seen as complex and layered networks of language varieties that correspond with all sorts of sociolinguistic parameters: geographically, socially, situationally, etc. defined varieties. As people belong to various social categories at the same time, their utterances simultaneously carry all sorts of social information: information about their regional background, their age, their gender or the peer group they belong to. Discursive modes carry along this diversity inherent in speakers' social identities, and it is quite obvious that the diversity of the linguistic means deployed increases in intercultural communication. Yet, precisely in a language situation as multilingual as the asylum application interview, monolingual ideologies still appear to prevail. The impact of these ideologies is particularly felt in the procedural imposition of unequivocal linguistic choice, which requires on the part of the applicant full competence in one particular standard code. The institution is quite straightforward in this: the applicant has to declare in what language s/he wants to do the interview and then there are basically two options: (a) direct interaction between applicant and official (basically Dutch, English or French) and (b) mediation by an interpreter (or more interpreters in case one or more mediate codes are required for source-target translation). In both cases not much attention is being paid to potential linguistic variation, fusion or mixing and this accounts for a great deal of what goes wrong in procedural interaction.

The denial of linguistic variation particularly turns into a problem where the identification of non-native varieties of world languages such as English, French and Arabic is concerned. After all, every language has to be seen as a complex of varieties, and variation increases with scope. World languages such as English or French display an enormous range of language varieties, for example: native varieties with differing degrees of mother-tongue interference, second or third language varieties, pidginized and creolized varieties. Yet only standard varieties qualify for procedural interaction. Moreover, the institution skirts the additional problem that, just like the variation within codes, the categorization and perception of codes may also vary as people move across different places. The interviewer's perception of a particular code does not necessarily parallel the applicant's perception of it. Potential variability in the perception of codes, however, is not taken into account in the procedure and this may have quite serious implications for the asylum seeker. What the speaker identifies as a particular language is often subject to interference from other codes from the speaker's repertoire to such an extent that it is no longer intelligible or even recognizable as such for the interviewer. The problem is, however, that the applicant is supposed to inform the authorities formally in advance about the language in which s/he wants to do the interviews and it is based on this language choice that the allocation of an interpreter is decided. The gap between language perceptions and formal statements about language on the one hand and actual practice on the other gives rise to situations in which the varieties of what is labelled as one and the same language are divergent to such an extent as to require interpretation. The selection of interpreters is similarly affected by broad language generalizations in the sense that variation within the language is also ignored here. The following example shows discrepancies in perceptions of English. The applicant is a young girl from Sierra Leone. She identifies her language as English:[3]

Extract 1
   (1) I: Urm . what is the language you speak in Sierra .. English
   (2)   .. no other languages
   (3) AS: I speak English
   (4) I: you speak English ....yeah

English is supposed to serve as a lingua franca here so the assistance of an interpreter is not required:

Extract 2
   (1) I: so I'm gonna ask you to sign . your document urm this
   (2)   is your document so you can . stay here in Belgium .
   (3)   for the meantime . ok and this is a paper you want .
   (4)   you choose English . urm to do your interview ok .

However, in the following fragment taken from the same interview the applicant tries to explain how in Belgium she was picked up from the streets by a stranger who wanted to help her, and her lack of proficiency in the expected variety of English is evident:

Extract 3
   (1)   I said ok but then when we get there . he said he help me xxxxxxx
   (2)   and he brought .. 2000 Belgian Francs he give it to me then . he
   (3)   said ok . xxx usay to go xx is not going to take me but but I don't
   (4)   xxxxxx is problem that he's going to call ..xxxx why didn't he tell
   (5)   me this before .
   (4)   then he said no xxx the person wanted me to do ..; that . I don't

---

[3] The abbreviations used in the transcript: asylum seeker (AS) and interviewer (I). Transcription symbols are: / for an intonationally marked clause boundary, dots for pauses, = for overlaps, *x* for unclear parts of the utterance and *** for the interviewer's typing work on the computer.

(5)   want him to do xxx he told to call the police xx he'll make that
(6)   you she's going to tell the police xxxxxxx he said you can't do
(7)   that .. how can I go into the person I said I don't know before
(8)   then I I will come I'll be searching for what I xxx I said is not sure
(9)   I said for me to do that. I'll xxxxxx to give me .. something . xxx
(10)   if I don't want .... x will go to his place then he no tok me that .
(11)   his his wife were there . that . he don't live there . I said aah .. he
(12)   told me I don't marry... before .. he said long die not the problem..
(13)   then I said let me go to and I wanted to go . h he have xxx urm he
(14)   xx to . xxx I said urm .. why but I was running . I didn't know he
(15)   called the police ....

This chunk of experiential narration shows that interpretation would be no luxury for officials who are not familiar with African Englishes – note also how the procedural replicability conditions affect the interpretation of interview data: recording or transcribing are considered time-consuming. Apart from the fact that the fragment represented is a piece of highly fragmented narration, it is told in a code that displays African English elements, containing pidgin and Krio (a West African creole mainly spoken in Sierra Leone) interference: 'usay to go' (line 3: 'where to go'), 'he no tok me that' (line 10: he didn't tell me that), 'he said long die not the problem' (line 12: 'he said (she has) died long ago, that's not the problem'). At the same time, however, the applicant displays an enormous variety of resources, ranging from Pidgin English forms ('he said he help me' (line 1)) to quite complex verb constructions ('I'll be searching' (line 8), 'I didn't know he called' (lines 14-15)). In short, what the applicant produces as 'English' – an African variety of English that is permeated by instances of language mixing and shifting – does not correspond at all with the kind of English expected in the procedure. Still, the procedure does not address potential variability in the use and the perception of English and this puts asylum seekers at a disadvantage in expressing themselves.

The following extract shows how English as a 'standard language' does not work as lingua franca for the intercultural exchange of information. The interference of elements from African varieties of English at various levels of grammatical structuring (phonetic, syntactic, lexical) may cause crucial and sensitive materials to be misinterpreted or lost. As an example, a short field transcript is given of the interaction between a young Sudanese girl and a young female interviewer:

Extract 4

(1)	I:	you just ran away .... Uhum ...... and what happened
(2)		to . you ran away ... so where to .
(3)	AS:	one man ...... one man .. carry me . help me ....
(4)	I:	Karami
(5)	AS:	yes
(6)	I:	it was a man or a woman.......
(7)	AS:	man ....

The exchange is rewritten in the following statement selected from the interviewer's report (my translation from Dutch):

> "A man named Karimi helped me".

The lack of a third person singular 's' combined with the West African English pronunciation of 'carry me' as /kari:mi:/ (line 3) causes the interviewer to interpret the word group as the name of the man (line 4). The asylum seeker, however, probably because of her low proficiency in English, fails to detect this misunderstanding in the interaction. In cases such as these, the code itself forms one of the main obstacles to negotiating intended and interpreted meanings in interaction. These kinds of misinterpretations however have serious consequences for the eventual decision-making process: inconsistencies between the information (names, dates, places) provided during successive interviews in the different stages of investigation can, in combination with other criteria, be used as grounds for rejection.

Institutional pragmatics
The displacement of narrative resources

This dimension of displacement in the procedural context is concerned with the way in which the transfer of internalized experiences to an institutional interactional space is given shape. The applicant has to fall back on the communicative materials s/he has at his/her disposal to function in a discursive space that is controlled by a legalistic genre in terms of linguistic/narrative/stylistic mode – the concept of genre being used here in the broad Bakhtinian sense as a discursive mode related to a particular social context. This is a genre of formality and abstraction that crystallizes into the legally established categories and standard rules of evidence intrinsic to institutional semiotic centres: temporal order, precision and detail, and textual coherence and consistency (Blommaert, 2001; Maryns and Blommaert, 2002a). These genre expectations are clearly reflected in the official guides socializing the interviewers into prevailing conventions for narrating events as they are expected to be mirrored back in the interview reports.[4] However, the genre requirements are not merely asserted in the report. As a way of anticipating the required reformulation of the applicant's story into a legally transparent case, officials are equally inclined to push for the use of the required genre conventions of the report in the course of the interview. This however collides with what the applicant is able to bring into the interaction. Repercussions of conflicting genre expectations will be highlighted in a discussion of the negotiation of time and space in the interaction.

Maybe one of the most articulate expressions of the gap between institutional standards and speaker production lies in the structuring of the narrative in terms of time and space. Whereas the procedural report requires exact time references and a chronological ordering of the events, temporality and time are very complicated concepts for refugees. Displacement leads to confusion about time. Detention in isolated cells, weeks or even months of hiding in the bush or days of hiding on a ship. blur any perception of time. References to places and events, on the other hand, serve as much more useful orientation tools for the asylum seeker. In this way, the spatial structuring of personal experiences in asylum seekers' narratives relativizes the organizing function of temporality in narrative and confirms the observation that "[a] narrative of personal experience is far more than a chronological sequence of events" (Ochs and Capps, 1996:25). Asylum seekers' stories are organized around place. Their

---

[4] Determination of refugee status: UNHCR Training Module 1989: 33-34:
Encourage claimants to provide as much pertinent detail as possible about the incidents that relate to their claims. Knowing when, where, why, whom, what and how can help distinguish between a credible story and a false one. Establish a time frame, linking dates with location: if contradictions emerge, ask for clarification. The interview report should contain:
1. the account of events given by the applicant in a chronological and understandable manner,
2. a separate assessment of his credibility by the interviewer which takes into account:the applicant's attitude and behaviour (frankness, spontaneity, hesitation, or reticence);the feasibility of the statements made.

main subject is the narration of displaced lives. Physical displacement turns refugee experiences into predominantly spatial trajectories and becomes indexical of the exile identity of the speaker (Malkki, 1995b; Blommaert, 2001).

The following example illustrates how difficult it is for asylum seekers to make exact references to time. The extract is taken from an interview with a Sierra Leonese girl; it is a highly fragmented passage containing a mixture of Krio and English. It represents a clear instance of 'trajectory telling' in the spatial sense of the term:

Extract 5

(1)	I:	ok .. and urm when did you leave the camp
(2)	AS:	now the camp I be *there* the day . the war attacker get
(3)		me back . so one Fula xx for take me . Mohammed Bah .
(4)		so he can take me *now*
(5)	I:	uhum
(6)	AS:	xxxxxxxxxxx
(7)	I:	yes
(8)	AS:	xx *then* x go x inside na Guinea …. So *now there* they
(9)		hold me back and tell me now let me now send me to
(10)		(rebel) but they aks me I said that na tell tell you I did
(11)		no for tell you . they send me na Salone
(12)	I:	yeah
(13)	AS:	the reason xxxxxx Sierra Leone I commot I be *there*
(14)		now camp xxx camp xx
(15)	I:	uhum
(16)	AS:	I be *there* na camp . so I be there na camp .xxxx I de
(17)		*now* go came in Guinea.. when we came in Guinea . for
(18)		there now . I they left me . they de go so they xx xxx xx
(19)		didn't take me . so I be with them *now* so usay they be
(20)		usay they be found hus .. usay they be me hus .. so I be
(21)		there na bush *now* . all the time there be ..say xxxx
(22)		come in Guinea …..
(23)	I:	it it it's ok …
(24)	AS:	ok ……………
(25)	I:	urm . so you stayed in Guinea in the camp ..
(26)	AS:	yeah
(27)	I:	ok …
(28)	AS:	from Guinea now
(29)	I:	yeah
(30)	AS:	now we left there now the man xx and they take care
(31)		of me

(32) I: uhum

(33) AS: so when xxxx

(34) I: = it it's still Mohammed Barry who is taking care of you

(35) AS: yes

(36) I: ja ……..

(37) AS: so we de go *now* … he carry me na ONE big field ..

(38)   xxx but inside xxxxxxxxx so I come inside BIG field…..

(39)   from there now I did see xx (car) so be xx(car) . are

(40)   military .. xxxxxxxx .

(41) I: uhum .. and then you arrived in Belgium …..

The interviewer's question is a question about time: 'when did you leave the camp?' (line 1). In the entire trajectory telling of the applicant, however, any precise temporal reference in terms of days, months or years is missing. Instead we get a narrative organized around a set of nonlinear references to different places: from a displaced people's camp on the Guinean-Sierra Leonese border, sent back to Sierra Leone, replaced to a camp in Guinea, and then transported to one big field (presumably the airport in Conakry, the capital of Guinea). Time references are expressed in adverbs such as 'there' (line 2, 8, 13, 16), 'now' (line 4, 8, 17, 19, 21, 37) and 'then' (line 8). The narrative clearly displays what Blommaert identifies as patterns of temporal and spatial deixis, i.e. "nonlinear references to here/there and now/then/always [which] make up the considerable complexity of such stories" (Blommaert, 2001:435). And indeed, it is very hard to unravel the intricate network of placing and displacement. Lines 2, 3 and 4 for instance contain very complex references to place: no fewer than three different locations are referred to in one utterance. The deletion of important linking words however makes it extremely difficult to draw a line between the places talked about. Further contextualizing work 'clarifies' – ironically enough in this context of complicated experiential narration and linguistic repertoires that are very hard to decode – the link between the places. The utterance can be rephrased as 'now the camp I be there *until* the day . the war attacker get me back *to Sierra Leone* . so one Fula xx for take me . Mohammed Bah . so he can take me *now back to Guinea*'. In this extract, the asylum seeker is to a certain extent given the chance to contextualize her answer to the question, yet her accessibility to both linguistic and narrative resources considerably reduces the possibility for interactional uptake. Like the asylum seeker in extract 4, this girl also expresses herself in a mixed variety of African English. Moreover, she basically relies on spatial references for narrative structuring. Due to her lack of access to institutionally expected linguistic and narrative resources however, the importance of her contextualization work is not being picked up as such by the official. The asylum seeker is interrupted (line 34). Her contextualization work loses its function, as it is not suitable for interactional uptake.

Event perspective
Experiential versus professional vision

This dimension of displacement in institutional encounters addresses contrasts in experiential and professional event perspective. In bureaucratic settings such as the asylum seeker's interview, applicants present their case as an individual one. Yet it is not treated as such in the procedure: the bureaucratic processing of individual cases always involves a measurement against comparative ones and standard professional ways of processing information. Bureaucratic processing practices in the Belgian asylum procedure display some remarkable features of what Charles Goodwin refers to as 'professional vision': "socially organized ways of seeing and understanding events that are answerable to the distinctive interests of a particular social group" (1994:606), the social group here being the professional group of public officials who have been socialized into particular bureaucratic practices, that is who have learnt to behave and act in ways that are institutionally acceptable. Goodwin addresses the politics of representation and illustrates the ease with which arguments can be turned around using discourse practices that are 'in place'. Goodwin explores the theory behind perception, perspective and representation and illustrates how professional vision displays itself in the discursive activities of (a) coding: transformation of the observed phenomena into professionally established categories; (b) highlighting of particular phenomena as salient and (c) producing representations of selected parts of reality. Such practices of gaining professional vision characterize the socialization of public officials into their bureaucratic way of seeing things.

The following set of data cases shows how experiential narration becomes subject to practices of coding, highlighting and representation in institutional discourse. The interviews selected for the analysis share a number of striking features in terms of communicative behaviour, linguistic resources and narrative structure. The applicants are female, between

18 and 25 and come across as very shy and insecure throughout the interaction. They speak softly and avoid any eye contact with the interviewer. Their linguistic resources are limited: they pick up very little from what the interviewer says and their utterances are confined to disconnected word groups in which hardly any grammatical relations are expressed. Their narratives are vague and share a particular pattern: short fragmented references to what happened in their home country ('fighting everywhere', 'everybody run', 'I cry for help', 'he bring me to the place', 'white man help me', etc.) are immediately followed by an elaborate narration of their experiences in the country of refuge. The actual transfer from home country to refuge country, however, is hardly documented. Also striking are the repeated references to the train station and to the protagonist's search for particular people there. Some of the girls explicitly mention that they are looking for a job in the neighbourhood of the train station in Brussels (which calls up associations with prostitution networks). What follows is an example of such a narrative that displays some of the characteristics described above:

Extract 6

(1)	I:	************************************** what
(2)		happened to you especially that urm the reb ... so you
(3)		just left . because of the fight .. what happened to you ...
(4)	AS:	nobody I stay with . my . my auntie .. run .. I don't see her
(5)		.....
(6)	I:	everybody urm just ... ran away
(7)	AS:	I don't see her yeah I don't say anybody saw her ... I
(8)		run too ....
(9)	I:	***************************** *********** so.
(10)		so you didn't see nobody . from your family and you've
(11)		also ran away .
(12)	AS:	yes
(13)	I:	and uuurm . nothing happened to you especially like
(14)		urm the soldiers or the rebels came to you and did ......
(15)	AS:	huuuum . don't urm .... When they're fighting we run
(16)	I:	you just ran away .... Uhum ...... and what happened
(17)		to you ran away ... so where to ....
(18)	AS:	one man ...... one man .. carry me . help me ....
(19)	I:	Karami
(20)	AS:	yeah
(21)	I:	it was a man or a woman.......

(22) AS: man ……..
(23) I: *************************** yeah but … how did
(24)   he help you . hee took you some place … or he gave
(25)   you money or ….
(26) AS: no took … me .. place
(27) I: and you don't know where ………… ****** .. and
(28)   then ……………. … and then . **********
(29) AS: then
(30) I: = what happened then he took you to a place .. and
(31)   what happened then ….
(32) AS: I urm .. bring me … tell me …. He is safe …. And
(33)   …… I cry .. for help
(34) I: huhum …………….. *** ((telephone rings))
(35) …………..***
(36)   so you cried for help.. uhum .. and hat happened then ….
(37) AS: man ….. brave man ….. say .. why cry … me ..
(38) I: uhum
(39) AS: why cry ….. I say … I'm Soudan .. I don't have . body
(40)   here .
(41) I: uhum
(42) AS   and … take me . to place and . save me yeah . this man
(43)   has said … you . people . helped with xxx ……………..
(44) I: ***
(45)   ******* uhum .. and then ………………….
(46) AS: he urm he come here ….
(47) I: so . he . he didn't bring you to a white man . or something
(48)   …..
(49) AS: no . bring me .. here that you will help me … people
(50)   help me …………….

For the interviewers doing one interview after the other, these recurring features turn into recognizable patterns. One or two of these features suffice to trigger off an entire category such as that of 'prostitutes' (line 47: 'he didn't bring you to a white man or something'). The working pressure at the Immigration Office combined with the frustration with the poor linguistic proficiency of the speaker, but above all, the predictable outcome of the case, make the official decide not to put too much energy in this kind of interview. This routine has an impact on the officials' attitude during the interaction itself. A priori conjectures about the identity of the applicant stimulates them to deal with the case very quickly and to listen with a 'bureaucratic' ear. This lack of attention to individual cases results in a self-fulfilling prophecy that decides the interpretation of the case. As soon as the narrative displays a few of the recognizable elements, all subsequent utterances are interpreted as fitting the category, irrespective of the applicant's attempts to express herself. In this way, crucial information might get lost. This is clearly shown in the following example where the applicant's contextualizing work is disqualified and re-oriented towards institutional categories. The data is taken from an interview between a quite determined female interviewer and a girl of Sierra Leonese origin. The applicant here is asked to explain her problem:

Extract 7

(1)	I:	ok .... now you can tell me your
(2)		problem ... your father .... Your mother .. your brother .
(3)		and your sister . they are killed ... ok? ....
(4)		he .... That's right....... They're all killed .. your
(5)		family ..... all killed ((sign for (kill')) ...... hen ... why
(6)		....
(7)	AS:	listen . my father . joined the .. politician .... in the law
(8)		urm . they see my my my father
(9)	I:	uhum ..
(10)	AS:	he choose the side of the ... politician
(11)	I:	uhum ..
(12)	AS:	that is my ....
(13)	I:	ok ..and what was the name of the politicians ..
(14)	AS:	I don't
(15)	I:	you don't
(16)	AS:	xxxx ..the law school...............................
(17)		....
(18)	I:	what's the your father . was he member of a political
(19)		party ... .

The interviewer doesn't really make an effort to understand what the applicant is trying to say. As soon as she picks up a familiar word that can pass for a legal trope, she starts to shower the applicant with bureaucratic questions. The applicant cannot provide names or information about political parties. She does, however, try to give more contextual information about her father's political involvement, his profession at the law school and his affiliation with a colleague pastor (extract 7): 'my father joined the politician .. in the law.. they see my father..' (lines 7-8), 'the law school' (line 16), and confirms in the next extract 'you know at the law school' (line 5) 'he was colleague pastor' (line 10). Experiential narration serves as crucial contextual information for understanding her case. However, as soon as she starts her explanation – which is metapragmatically framed by the imperative 'listen' (extract 7, line 7) – she gets interrupted. The interviewer simply does not listen. The interviewer's communicative behaviour links up with the labelling practices and self-fulfilling prophecies as analyzed earlier, as can be seen in the following piece of interaction:

Extract 8

(1)	I:	the name of the pastor … you know his name
(2)		…………………….. what was the name of the pastor
(3)	AS:	x pastor (ok) ………………………….
(4)	I:	you know his name
(5)	AS:	you know at the law school ……..
(6)	I:	yes . you had no school but ….. you know . the name .
(7)		of the pastor
(8)	AS:	no
(9)	I:	no you don't know
(10)	AS:	he was colleague pastor pastor

Instead of giving the exact name of the pastor, the applicant launches into another attempt at explaining the pastor's connection to her father and the law school. Yet this information is interpreted by the official not as an explanation of her father's involvement in the law school, but as a statement about her own school experience. Misinterpretation here is rooted in the metapragmatic framing statement 'you know' (line 5) which triggers another one of the applicant's attempts to explain her case. The African English pronunciation of the verb 'know' as /no/ is central to the official's misinterpretation. A phonetic transcription of the entire utterance might be useful to illuminate what the interviewer eventually picks up: /ju: *no*: at di: la: *sku:l*/. Only what are interpreted as 'no' and 'school' survive the transmission. After all, limited school experience serves as one of the typical features of the described 'category' of refugees: the fact that one never had any schooling is often used as a reason for not having to give detailed information about timing, places or political situations, as in the following fragment taken from an interview with a Somalian girl:

Extract 9

(1)	I:	which year
(2)	AS:	well me no de go school I no

(3) I: no no but long ago
(4) AS: I no go school yes . they don't tell

The public official's interpretation of the utterances in extract 8 appears to be framed against situations such as the one represented in extract 9, in which reference to limited schooling has to account for the applicant's failure to provide detailed information. Differential patterns of accessibility to linguistic and narrative resources only encourage such interpretations. Despite the fact that the applicant indeed has something to tell, her explanatory attempts get lost in the official's biased interpretation of the discourse. The interviewer associates information from different contexts that contribute to a preconception about the applicant's belonging to a particular category of refugeeness. Such contexts are:

- The context of rehearsed narratives identified in intertextual links between linguistic, stylistic and narrative particularities of asylum seekers' stories and its connection with the above described climate of reluctance towards political refugees.
- The context of the further legal support of the case. The interview at the Immigration Office is the first one in the sequence of interviews that make up the procedure. It is the only interview, however, in which the applicant cannot fall back on the assistance of a lawyer. As soon as the lawyer comes in, these female applicants disappear from the institutional scene. They hand in a request for appeal but from then on they no longer turn up for the interviews. Strikingly enough, in their request for appeal, the names of particular lawyers turn up time and again.
- The context of recurring public discourses about the illegal trafficking of refugees and related internal staff notes about the ways in which applicants are being prepared for the interview by their trafficker. This applies both in terms of narrative content (what to tell) and in terms of communicative behaviour (e.g. the instruction to stick to vague notions of English in order to hide one's real linguistic identity), directed towards a delimitation of their potential for identity work in the narrative.

This involvement in particular contextual domains, however, is confined to the institutional side. The way in which "differential access to these contexts as well as to the circulation between them alienates applicants from the (de)construction of their own identity" (Maryns and Blommaert, 2002b:3; Briggs, 1997b) gives rise to hidden asymmetries in the possibility to determine what counts as reality.

Conclusion

In my discussion of displacement in asylum seekers' narratives, I concentrated on institutional discourse practices from the perspective of contextualization and mobility. On the basis of the hypothesis that a lot of what is shared in 'local' interaction needs to be made explicit in 'translocal' communication, I explored the importance of contextualization and performance in institutional encounters. Analysis pointed in the direction of a lack of contextualization space in the asylum procedure and a predominance of univocal categories, categories that are much easier to deal with than the complex diversity of people entering the procedure. In each of the three cases analyzed, it was shown how the production of contextualizing discourse was suppressed, lost its functionality in the interactional and textual transfer and got misinterpreted, with far-reaching consequences for identity attribution. A great deal of the interpretation – re-and decontextualization – of the asylum seeker's discourse however was not made sufficiently explicit to the asylum seeker and was appropriated in ways that were far beyond the asylum seeker's concerns.

The cases analyzed revolve around mobility: mobility of relations between linguistic, narrative, pragmatic resources and intended functions or meanings to different sense-making spaces. And mobility is a matter of accessibility to contexts of discourse. Hidden asymmetries in the ability to decide what counts as reality are rooted in differential accessibility to contextual spaces and strategies to regulate the circulation of the meanings produced between contexts. The procedure to a certain extent presumes equality yet from a critical perspective this assumption of sharedness could as well be seen as an ignorance of variability resulting in a unilateral imposition of institutional sayability and interpretability criteria. Conversational narrative performances are "dependent on local definitions of and expectations about narrative functions and tellability" (Georgakopoulou, 1997:11). This illustrates Briggs's observation that:

> [a] first general point about conflict narrative is that it is difficult to sustain the premise that there can be narratives independent of the situations in which they are told. The content and conduct of conflict narratives are linked through the circumstances of a particular telling, and they are further intertwined with a particular web of narrator, audience, purposes, and expectations. (1997a:42)

In short, successful transfer of speaker resources makes their communicative output 'work' well. This kind of 'preferred' transfer however is far from obvious in the asylum seeking procedure.

Even though initially the asylum seeker has the opportunity to tell his/ her story, the fact that the institutionally re-entextualized version is all that matters in the end considerably reduces the asylum seekers' rights to recount their version of what happened.

References

Agar, M. (1985) 'Institutional Discourse', *Text* 5 (3):147-68.

Blommaert, J. (2001) 'Investigating Narrative Inequality: African Asylum Seekers' Stories in Belgium', *Discourse & Society* 12/4:413-449.

Briggs, C. (ed.) (1997a) *Disorderly Discourse: Narrative, Conflict and Inequality*, New York: Oxford University Press.

------ (1997b) 'Notes on a "Confession": On the Construction of Gender, Sexuality, and Violence in an Infanticide Case', *Pragmatics* 7/4:519-546.

Drew, P. and J. Heritage (eds.) (1992) *Talk at Work. Interaction in Institutional Settings*, Cambridge: Cambridge University Press.

Georgakopoulou, A. (1997) 'Narrative', in J. Verschueren, J.O. Östman, J. Blommaert and C. Bulcaen (eds.) *Handbook of Pragmatics* (pp. 1-22), Amsterdam: John Benjamins.

Goodwin, C. (1994) 'Professional Vision', *American Anthropologist* 96 (3):606-633.

Gumperz, J. (1982) *Discourse Strategies*, Cambridge: Cambridge University Press.

Kristeva, J. (1991) *Strangers to Ourselves*, New York: Columbia University Press.

Malkki, L. (1995a) 'Refugees and Exile: From "Refugee Studies" to the National Order of Things', *Annual Review of Anthropology*, 24:495-523.

------ (1995b) *Purity and Exile*, Chicago, IL: University of Chicago Press.

Maryns, K. and J. Blommaert (2002a) 'Pretextuality and Pretextual Gaps: on De/refining Linguistic Inequality', *Pragmatics* 12/1:11-30.

------ (2002b) 'Conducting Dissonance: Codeswitching and Differential Access to Context in the Belgian Asylum Procedure', Paper, International Symposium on Bilingualism, Vigo, October 2002.

Ochs, E. and L. Capps (1996) 'Narrating the Self', *Annual Review of Anthropology* 25:19-43.

Sarangi, S. and S. Slembrouck (1996) *Language, Bureaucracy and Social Control*, London: Longman.

Silverstein, M. and G. Urban (eds.) (1996) *Natural Histories of Discourse*, Chicago, IL: University of Chicago Press.

Urban, G. (1996) 'Entextualization, replication and power', in M. Silverstein and G. Urban (eds.) *Natural Histories of Discourse* (pp 21-44), Chicago, IL: University of Chicago Press.

The Registration Interview
Restricting Refugees' Narrative Performances

MARCO JACQUEMET, *University of San Francisco, USA*

"Refugees should stay home".
Italian Senator Umberto Bossi, leader of the Lega Nord,
an anti-immigrant political party.

Introduction

In 2000 the United Nations High Commission on Refugees' office in Tirana, Albania, held responsibility for granting refugee status to Kosovars seeking UN protection and aid. By then, almost a year after the Kosovo war had ended, it had become apparent that a large number of the people claiming to be refugees had never set foot in Kosovo and were in fact Albanian citizens. One of UNHCR's responses to these bogus claims was to alter the registration interview radically: would-be refugees were no longer allowed to tell their stories in free and unobstructed narratives but had to be thoroughly quizzed on their local knowledge of Kosovo (toponymy, local terms, and cultural labels). Using data gathered in the UNHCR Registration office in Tirana, this paper discusses the link between narratives and credibility, explores the problematic nature of turning the interview process into a judicial process, and assesses the sociopolitical and humanitarian consequences of restricting refugees' narrative performances.

Tirana, Albania[1]

Winter 2000. The southwestern Balkans were in a suspended state of calm, as if someone had pushed the pause button in a war video game. The

---

[1] The research for this chapter was conducted in Tirana, Albania, from December 1999 to June 2000 with the aid of a Wenner-Gren Travel Grant and a Sabbatical Leave Fellowship from Barnard College, New York. Final write-up was supported by a Summer Research Grant from the University of San Francisco. I would like to thank these institutions; my field assistants, Idlir Azizi and Ilirjana Stringa, for their help in transcribing, translating, and editing the transcripts; Roz Morris (Columbia U), Caz Philips (Barnard), Lesley Sharp (Barnard), Radhika Subramaniam

legions of NATO officials and journalists who watched the war from the relative safety of Tirana had, for the most part, cleared out. To the north, NATO air power had succeeded in chasing Serbian forces out of Kosovo. This region of the Yugoslavian Federation, in which NATO had engaged its military power to protect the Albanian majority from Serbian 'ethnic cleansing', had become a somewhat autonomous zone under international protection. Though the border between Kosovo and Serbia remained sealed, communications and transport between Albania, Kosovo, Macedonia, and Montenegro had improved dramatically since the war's conclusion in July 1999.

Meanwhile, the swell of people passing through the United Nations High Commission for Refugees (UNHCR) Registration Office in Tirana to apply for refugee cards had subsided. Still, the appointment schedule was filled to capacity. Each morning five or six families patiently waited their turns. One by one, each family was invited into a small inner office to be interviewed by UNHCR staff who would determine the legitimacy of the applicants' asylum claims.

In the warmth of this office the asylum-seekers sat down next to an interpreter, across the table from a UNHCR officer. During the interview they heard the hum of computers in the background, as well as the noise of power generators in the backyard – the international community's audible affirmation of power and autonomy from a local government unable to deliver electricity. Outside the UNHCR office, Tirana was a mess. Because of the need for heating during the freezing Balkan winter, the energy supply was spread thin. Electricity was available just two to three hours a day. Since the former Communist regime chose electricity to be Albania's sole form of energy, this meant that one could do practically nothing outside those hours. People could not heat their homes, cook, run water to wash dishes or clothes (because pressure was maintained by electric pumps), take warm showers, watch television, or use other electronic appliances.

As a result it seemed that everybody in Albania wanted out. For a brief period during the Kosovo war, the invasion of Albania by NATO military personnel, international news organizations, and aid agencies had allowed Albanians a taste at home of the Western life they had previously only glimpsed on the TV screens or heard about from returning migrants. Anybody who could speak a foreign language was hired for $100 a day by

(Connect/ArtsInternational), Paul Silverstein (Reed), Christopher Kamrath (USF), and Johnnie Johnson Hafernik (USF) for their comments, and Dawn Cunningham for her insights and editing.

foreign news media. Spare rooms could be rented to foreigners for $50 a day. Drivers were in constant demand. Money was finally flowing in a country where the average pension was $60 per month. However, by fall 1999 all of this was gone, leaving behind only a handful of agencies in need of Albanian workers. Even shadowy entrepreneurs trafficking in dope, humans, and weapons had moved their operations to Kosovo – by then the ultimate lawless zone.

Before the war, Albanians who could not leave by legal means were left with only one option: to take the *gommoni*, rubber speedboats that could bring them to Italy in two hours, but were also liable to lose their passengers overboard in the choppy Adriatic waves. Even once would-be migrants made it to Italy, they were often intercepted by the Italian police, interned in prison-like camps, and sent back at the earliest opportunity. But with the Kosovo War, Albanians found a new avenue: they could try to pass for Kosovar refugees. By the winter of 2000 a growing number of Albanians, locked out of rich countries by immigration restrictions, increasingly resorted to scoring an asylum card as the only legal means of achieving the right to migrate.

This was perhaps the most ironic development of the Kosovo crisis, and the most telling evidence of the quality of life in Albania. Among the asylum applicants in the UNHCR Registration Office on any given day there may have been a number of Albanian citizens desperately seeking to be recognized as Kosovar refugees. While most people designated as 'refugees' have had this label imposed upon them, Albanians sought it out and, when they attained it, saw it as a godsend. Besides a weekly allowance of food and cash for lodging, refugee status brought the right to medical treatment (in the most urgent cases, even air evacuation to a European Community hospital) and, most importantly, the chance to be resettled abroad in Western Europe, the United States, or Canada.

As a result, the UNHCR mission in Albania had evolved from providing legal documentation to refugees and mediating between refugees and humanitarian organizations, to investigating the asylum-seekers' claims to be Kosovar refugees. The priority of the Registration Office (for both staff and interpreters) became identifying bogus claims for this status filed by Albanian citizens. Every interview conducted by the office's staff and interpreters included careful screening of the identity of the asylum-seekers – a process that depended heavily on the interpreters' fluency in multiple Albanian dialects as well as in English.

In their interactions with asylum-seekers, caseworkers and interpreters made a point of never asking the would-be refugees to tell any stories of their ordeal. During the interview, they abandoned their curiosity for narratives in an effort to determine the asylum-seeker's objective link to Kosovo. In short, stories were denied a role in the determination of the refugees' status. Refugees perceived this denial both as a lack of trust on the part of the caseworkers and as a sign that their suffering did not count in this bureaucratic encounter. This in turn caused serious problems in refugees' perception of the asylum process and, more importantly, in their ability to utilize their encounter with relief workers as a therapeutic moment in the search for closure of a usually traumatic experience. As a result these interviews were experienced as confrontations rather than as exchanges based on trust, and some refugees found themselves resorting to angry posturings to vent their frustration with the bureaucratic handling of their case.

In documenting such a denial of narratives, this chapter first addresses the link between stories and credibility, then looks at the UNHCR's treatment of refugees' attempts to launch a narrative performance. Finally, it discusses how the denial of narratives was interpreted by refugees as a symptom of the relief organization's lack of 'humanity', resulting in an antagonistic stance that hindered any chance for an open and frank exchange, which led to serious consequences for the entire asylum process.

Narrative Performances and Credibility

The link between refugees' stories and their referential value is fraught with ambiguity and paradox. As Knudsen remarked in his contribution to *Mistrusting Refugees*, after the first interaction with the asylum process, refugees learn that a carefully crafted interview is a ticket for an easy certification process while a mismanaged one can cause delays, even application denials: "Any incongruity has serious consequences if judged to be a deliberate deception intended to advance one's position in the departure queue. Inconsistencies must, therefore, be minimized, not only in the personal data reported but also in the life history presented" (1995:22).

Refugees must manipulate their experience – inevitably messy, complicated and confusing – to provide a straight, simple narrative reality perceived to fit the requirements of the asylum process. The resulting narrative performances are scattered along a continuum between understatement and overstatement. Quite often, refugees tend to understate their experience. Val Daniel, in his research on Tamil refugees, pointed out the "unshareability and incommunicability of pain and terror" (1996:139): the telling of an act of torture or execution is believed to be too monstrous for words, the experience to be unlike any other, making it impossible to relate. Asked to explain their ordeal, refugees rely on stock narratives that couch that pain in acceptable scenarios that can be shared with people who have not experienced their unutterable suffering.

At the same time, we find many cases where these narratives are overstated. For instance, the British writer Caroline Moorehead, one of the country's most eloquent defenders of asylum rights, was reported in the *New Yorker* to be saddened by the fact that each refugee, knowing the odds against asylum – knowing that asylum itself involves a kind of triage – has to describe a past that is more horrific than the one his compatriot, and often his friend, has just recited to the person who will assess their cases (Kramer, 2003).

Either understated or overstated, refugees' stories run the risk of losing a measure of their truth, of their integrity, and thus of their credibility. This is partly due to the fact that these stories are not shared casually with friends, but are told to strangers in institutional settings invested with the infinitesimal techniques, tactics and devices through which authority, legitimacy, and dominance operate.

How should the international agencies in charge of refugees respond to this conundrum? Should they simply trust the refugees? Should a therapeutical concern for the healing power of narratives overwrite a bureaucratic concern for precise information and accurate facts? Or should they altogether cease listening to the refugees' stories?

In 2000 the UNHCR office in Tirana opted for the latter. Its decision not to rely on narratives reflected a common-sensical suspicion on the part of UN officers of the power of stories. To explain this suspicion we can point to three phenomena which constitute the inner workings of narrative performances: *persuasion, entextualization,* and *participation framework.* In other words, the motives at the basis of UN officers' refusal to collect stories stemmed from a resistance (more or less below the level of awareness) to the structural and rhetorical capabilities of narratives.

First, stories persuade by appealing to a human need for syntagmatic coherence. Stories string individual and separate facts into a compelling isotopic plot, able to increase the credibility not only of the entire narrative but also of single facts (Greimas, 1982). Defence attorneys, for instance, are known to encourage their clients to provide testimony in a narrative form, precisely to enhance their credibility (O'Barr, 1982; Jacquemet, 1996; Hirsch, 1998; Conley and O'Barr, 1998; Taslitz, 1999). By refraining from assessing refugee narratives, the UNHCR sought to establish 'objective' criteria for the assessment of each individual 'fact', evaluating each case by running through a checklist of facts instead of listening to the narrative development of a personal history.

Second, as Briggs argues in his study of conflict talk: "the art of con-necting words to form narratives provides humans in a wide range of societies with powerful tools for creating and mediating conflict and in doing so, constituting social reality" (1988:272). Stories constitute social reality through the process of *entextualization*, that is: "the process of ren-dering discourse extractable, of making a stretch of linguistic production into a unit – a text – that can be lifted out of its interactional setting" (Bauman and Briggs, 1990:70). Through distinctive features of narration (framing devices, reported speech, metalinguistic statements) stories not only recreate and comment on prior events, but in the process allow a particular recollection of these events to become a text, transposable to a variety of different contexts. In institutional settings, this means that sto-ries can be lifted from their interactional context to enter the public record, thereby acquiring legal force.

Finally, narrative performances such as storytelling allow participants to reframe and transform social relations. As Goodwin (1990) pointed out, stories operate on the *participation framework* of the people involved in the performance. In many cases, stories can dramatically alter the rela-tionships among participants, making it possible for people to align themselves with particular narrators and be recruited into the storytelling performance to declare their position vis-à-vis the characters and events in the story. Storytelling thus has the capacity to transform power alli-ances among participants, to force them to take sides: stories are in fact addressed to everybody in reach, and these people become an active audi-ence charged with the task of evaluating the story and declaring their disposition towards the matter under examination.

These three factors (persuasion based on isotopy, entextualization, and participation framework) would considerably reduce the power of an in-terviewer to control and unilaterally manage a verbal interaction. This is, in my opinion, the reason for the UNHCR's policy against allowing refu-gees to engage in open, unobstructed narratives. But how was this discouragement of stories achieved in the on-going flow of an institu-tional interview?

In the next section, I will look in detail at the interactional strategies and verbal tactics used between UNHCR agents and asylum-seekers in the aftermath of the Kosovo War. After introducing the socio-political context of these interactions, I will explore UNHCR's tactics for stopping stories by examining micro-sequences of institutional encounters during the asylum registration process.

The Registration Procedure

The registration process is one of the technologies of power set up by humanitarian relief agencies for managing mass displacements of people. Together with the refugee camp (see Malkki, 1995), the registration process establishes an ordered, replicable, and consistent operation that depends on smooth interactional routines to achieve its goal of surveillance, discipline, and control. In this way, the registration process may be considered a discourse practice. As we know from Foucault (see for instance his inaugural lecture at the Collège de France, 1981[1972]), discourse practices do not necessarily seek to depict the world: rather, they dictate the world by mobilizing tactics of social indexicality and strategies of social inequality advantageous to the dominant group(s) in charge of institutional decision-making.

The Caseworkers

The UNHCR international staff in Tirana in 2000 came from all over the world – Spain, Uganda, Peru, Japan. Most of them were young, and were on their first or second UN mission, in many cases under temporary contracts renewable every six months. The majority had been hastily recruited for Kosovo emergency and had been quickly deployed to the field after minimal training (in most cases provided by individual nations and not by the UN).

Their duty during the registration process was to find a clear and substantial connection between the asylum-seeker and his/her purported Kosovar origin. They routinely spoke in English (the official language of this global organization) for internal communication, to direct their local staff (all fluent in English and usually another international language), and to communicate with the interpreters.

Their lack of cultural and linguistic awareness was at times quite pronounced. Behaving like post-colonial players, they seemed unable to grasp and understand the complexities of local interactions, and as a result relied heavily on their staff, and especially on the interpreters, for almost all their dealings with the refugees. This placed a heavy burden of responsibility on the local staff and again especially on the interpreters, who were left squarely in charge of the registration process.

The Interpreters

The UNHCR interpreters, Kosovar refugees themselves, played a pivotal, though often unrecognized, role in managing the interaction between asylum applicants and the international community represented by the UNHCR. They were the most transidiomatic of speakers among Kosovar refugees. They were fluent in the Gheg variety of Albanian spoken in Kosovo, able to detect its differences from the Gheg spoken across the mountains in Northern Albania, conversant in Albania's standard language, and effective in an English-language environment. All were male and most came from an urban, college-educated milieu. They were recognized as 'community elders' by both refugees and the UNHCR, although in some cases they were still in their twenties.

At the peak of the registration drive during the Kosovo war, the UNHCR employed twelve interpreters, who were scattered all over Albania: near the checkpoints at the Kosovo border, in the refugee camps and in the temporary offices opened by the UNHCR in the main Albanian towns. At that time registration interviews were hastily conducted while the interviewees were waiting in line for food or shelter. The interviews lasted five minutes at the most – a short time indeed to determine whether someone really came from Kosovo, if s/he belonged to a Kosovar family, if s/he was a Kosovo Liberation Army member.

Once the emergency ended, all interviews were moved to the UNHCR headquarters in Tirana. Only the best of the interpreters were retained, and were given more time and responsibility for addressing asylum requests. Interpreters were also in charge of scheduling interviews and helping asylum-seekers fill out the many forms required prior to the interview.

These pre-interview screenings were somewhat problematic, since they inevitably biased the interpreters' assessment of the asylum-seekers. Instead of relying on hard evidence, in most cases interpreters' first impressions were heavily influenced by such communicative factors as accent, looks, or politeness. From the moment the asylum-seekers approached them to set up interviews, the interpreters turned into communicative detectives – they tuned their ears to accents, checked clothes and communicative behaviour, and observed women's gazes and postures. As a consequence, before the interview proper had even started, the interpreters in many cases had already made up their minds, often based on the conviction that they had detected the 'wrong' accent (i.e. a North Albanian accent when speaking Gheg) or other non-Kosovar clues. This bias was then carried over into the interview proper, with potentially life-changing consequences.

The Interview

The interview itself was based on a well-oiled routine. The UN caseworker would ask short questions, through the interpreter, to determine an applicant's name, date of exit from Kosovo, prior contacts with relief organizations, and number and whereabouts of close relatives. Together, officer and interpreter would also check the authenticity of identity documents (if they had not been lost or destroyed at the border by Serb police). Then the UN officer would turn the entire proceeding over to the interpreter, who took the initiative in evaluating the applicant's claim of being Kosovar.

This relay was usually achieved by the caseworker (C) asking the interpreter (I) to ask the would-be refugee (R) a question about Kosovo's toponymy:

03/08/00²

R=young man
C ↔ I
01   C   so can you ask him some questions about this part of kosovo?
I ↔ R
02   I   pa thuma tash ndonjë fshat të rrethinës së malishevës aty?
         (now, can you name any village of the malisheva area?)
03   R   po (..) është- belanica/ thuj mbas qysh i thone belza- baja-
         (yes..there is- belanica/ and after it I say belza- baja)
04   prejucaki- seniti- është:: (..) si e ke emrin- është klecka një-
         (preucaki- seniti- then:: .. what's its name... klecka, this is a-)
05   një lagje komplet në prizren- sa thashë unë- pese t´i thashe-
         (a- large neighbourhood in prizren- how many I mentioned-
         five?)
06   (..) pastaj vjen durgazi- vjen bllaca- vjen kemecia- asht-
         (... then there's durgazi- then bllaca- then kamenica- that's it)
C ↔ I
07   C   yes he knows well that region.

The interpreter/questioner would initially limit himself to probing the

---

² The transcripts identify the date of the interview, the gender and age of the refugee, and the primary axis of conversation (caseworker-interpreter: C ↔ I, interpreter-refugee, I ↔ R, or multi-party C ↔ I ↔ R). The interpreters' English turns are left in their original form. I use the following transcription conventions:

=	latching turns
=/=	overlapping turns
CAPS l	oudness
(text?)	difficult to hear
(xxx)	impossible to hear

applicant's knowledge of his/her alleged area of origin. Most people, such as the man above, would answer this query with a long list of toponyms. If an interpreter did not know the applicant's home town, he would compare the applicant's description with the sketches of villages and towns drawn by other refugees at the request of the UNHCR. Or he would ask about the nearest large town, the villages that one passes en route to that town, or the name of the most important mosque or bridge in the area. Here again, he would often consult maps drawn up exclusively to verify the answer's accuracy.

If, in the pre-interview screening, the interpreter's first impression of dealing with a compatriot had been positively reinforced by the applicant's responses, the interview was conducted in a relaxed mood. Sometimes the interpreter would preface questions about Kosovo with disclaimers about the need to follow 'procedure'; at other times he might even suggest the right answers. A smooth interview would, in this case, last only a few minutes.

On the other hand, if an interpreter suspected the accent, behaviour, or look of the asylum-seeker, then the interview quickly turned into a rigorous interrogation. Family members were separated and interviewed in succession. Knowledge of local geography and Kosovar practices were probed over and over again. Some people, unable to answer, blamed their ignorance on the isolation of their lives. Women, in particular, would claim never to have left their houses after their wedding days (a claim eagerly corroborated by their husbands, who proudly confessed that they were 'religious fanatics').

If people were unsure about toponyms, the interpreter would test knowledge of local farming and cooking terminology, or Yugoslavian bureaucratic practices. After the interpreter was satisfied, he would give the officer a synopsis, in English, of his questioning and the applicant's responses; sometimes he would give his assessment alone of the case (as in line 7 above).

The majority of the asylum-seekers were somewhat puzzled at having to describe their town or region to prove that they came from there, and sometimes did not comprehend the connection between this line of questioning and their asylum application.

03/09/00
    R=young woman
    C ↔ I
    01   C   can you ask her some questions?
    I ↔ R

02   I   yes- mirë si ashtu thotë- na thuni ca lagje të gjakovës-
           (yes- well, how- so she says- name us some neighborhoods in
           giakova)

03   diçka për gjakovën
           (some things about gjakova)

→   04 R   do të dij ça kam bërë atje?
           (does she want to know what I did there?)

→   05 I   JO. lagjet lagjet e gjakovës
           (NO- neighborhoods, neighborhoods of gjakova)

06   R   rrugët?
           (streets?)

07   I   rrugët- mëhallat- mund t´na i thush?
           (streets- city quarters- can you tell us?)

08   R   po
           (yes)

Most asylum-seekers, such as the university student interviewed above, thrown off by the topographic inquiries, instinctively sought to provide autobiographical narratives (line 4, where she asks whether they wanted to know some narrative details of her life in Gjakova). However, as we already mentioned, the UNHCR was not interested in narratives, and the interpreter was quick and forceful in rejecting the asylum-seeker's offer of personal stories (line 5). This active discouragement of narratives stood in striking contrast with asylum-seekers' expectations about the registration interview: that the entire process of becoming a refugee would entail the reconstruction of their past lives and the deliberate, exquisitely detailed telling of the story of their ordeal. In this case, the university student could only reply to the interpreter's questions with a meek "yes" (line 8) before producing a list of Giakova's streets.

Yet the power of syntagmatic coherence was often too great to resist and some applicants, even in recalling toponyms, managed to give detailed narrative descriptions of the area, walking the interpreter through the village streets: at the left is the mosque, the market is down on the right, home is just on the other side of the stream.

Preventing Stories

Both caseworkers and interpreters put considerable effort into trying to prevent asylum-seekers from relating unobstructed narratives. The caseworkers' main concern was to restrict the interview through punctual and detailed questions with the goal of determining the asylum-seeker's link

with Kosovo. This concern was readily apparent in one of the first encounters I observed, in which a young woman arrived at the office with an
identity card (supposedly, but unverifiably hers – identity cards produced
during the war did not have pictures) cut in two. She asked to have a new
one issued to her. The caseworker, suspecting identity fraud, decided to
interrogate the woman regarding the card. After asserting that it had been
cut during a car accident, she tried to launch into a narrative that would
provide some credibility to her claim of being a refugee:

02/07/00
    R=young woman
    (..)
    I ↔ R
    08   R   jo jo jo- kur kina ardhë në shqipëri- na kanë- kanë sjellë në
                   (no no no- when we came to Albania we were pushed to
                   Albania)
    09   shqipëri serbët- na kanë- qit nëpër rrugë- nëpër mal kish pasë
                   dhe
                   (by the Serbs- they- drove us away- into the mountains-)
    10   një minë- asht ra mixha jem baba-
                   (a mine was there – my uncle and father stepped on it)
    C ↔ I
    11   I   she explain something during the war how they came here –
    12   Albania
    13   (..) and she said on the mine my father cut the leg-
    14   C   yeah
    15   I   and my uncle lost his life
    16   C   and?
    17   I   he were- he was died.
→   18   C   and what's the relation with this card?

By bringing the young woman back to the issue of the card (line 18), the
caseworker seeks to avoid the open-ended development of the narrative.
At the same time, this move might be read as demonstrating callous disregard for the highly traumatic story being told by the woman. Note also the
interpreter's freedom in relaying the events, where the statement "my uncle and father stepped on a mine" (line 10) is rendered as a wounded
father (line 13) and a dead uncle (line 17).

While in the case above control of the interaction was mostly achieved
by the caseworker, in most cases the task of stopping storytelling fell heavily
to the interpreters who, because of their interactional role, represented the
first line of defence against unobstructed narratives. The simplest way to

prevent storytelling was achieved by implementing a strict question and answer format:

02/07/00

    R=adult male

    C ↔ R

    01   C but did you obtain a- uh passport in kosovo?

    I ↔ R

    02   I   po ju a keni marrë pasaportë në kosovë a keni marrë pasapor-=
                 (did you obtain a passport in Kosovo a passport did you)

    03   R =janë djegë
                 (they are burned)

    C ↔ R

    04   C before the war

    I ↔ R

    05   I   PARA lufte/ para lufte para lufte a keni pasë ju pasaportë?
                 (BEFORE the war, before the war did you have a passport?)

    06   R po po
                 (yes yes)

    07   I   po po apo jo?
                 (yes, yes or no?)

    08   R po pasaportë-
                 (yes passport)

    09   I   keni pasë?
                 (did you have one?)

    10   R kemi pasë e janë met andej ato hupë
                 (we had them but we left them behind, they are lost)

    I ↔ C

    11   I   he repeat the same thing,

    12   we lost the passport, we lost the documentation

Most of the time asylum-seekers tried to expand the question and answer format into a more conversational structure, which in most cases meant trying to launch a narrative explanation of their case. However, the ever-vigilant interpreters were quick to stop any attempt at storytelling in its tracks. As soon as an answer departed from the expected script and especially if it seemed to lead into a story, the interpreter promptly redirected the asylum-seeker to the solid ground of well-known toponyms:

01/28/00

    R=man in his forties

    C ↔ I

    01   C can you ask him some question about the region?

02   I   yes
I ↔ R
03   tash a mundet me thanë diçka për uh uh- rrethin e deçanit-
          (now can you say something about uh uh-deçan county-)
04   katundet rreth decanit a mund i thuni?
          (the villages around deçan can you name them for me?)
05   R   iznici-raxhaja-ralia-deri deri (..)
          (iznici-raxhaja-ralia-deri deri..) [pause]
06   në plavë e në guci e i kam shtëtit unë e =jam ken-=
          (up to plava and gusi I have been there because I went to-)
→ 07   I   = hajde =
                                                       (come on!)
08   thumi katundet e rrethit të deçanit
          (name me the villages in deçan county)

In the case above, as soon as the asylum-seeker moves to launch a narrative (see the two story preface cues in line 6: 'because' and 'I went' mark
the motive and deictical pronominalization for the story), the interpreter
quickly overlaps (=), interrupts the other, and directs him to stick to the
question. Metalinguistic awareness, ever present in any good interpreter's
bag of tricks, is here so heightened that the interpreter recognizes story
cues as soon as they emerge. He is thus able to pre-empt the actual launching
of the story, thereby avoiding the more difficult task of stopping a narrator
in the middle of his performance.

As Goodwin (1990) reminded us, stories have the power to engage
participants in a speech event and impede early unilateral exit from the
event. Particularly in the case of a one-on-one interaction, obligations
imposed by the interactional order (such as those described in Goffman,
1974) make quite difficult for the listener to interrupt the storytelling without serious face loss for everybody involved. It is much easier to halt a
story before its full emergence by resorting to metalinguistic directives
(such as the "come on! name me the villages" in lines 7-8) that successfully restore control of the exchange to the interpreter.

Another tactic used to halt refugees' attempts to launch narratives was
offered by the particular sequential organization of turn-taking set up by
the need to interpret. Other researchers (Berk-Seligson, 1990; Davidson,
2000) have already pointed out the gate-keeping role played by interpreters. Rather than serving as a neutral conduit between case worker and
asylum-seeker, the interpreter is an active participant in the exchange,
maintaining parallel and related conversations with the other two partici-

pants, keeping each informed of the other's general drift. In the material under study here, this role is boosted by the interpreter's power to silence one of the other speakers (that is, the asylum-seeker) by simply ceasing to translate and selecting the caseworker as next speaker:

01/28/00

    R=old man
    I ↔ R
    01   R   jo unë po t´thome se unë jam shëtit e jam kon atje- për-
                (no I am saying I have been around and I was there-for-)
    02   më ka rasti që të ngrihem q´aty-
                (I had the chance to go up there-)
    03   I   jo uh- të rrethit të deçanit katundet
                (no uh-{tell me about] deçan county, the villages)
    04   R   t´i thashë- këvralla- elebi- s´jam marrë me atë punë unë veç-
                (I told you: këvralla,elebi- I didn't just walk around but-)
    05   (xx) në postë jam =marrë me-
    →   (once in the post office I dealt with-)
    I ↔ C
    06   I   =he doesn't know.

In the case above, as soon as the asylum-seeker begins a story (line 5), the interpreter quickly overlaps and interrupts him by switching to English and directly addressing the caseworker, producing a realignment in the participation framework. Moreover, the interpreter does not limit himself to addressing the caseworker, but uses this opportunity to assess the communicative performance of the asylum-seeker (line 6). This behaviour on the part of the interpreter points to his role as 'interpreter-judge' (a label devised by Davidson in his study of interpreters in medical encounters, 2000): instead of serving as an advocate for interpreted asylum-seekers, the interpreter acts as an informational gatekeeper, assuring a smooth interactional routine while maintaining a role of prominence in the exchange. His interpreting competence allows him not only to control the flow of the interaction but also to pass judgement on the asylum-seeker being interviewed.

The next case, a stringent interrogation of a young woman claiming to have been attacked by Serbian soldiers, clearly shows the interpreter's personal involvement in determining the asylum-seeker's credibility. Here again, as soon as the asylum-seeker attempts to initiate a story involving Serbian policemen, the interpreter stops her by asking a fact-seeking question regarding their uniforms:

02/07/00
  R=young woman
  I ↔ R
  01   I   çfarë uniforme kanë pasë?
           (What was their uniform?)

  02   R   kur na-
           (when we-)

  03   I   çfarë ngjyre kanë pasë?
           (What color?)

  04   R   ngjyrë- unë kur jam ardhë vetëm për shqipni kam pa ma së
           shumti serb-
           (color- while coming to Albania I saw mostly Serbians-)

  05   ata ishin me ngjyrën- qashù ngjyrë ushtarake-
           (they had the color- a military color, like this)

  06   I   çfarë?
           (which?)

  07   R   sikur ajo ngjyra [points to green sweater]
           (like that color)

  08   I   kjo? [points to green sweater]
           (this one?)

  09   R   e si ajo-
           (yes like that-)

  I ↔ C
  10   I   this kind of color [points to green sweater]
  11   the uniform- uniform
  12   C   uh uh- serbian force/
  13   I   serbian police
  14   C   uh uh

  R ↔ I ↔ C
  15   R   edhe me maska në kry-
           (and with masks on their heads)

  16   I   and with some masks=
  17   R   =ne na kanë vjedh- kur kemi ardhè këndej na kanë vjedhé=
           (they robbed us- when we came here they robbed us=)

  18   I   =but is not true

After having forced the young woman to identify the colour of Serbian
police uniforms (lines 1-9), the interpreter dismisses the case as a false
claim (Serbian police uniforms, he knows, are black). He quickly loses
interest in this case and ends up declining to translate the asylum-seeker's
last turn (line 17), offering instead his assessment of the mendacity of the
interviewee (line 18).

Against the Procedure

Most of the asylum-seekers in Tirana resented the UNHCR procedure, finding it a demeaning and final trauma in their already traumatic adjustment to life as a refugee. They were particularly shocked by the implicit lack of trust underlying the registration interview. Moreover, the apparent callousness with which they were asked to recall toponyms of an area severely damaged by war made a deep impression on them. The refugees' perceptions of the lack of trust and callousness of the UN officers gave rise to the most common complaint about the interview process: its utter disregard for refugees as human beings.

This perceived lack of interest for refugees as human beings features prominently in the next case examined here, the clamorous and at times quite emotional outburst of a man in his forties, well-known in the UNHCR offices for his self-appointed role as protector of refugee rights. This 'procurator' (P), a 'certified' Kosovar refugee himself, had taken up the cause of an elderly couple denied refugee status because they failed to provide any factual information linking them to Kosovo. After having learned from the couple about the denial, he burst with them into the UN office demanding an explanation for the dismissal of their case:

31/01/00

    I ↔ P

  01 I   ashtu- sipas procedurës-
              (so- according to the procedure)

  02 P   po sipas procedurës- PERSE- PERSE?-
              (according to procedure- WHY-WHY-)

  03   DUHET ME DITE PERSE ARESYEN UNE
              (I HAVE TO KNOW THE REASON)

  04   procedurën PO e LEXOJ- PO PSE?-
              (I READ THE procedure- BUT WHY?)

    I ↔ C

  05 C   ok-if he (xxx)

  06 I   he say why-

  07   I follow the procedure and at the end

  08   they are not resulted to be kosovars- then why?- why?

  09 C   because we cannot find their link with kosovo

    I ↔ C ↔ P

  10 I   sepse nuk mund të gjejmë lidhjen e tyre që kanë me kosovën/
              (because we can't find the link they have with kosovo/)

  11 P   po more- po more- po kjo është e palogjikshme-
              (yes sir- yes sir- this is illogical)

12   I   it's- it's illogic- they are kosovars

13   P   po- po- kein logic hier- wie verstahen/
         (ok ok, there's no logic here, understand?)

14   keine logik
         (no logic)

15   (..)

16   po- keine logik-
         (right, no logic)

17   po kjo s'ka një logjikë mre burrë-
         (but this is illogical man)

18   qysh bohet- po këto nuk janë buburreca mor-
         (how can that be- they are not fleas-)

19   janë dy njerëz të thjesht- t'vjetër-
         (they are simple people, simple, old)

20   C   if they are (xxx)

21   P   bitte?

22   C   i think- we have already told you

23   I   ne iu thamë-
         (we told them)

24   C   what we can tell you?

25   I   çka mund t'ju themi?
         (what can we tell you?)

26   P   mor në rregull- atëhere thuj që ne jemi të pakënaqur-
         (well all right- then tell her we are not satisfied-)

27   që kundërvenia juaj nuk ka logjikë
         (that her way of confronting [refugees] is illogical)

28   I   we are not satisfactory

29   C   yes

30   (..)

31   C   but I have to work up here-

32   P   përgjegjësinë- KUSH E MERR PËRGJEGJËSINË-
         (responsibility- WHO HAS THE RESPONSIBILITY?)

33   I   ajo thotë kam punë të tjera thotë-
         (she says I have other work to do she says)

34   C   so please go to OFR

35   P   në rregull- thuj- thuj- ne nuk e meritojmë këtë mënyrë-
         (all right- tell her- tell her- we don't deserve this attitude)

36   I   we are not deserving to be treated like this

37   P   und I say you goodbye
     [P storms out of the office]

The UNHCR caseworker's response to the procurator's outburst is typical of bureaucrats trying to shield their work from criticism: she appeals

to a higher form of authority, in this case the 'procedure', (which the interpreter promptly translates, line 1) of establishing a link to Kosovo through detailed questions (line 9). By citing an abstract, impersonal principle, the caseworker is trying to dilute responsibility for her own decision (on the concept of responsibility in verbal exchanges, see Hill and Irvine, 1992).

This strategy is countered by the procurator's claim that the procedure is illogical (line 11, reinforced in his next turn by code-switching to very rudimentary German, 'keine logik') and does not allow for a humane treatment of the asylum-seeker (lines 18-19: "they are not fleas / they are simple, old people"). The appeal to necessary procedural steps is interpreted as evidence that the caseworker has an 'attitude problem' (line 35), and that she turns a request for help into an "illogical way of confronting [refugees]" (line 27). Any attempt at establishing rapport between caseworkers and asylum-seekers is clearly compromised.

The perceived disregard for the humanity of refugees is again displayed in the final case examined here, an interview with a Kosovar lawyer (one of the few educated individuals whom I observed undergoing the procedure). After having described (correctly) the toponymy of the area around Prishtina (Kosovo's main city), the lawyer objects vigorously to the UNHCR line of questioning:

03/05/00

I ↔ R

01   R   kështu që ndihem shumë i ofendum
            (well, I feel very offended)

02   I   për çka?
            (what for?)

03   R   për pyetjet rreth prishtinës për fshatrat e ma tjerat-
            (for the questions about Prishtina and villages and so on)

04   kam marrë me qindra njerëz/
            (I sheltered many people in my house)

I ↔ C

05   I   and I- I feel that uh- my feelings is- is that

06   I am like offenced- offenced-

07   C   uh uh

08   I   from this- kind of questions

09   C   uh uh

10   I   you know- because you are not believing to my words

I ↔ C ↔ R

11   R   uh- më fal- jam ofendum-
            (excuse me but I'm offended)

12   I   yes he says I'm offenced

13   R   jam i vetmi avokat këtu që kam qenë (xxx)
         (I am the only lawyer here that has been xxx)
14   I   because I am a lawyer-
15   R   në kosovë- i vetmi avokat jam që jam i akuzum/
         (in kosovo- the only lawyer who's been accused)
16   I   and he:: was charged in kosovo
16   R   baza e akuzes është= se i kam =
         (the charge is I had)
17   C   =uh sorry sir=
18   I'm sorry sir but we have a procedure
19   we believe you but we follow procedure
20   (..)
21   R   ska problem
         (well... no problem)

This exchange features not only the case worker's ready invocation of 'procedure' to avoid personal responsibility for her questions, but also the interpreter's awareness of the UNHCR office's underlying mistrust of asylum-seekers.

When the lawyer/refugee vents his displeasure with the interview and tries to recount his experience with political dissent before the war (line 4), the interpreter quickly identifies for the caseworker the basic issue behind the lawyer's displeasure: the lack of trust (line 10). While other refugees made this point explicitly, the issue of trust does not come to the foreground in the lawyer/refugee's complaint. He seems mainly interested in telling his story, rather than complaining about the lack of trust. Nevertheless, his second attempt to begin a narrative is cut short by the intervention of the caseworker, again with an appeal to the need 'to follow procedure' (line 19).

By appealing again to procedure, the caseworker tries to minimize responsibility for her own questions, and their underlying implication of mistrust. The issue, as implied by the caseworker, is not suspicion of the present interviewee, but a more formal principle of equal treatment for everybody which, as in any institutional setting, is guaranteed through universally applied procedural means.

It is interesting to note that both the caseworker's and the interpreter's responses prevent the refugee from telling his story of political dissent that started well before the war. Twice silenced, by the end this interviewee can only give up on his narrative, and after a pregnant pause (line 20), acknowledge the authority of the UNHCR office over the interview process.

Conclusion

> Refugees should not be seen solely as a burden. Without underestimating the humanitarian and security issues related to the presence of large refugee populations, it must be recognized that refugees are not merely the beneficiaries of humanitarian aid. They can make positive contributions. Rather than marginalizing refugees, our challenge is to find ways of empowering them, so that they can contribute to our societies. We must ensure respect for the individual dignity and worth of each and every refugee.
> (Ruud Lubbers, United Nations High Commissioner for Refugees, in a speech to the UNHCR headquarters in Geneva, December 12, 2001)

Why should we care that asylum-seekers in Albania were systematically denied the chance to tell their stories in the UNHCR registration procedure? After all, most people applying for refugee status have endured experiences far more traumatic than the interviews examined above.

The UNHCR in Tirana made it a practice to discourage the refugees from sharing narratives. But if it wanted to do so, it should have clearly spelled out its reasons to the interviewee, to allow them to make sense of the proceedings.

Storytelling is precisely one of the practices refugees have for making sense of their experience, by exploring traumatic events in front of an audience and hearing comforting responses. Refugees use storytelling to locate themselves in a specific space and time, countering on the symbolic plane the material dislocation they have had to endure. By denying asylum-seekers the opportunity to tell their stories, the UNHCR office may have succeeded in saving time on interviews and avoiding the persuasive force of narratives, but this policy carried hidden costs for both itself and the refugees: the agency lost credibility as an advocate for displaced people and the refugees lost the opportunity to use the interview as the first step in their road to recovery.

Through its 'procedure', the UNHCR may have caught some bogus applicants, but in so doing it may have seriously jeopardized its relationship with 'true' refugees. By abruptly launching a barrage of questions without proper framing, that is, without giving the interviewees any explanation about why they were being asked to recite Kosovar toponyms or why they were not allowed to engage in storytelling, the UNHCR turned a neutral conduit (the interview) into an absurdist (and at times antagonistic) exchange. With their future on the line, the refugees were subjected to judiciary techniques that made very little sense to them, except that they knew that a wrong answer could lead to a denial of their application.

The abrupt switch to factual questions very soon into the interview did more than just signal to all asylum-seekers that they were 'suspects' in the eyes of the UNHCR and that their stories were irrelevant: it disempowered them, turning them into automatons asked to recite toponymic lists. Moreover, deprived of a clear explanation of the proceedings, the refugees left the UNHCR office baffled and frustrated. In other words, by being reduced to automatons and kept in the dark about the UNHCR's rationale for handling these encounters, they were denied their agency.

If the UNHCR is sincerely concerned with "finding ways of empowering" the refugees and ensuring "respect for their dignity" (in the words of its High Commissioner quoted above), its officers need to do a better job of explaining their methods and procedures to people seeking their help. In Tirana such an explanation was never properly offered, and as a result the UNHCR came to be perceived by refugees as an institutional, insensitive body of bureaucrats, disinterested in their agency and their suffering.

References

Bauman, R. and C. Briggs (1990) 'Poetics and Performance as Critical Perspectives on Language and Social Life', *Annual Review of Anthropology*, 19:59-88.

Berk-Seligson, S. (1990) *The Bilingual Courtroom: Court Interpreters in the Judicial Process*, Chicago: University of Chicago Press.

Briggs, C. (1988) 'Disorderly Dialogues in Ritual Impositions of Order', *Anthropological Linguistics*, 30:3-4:448-91.

Conley, J. and W. O'Barr (1998) *Just Words: Law, Language, and Power*, Chicago: University of Chicago Press.

Daniel, V. (1996) *Charred Lullabies: Chapters in an Anthropology of Violence*, Princeton: Princeton University Press.

------ and J. Knudsen (eds.) (1995) *Mistrusting Refugees*, Berkeley: University of California Press.

Davidson, B. (2000) 'The Interpreter as Institutional Gatekeeper', *Journal of Sociolinguistics*, 4 (3):379-405.

Foucault, M. (1981) 'The Order of Discourse', in R. Young (ed.) *Untying the Text: A Post-Structuralist Reader* (pp.108-138), London and New York: Routledge and Kegan.

Goffman E. (1974) *Frame Analysis*, Cambridge, Mass: Harvard University Press.

Goodwin, M.J. (1990) *He-Said-She-Said: Talk as Social Organization Among Black Children*, Bloomington: Indiana University Press.

Greimas, A. J. (1982) *Semiotics and Language: An Analytical Dictionary*, Bloomington: Indiana University Press.

Hill, J. and J. Irvine (eds.) (1992) *Responsibility and Evidence in Oral Discourse*, Cambridge: Cambridge University Press.

Hirsch, S. (1998) *Pronouncing and Persevering: Gender and the Discourse of Disputing in an African Islamic Court*, Chicago: University of Chicago Press.

Jacquemet, M. (1996) *Credibility in Court: Communicative Practices in the Camorra's Trials*, Cambridge: Cambridge University Press.

Knudsen, J. (1995) 'When Trust is on Trial: Negotiating Refugees Narratives', in V. Daniel and J. Knudsen (eds.) *Mistrusting Refugees* (pp.13-35) Berkeley: University of California Press.

Kramer, J. (2003) 'Refugee: An Afghan woman who fled tyranny on her own' *New Yorker*, January 20:64-73.

Malkki, L. (1995) 'Refugees and Exiles', *Annual Review of Anthropology*, 24:495-523.

O'Barr, W. (1982) *Linguistic Evidence: Language, Power, and Strategy in Courtroom*, New York: Academic Press.
Taslitz, A. (1999) *Rape and the Culture of the Courtroom*, New York: New York University Press.

Stories from the Court of Appeal in Literature and Law[1]

ROBERT F. BARSKY, *Vanderbilt University, USA*

> Yet if one looks closely one sees that there is no essential difference between a beggar's livelihood and that of numberless respectable people. Beggars do not work, it is said; but, then, what is work? A navy works by swinging a pick. An accountant works by adding up figures. A beggar works by standing out of doors in all weathers and getting varicose veins, chronic bronchitis, etc. It is a trade like any other; quite useless, of course, – but, then, many reputable trades are quite useless. And as a social type a beggar compares well with scores of others. He is honest compared with the sellers of most patent medicines, high-minded compared with a Sunday newspaper proprietor, amiable compared with a hire-purchase tout – in short, a parasite, but a fairly harmless parasite. He seldom extracts more than just a bare living from the community, and, what should justify him according to our ethical ideas, he pays for it over and over in suffering. I do not think there is anything about a beggar that sets him in a different class from other people, or gives most modern men the right to despise him. George Orwell, *Down and Out in Paris and London*: (1972:169)

Millions of people are forcibly dislocated and relocated each year, the result of famine, war, natural disaster, unemployment or fear, transforming ordinary people who had always considered themselves 'citizens' or 'workers' of some country or another into unfamiliar marginal beings, described by legal and social categories such as 'homeless', 'refugee', 'illegal' or 'in flight'. For the least favoured members of society, who find themselves in this situation, Western societies offer various versions of social welfare, unemployment insurance or, in more extreme situations, refugee determination boards; but in order to gain benefit from these apparatuses, people in these extreme situations have to tell their 'life story'

[1] I would like to thank Denise Helly and Richard Janda, who inspired this work, as well as the SSHRC, Multiculturalism Canada, and the Quebec Court of Appeal, who funded it. A much-abbreviated version of this text was given at a talk at the French and Italian Department of Vanderbilt University in March of 2003, and I'm grateful to have had, and to have, the opportunity to be affiliated with that institution. Thanks as well to Patricia Foxen, for her on-going and precious input.

in unfamiliar settings to strangers who have been charged with offering assistance. In Western society, the helping organizations which are the forums for these stories are deemed 'administrative' rather than judicial, which makes them flexible, but also fickle to the wills and whims of governments who can strive for versions of social inclusion or exclusion, depending upon whether the emphasis is placed on (say) integration and well-being (the New Deal, Medicare, universal human rights), or security and state interest (the Patriot Act, Homeland Security, the Criminal and Alien Removal Act). The streets of American cities are peopled with beneficiaries of policies aimed at ameliorating the conditions of the underclasses, but as marginalization comes to be equated with security risk, the Boards and procedures designed to alleviate suffering are becoming screening areas for security risks, making the already complex process of finding relief all the more ominous. This trend raises the stakes for the claimant who is in need of assistance, which begs the question of what kind of forum is best suited to hear claims, and also whether forums for appealing unfair rulings should be rigidly judicial or more informal. Drawing from three different sources of such appeals, refugee hearings, interviews with homeless persons and literary renditions of displacement, I will argue that whatever the risks, decision makers should err on the side of fairness, generosity, caring, and leniency. Particularly in the case of the poor and the disenfranchised, it is better to allow claimants to tell their story in their own way, and to provide them with the means to do so – in the form of proper counsel and reasonable allowances for occasional missteps – rather than to turn them away on the slightest pretext on the basis of some misguided sense of 'security'. It is not because the suffering 'other' doesn't resemble the vision we'd like to have of the collective 'self' that we are in any way justified in supporting repressive treatment of those who need our assistance.

In the US., those in dire straight seek this assistance from both formal and informal networks because the range of government social service aids is simply too restricted, particularly in comparison to more generous social welfare states. In Canada, for example, efforts have been made to offer formal restitution for those who have fallen through the cracks of the existing economic template and, although the relative levels of assistance are far greater than in the US., many people nevertheless slip through the social security net and then fail to exercise their right to attain restitution, getting down to levels of social assistance which are as low as their American counterparts. The problem in both systems, over and above uneven distribution of resources and intrinsic inequalities, is that those who are most in need are often either unaware of the programmes which can assist them, or have been pushed beyond the reach of existing judicial or administrative helping organizations. This leads to the perverse truism that the more foreign someone is to the administrative system charged to deal with their case (because of country of origin, culture, physical or mental handicap), the more difficult it will be for this person to receive adequate assistance in the first instance. And the wrongs committed against these marginalized human beings are seldom overturned because the small number of appeal mechanisms that exist in administrative organizations, like welfare offices or refugee determination boards, are resistant, or not adequately equipped, to hear appeals for manifestly founded claims. The evidence for this neglect is found in the stories told by America's outsiders – immigrants, refugees, welfare claimants, and homeless people – in courtrooms, in everyday conversations and in fiction written by authors who try to represent their experience in these realms.

Data and Objectives

In much of my work I have tried to give voice to the authors of stories by 'outsiders' by collecting legal and literary narratives which dramatize the problem of finding a forum for properly representing the suffering self to a judicial or administrative body charged with offering sufficient aid to prevent or address situations of social marginalization (Barsky, 1994; 2001). In this chapter I'll expand upon this work by examining how narratives allow us to analyze reasons for the failure of administrative tribunals, and to assess the best means of redressing these concerns. The primary data will be drawn from two sources, one fictional and one non-fictional, and the analysis will be based on an approach to theories of outsider law, life-story research and discourse analysis theory that I describe below. My use of fictional and non-fictional examples suggests a link between discursive practices of everyday life[2] and depictions of it in what Mikhaïl M. Bakhtin calls the 'dialogic novel', best represented by the works of Dickens and Dostoyevsky. Discourse in fictional texts can be free and open in part because there is no pre-ordained strategy for adequate representation, which gives free reign to a multiplicity of voices and strategies of representation, and in part because characters can be autonomous and

---

[2] A range of research demonstrates the ways in which everyday stories are similar to fictional stories. See for example Corradi, 1991; Linde, 1993; Norrick, 1998; Polanyi, 1985a; 1985b. Related work discusses the ways in which stories are subjective reconstructions of personal experience, for example J. Bruner, 1990 and 1991.

uncoerced, thus producing "a plurality of independent and unmerged voices and consciousness, a genuine polyphony of fully valid voices" (Bakhtin, 1984:6). For the theme of marginal outsider voices seeking retribution, another more pragmatic reason to look to fictional narratives is the blurring of the line between fiction and non-fiction; in immigrant novels, for example, the author needs to constitute him or herself entirely, speaking to a context in which cultural markers are unfamiliar or strange. Immigrant authors might also feel frustrated in their attempts to represent themselves to host country organizations and therefore turn to fiction as a way to tell their story better; for this reason some of the examples for this chapter are derived from fictional narratives, generally autobiographical, describing experiences of displacement. The texts were isolated in the context of a larger study concerning how immigrant writers, who published novels or collections of short stories in Quebec since the 1980s, narrate integration into, or participation in, Quebec society. The corpus includes novels and collections of short stories published in Quebec and written by authors from the Middle East, North Africa, Latin America and the Caribbean, who describe refugee and immigrant encounters with First World adjudicators. The experiences described in these texts find echoes in similar texts written in Canada and the United States, but to be specific about sources of possible aid, and similarities to narratives of street people in the same region, I have limited this research to Quebec. Furthermore, although this corpus fits loosely under the rubric of immigrant literatures, it grows out of a multiculturalism program, specific to Canada, which funds fiction written by immigrants (via Multiculturalism Canada's 'Book Publishing Industry Development Plan' and through initiatives such as 'The Multiculturalism Programme' of the Department of Canadian Heritage). This approach to integration, described by Neil Bissoondath (1994); Linda Hutcheon (1990); Will Kymlicka (1996; 2001) and Charles Taylor (in Taylor and Gutmann, 1996) has been the subject of lively debates within the literary and cultural communities for its relative benefits and failings.

The non-fictional texts are from interviews I conducted with people who, although eligible for social aid, have been mistreated by commissioners employed by the Ministère des Affaires Sociales in Quebec and who as a consequence have found themselves living, and dying, on the streets of Montreal. The latter study was initiated by a leading Quebec judge and the Vice-President of La Commission des Affaires Sociales, who grew alarmed by the number of manifestly legitimate cases that were finding their way into appeals, and therefore the obviously high level of injustice at lower levels of the social assistance bureaucracy. The project was divided into two streams, the first constituted by interviews and opinion surveys undertaken with the bureaucrats responsible for lower-level decisions, and the second by interviews with people who were living in the streets of Montreal. For the latter I interviewed thirty-two homeless people, attempting to correlate motives with actions, looking at the question of how they landed up in the streets in the first place, and what kind of aid they had applied for, and received, since. These interviews would last for anywhere from fifteen to sixty minutes and the specific questions were adapted to individual cases, given the vast range of persons interviewed in terms of age, addiction, mental health, and so forth. All of these interviews were taped, in exchange for which I offered compensation, as well as information about the appeal system, in the hope that the interviewees would exercise the right to change their plight. The transcriptions cited are, unfortunately, all that remains of the experience. The rest: the troubled faces, the sad demeanours, the apparent malnutrition, and the incredible pain that was transmitted in the face-to-face encounters were lost in the transition from spoken word to written text. But a look at any one of the thousands of homeless persons in our society transmits this pain, and a few words exchanged during brief encounters with them will provide a glimpse of their plight. Since the stories they tell are frequently similar to those recounted by Convention refugees who have sought asylum, I'll also make reference in this chapter to some of these narratives and to methods for their assessment.

The logic of examining these particular fictional and non-fictional narratives together is that they emanate from similar time periods in Quebec, and have common themes. All of the narratives describe a dislocation from one realm in which considerable obstacles led to some kind of personal disaster, and a subsequent relocation to some other realm via the intervention of an administrative process – with varying results. I have selected passages which specifically treat the confrontation between persons in need and the administrative organization charged with assisting the claimant. Like the stories told by refugees in formal hearings, these narratives are 'life stories' from people who are the most marginalized because of their cultural, linguistic and physical 'outsiderness'. They are also extreme examples of narrative construction in which the success of the story told will have a concrete impact on the integration of the claimant into the host society. For the homeless person the appeal can raise the level of sustenance to the point where s/he could rent an apartment, for the refugee the claim can allow for status in the host country, and for the novelist the narrative offers the occasion for a free and open recounting of the displacement and attempted integration into the host country. I'll consider these narratives using similar presuppositions if only because the boundaries between the truth of such stories is always open for question, and fiction often offers a far better forum for telling the 'actual story' than a rigid legal hearing.

Renouncing Identity and Seeking Rebirth in Administrative Settings

People 'tell stories' for different reasons and with different ends, but in administrative settings like the refugee determination hearing room or the Social Security office, claimants are looking for an adequate forum for the recounting of their story. Novels and short stories describe similar situations, but without the power structure of an actual hearing, or the chance of an 'outcome' at the end of the narrative (except, perhaps, for the reader's response to the text). Juxtaposing fictional and non-fictional renderings of this same process allows us to consider both candid and coerced versions of similar sentiments. For instance, in the face of an official decision-making body, claimants are apt to 'construct' themselves as adequate claimants, which can lead them to renounce their previous self and create, successfully or not, an 'other' deemed appropriate for the cause. For instance, *Le Printemps Peut Attendre*, by Andrée Dahan (1985), describes Maya's attempt to adequately represent herself in Quebec society after she has been selected to receive immigrant status by virtue of a successful application from her country of origin, Egypt. Maya is expressly attempting, through her relocation to Canada, to re-invent herself as financially and professionally successful in Quebec, and, in the process, she is setting out to free herself from the limitations of her native country. What she does not recognize is that such advancement comes at the cost of a literal rebirth in the form of a new person, an immigrant willing to assume the appropriate postures for acceptance:

> Maya knows now that her past can no longer serve as a reference point, that she, an immigrant, thirty-years-old, with a successful career in teaching of biology and six years of experience, ambitious, selected by the Canadian Department of Immigration, chosen from a larger group, in short, chosen by virtue of her passed past, must now renounce this past, to die in one form to be reborn in another, as a child who dies as an adult, and an adult as an elderly person (31, my translation).

Having relied upon her earlier qualifications and experience for the process of entering Canada, she must now in some ways renounce them. This experience is described in the novel in terms of a kind of symbolic suicide, since Maya must die as the person she was before immigrating in order to be reborn as a teacher in the Quebec secondary school system.

This theme of the renouncement of a former identity for a kind of professional rebirth is present in most of the works in this immigrant literature corpus. In Nadia Ghalem's short story *Le Recommencement*, and in Mona Latif-Ghattas *Le Double Conte de l'Exil* (1990), we encounter descriptions of male characters who cannot find work because they either don't understand the need to construct a 'productive other' (Barsky, 1994) or refuse to do so for reasons relating to memory, pride or obstacles intrinsic to life in the host country. For example, in *Le Recommencement*, Mourad is frustrated by the Canadian bureaucrats who continuously refuse his applications, offering neither proper assistance nor recognition of his many professional qualifications. He virtually echoes Maya's sentiments when, following another rejection, he says that: "He should have fought harder, not accepted just anything, re-launched the debate", as a way of showing his tenacity in the face of home country obstacles. As he states: "I have come here for this, I have expatriated myself for this very reason"; instead, "a young and intelligent man is sent into the streets, and into a state of despair" (26, my translation). This dramatic reversal of expectation, based upon the narrator's resistance to the norms and requirements of the host country, leads him to fight in order to claim a place which he feels is rightfully his in the host society. From the perspective of literature and law, an appropriate domain for the elaboration of such issues, what is most interesting is that Mourad's appeal is not heard in the Quebec Appeal Court where it belongs, but in fiction; as such, the line between Nadia Ghalem as immigrant author and Mourad as immigrant claimant is blurred, and the place of appeal becomes a (government-funded) literary text.

Resisting the Appeal Process

The phenomenon of failed or displaced narrative construction is endemic to the administrative apparatuses designed to accept, assist and integrate people into Canadian society; the problem has been exacerbated with the growing move towards neo-liberalism and neo-conservatism throughout the Western world. Whereas previous commissioners dealing with workplace abuse, social welfare, or refugee acceptance used to be largely associated with social work or some other 'helping' area, they are now more likely to be hired as bureaucrats whose aim is to control the growing flood of applicants. Unfortunately, given the nature of the relationship between the claimant and the State, the decisions of these Commissioners are often left unquestioned, as in the case of Jean, a homeless person who found himself on the streets after a decision (by the Social Affairs Commission, la Commission des Affaires Sociales) to cut his social welfare by $100/month. I asked him why he didn't file an appeal, to which he replied: "This is what happened to me. In my own mind, I was going to see a lawyer. But I didn't do it. My ideas weren't in that place. In other words, my ideas were not there, they were far away, they weren't there". Mourad's fictional narrative, and Jean's real-life case, are but two examples of experiences by claimants who have chosen not to exercise their rights; but if they don't then no one will help them, and if they don't seek professional advice they probably won't succeed in their appeal even if they do at some point choose to launch one. This situation is due to the fact that amongst those who do seek appeals there is a disproportionate number of better-connected and wealthier claimants, which has led to a growing number of lawyers in administrative hearings, higher levels of professionalization, a greater division between the haves and the have-nots, and an increasingly antagonistic relationship between claimants and State. This adversarial relationship has originated the spreading of a 'word on the street' that it is best to avoid administrative care-givers, such as social welfare offices, because people can be punished for making claims there. Current administrations in the refugee domain are also trying to pass on the same message. In response to my suggestion to fill out the forms needed to make an appeal for a revision of the decision to cut his social welfare, a street person named Jimmy said: "Are you kidding? They'll cut you completely". These fears are often rationally unfounded, but they do reflect the claimant's own experience, his or her assessment of how things work, compounded with mental illness, strange experiences of street life, or the belief that commissioners really do have the legitimate job of protecting state finances. This final point represents one of the conclusions of the study, that a discourse of fear and impotence by people on the street often illustrates how 'mainstream discourse' becomes accepted and interiorized by them, and that their narratives reflect this interiorization. "That they cut me off is not an injustice", says Jimmy. "Those guys, they have their own things that they have to do, whether it is an injustice or not". As perverse as this may sound, Jimmy is agreeing with the ruling, rather than appealing against it, because he has accepted his role as that of one who abuses state finances, even though it should be made clear to him that he has the right to accept assistance to improve his plight. One concrete suggestion that stems from this research, therefore, is that publicity campaigns about the role and value of social assistance should be launched to send out a message that social assistance is an acceptable programme in our society. This can serve to break down the fear felt by claimants like Jimmy who clearly expressed it in the interview I conducted with him. Below, I reproduce his response to my question about why he wouldn't appeal against decisions made by his Commissioner:

J. I am too scared.

Q. *How come?*

J. Because you might appeal today, and tomorrow you'll get nailed for that. They'll make your life a little harder. Do you understand? Especially if you lose your identification card. Then you are screwed.

Q. *So you feel that they might come back at you, if you appeal?*

J. Definitely. They've got the message from Quebec, they are cutting and cutting, and any excuse to cut you in any way - - if you agitate them in any way, especially when you are trying to find out your own rights, because they say, you don't have to worry about your rights. You're getting a cheque, at least you are getting something. At least your rights are not being violated. So you leave it at that. And you don't bother with them.

Q. *Do you know other people who have appealed, and have had problems?*

J. I have one guy named Greg, from Alberta. He had been here for quite a while. He couldn't get the things that he needed. Like the last day of school, the last day of his job, the name of his boss, all of the little things that you cannot seem to get. Do you know what I mean? You don't screw around with welfare. Especially if you are right and they are wrong. And if you haven't got a phone number, just forget about it. They'll get a hold of you when they want you, by sending you a letter. But if you want to get a hold of them because you need some assistance, forget about it.

Q. *Have you ever had the assistance of a lawyer? Did you know that you have the right to one?*

J. Not at all. Not at all. You go in there, and you get out as quick as you can. That is their policy. Especially when they are cutting, like now sir. They are cutting dramatically now, do you know what I mean? Left and right. It ain't the good time to be walking in with a lawyer. They'll look at you and say, what are you complaining about? At least you are getting something. Instead of getting nothing. That is how it is.

In the literary corpus we find stories that are similar to Jimmy's narrative when he describes how he hides his identity to avoid 'getting caught' but, probably because fictional characters have no status to lose, there are also many candid descriptions of the masks that people don in order to succeed. In a short story by Marilù Mallet called *How Are You?* (1986), Casimir, an ambitious Polish immigrant, decides to evoke false Jewish roots in his own narrative construction in order to seduce a wealthy although undesirable Jewish woman living in Toronto, and become 'married and a manager'. "When I receive my citizenship, I'll change my name, for there is anti-Semitism in these parts.... I could go and see my mother in Poland and, one of these days I'll work on Wall Street" (81, my translation). In Arnau's *La Mémoire Meurtrie* (1988) the main male character, a young French immigrant, constructs himself as an author even though he's never had any literary pretensions or interests, as a means of escaping the tedium of odd jobs. In Naim Kattan's novel *La Fiancée Promise* (1983), Meir, a Jewish immigrant from Baghdad, is employed according to his qualifications, but only thanks to members of the Iraqi community in Montreal who he pursues to these ends. In virtually all other cases described in the corpus, the goal of professional integration is frustrated because of the main character's initial dislocation and the subsequent failure to relocate, which often takes the form of a failed attempt at constructing an appropriate other – a self for his or her new Canadian identity.

Marilù Mallet's short story *La Mutation* (1986) adds another dimension by suggesting that part of the problem of adequate representation and construction relates to the stress that individuals feel under the pressure of the need to adapt and succeed in unfamiliar surroundings. This story describes how a couple of immigrant parents move to the Montreal workplace in order to make ends meet, and as a consequence are forced to place their two years old son Pepito in a French language day care centre. The result is that the child, left to his own devices, is befriended at the daycare by an immigrant janitor. The parents notice that their little Pepito isn't learning either French or English, but is instead making strange and unrecognizable sounds, but they justify themselves as follows: "With all of our obligations, we were not worried right away. We were in a new country, and we needed a minimum that a respectable family would have in this type of society: the fridge, the car, and all those other machines that make for comfortable development. This lead us to abandon Pepito in a daycare" (49, my translation). Those alien sounds turned out to be not signs of mental retardation, as the doctors and psychologists suggested, but the outcome of Pepito's contact with Hungarian, the language of the janitor.

Residual Horrors

Numerous characters described in these novels and short stories have left their countries of origin because of political oppression, war, or torture, and carry with them the effects of their persecution and suffering. This brings some of these narratives into line with the Convention refugee hearings, in which claimants are expected to construct themselves according to the categories of persecution set out in the 1951 Convention by telling the 'whole' story of the persecution that led them to the claim. In recent years, the grounds for appealing Canadian Immigration and Refugee Board decisions have narrowed, so that a claimant who, for example, is unable or unwilling to recount the horrors of his or her torture, or who does so with the inevitable inaccuracies instilled by torture or fear, will be deported without appeal (a kind of 'Cordelia' effect). Since refugee hearings, like social welfare, fall under the aegis of administrative law, their workings can be easily modified by officials, and also cordoned-off from public view. This makes the public increasingly unaware of the dynamics of this process, and renders fictional accounts all the more important. Ariel Dorfman's play *Death and the Maiden* (1994), which was adapted by Roman Polanski into a film by the same name, dramatizes the story of a rape victim's attempt to exact a confession from her alleged attacker (who has by chance befriended her husband due to a roadside mishap) by making the painful and heroic effort of describing what happened to her while in prison in an unnamed Latin American country.

Many victims from the corpus of fiction avoid confronting their past in this way as well, as we see in Dany Laferrière's *Éroshima* (1987), in which the narrator never refers to the Duvalier regime which drove him to Canada, and in which the Japanese women he meets refuse to recall the horrors inflicted and suffered by their parents and grandparents during the Second World War. "Hoki has never wanted to talk about 'back there'. 'Back there' means Japan. She says, 'I was born in Vancouver. I'm a North American woman...' 'Then why these sudden onsets of despair?'" (31). In Ghalem's short story *Le Recommencement*, we witness the flip side of this phenomenon, in which the memory of warring Algeria impedes a recently-arrived immigrant's ability to construct himself as a citizen of Canada: "Every time fate brought this type of blow, he heard the shots, the explosions and the cries of the war in Algeria" (27, my translation). For him, the problem is not that he cannot integrate into Quebec, but rather the sentiment that he should return to Algeria, where he'll be more 'useful'. He says: "Over there I am at home" (36, my translation). Other examples of how memory impedes adequate narrative reconstruction are found in Mona Latif-Ghattas's *Le Double Conte de l'Exil* (1990) and Jorge Fajardo's *Votre Manteau Mouillé* (1990). In Fajardo's novel, written in the form of an elegiac letter composed when the narrator learns that his mother has died, we find a character who created a kind of barrier between himself and the country of origin, Chile, to protect himself from the residual sentiments. The change that he describes is his own gradual resistance to Chile, a process that occurs concurrently with his mother's increasing submergence in Chilean society. His displacement has led him to lose track of his country and of his mother, which has in turn made him better able to tolerate the fact that he now lives in Canadian society; but it also makes him reluctant to return home, even when he learns that his mother has passed away, because he simply feels emotionally unable to go through the administrative steps required to travel back home for the funeral.

Just as residual memories can prevent people from telling their stories, so too can customs or habit affect people's willingness to make appropriate claims. This theme recurs throughout the corpus of narratives recorded from homeless persons:

R. I used to receive money from the government, but I lost my identification.
Q. *How did that happen?*
R. I was intoxicated.
Q. *And now there is no way to get assistance?*
R. I may be able to receive money if I go to Préfontaine, where I applied. They know me. They took photos of my I.D.. Then I went to Atwater, and lost my I.D. So I would have to go back to Syracuse to get my I.D. Where I would have to apply. So I am frustrated. But they have photocopies. They know me. I will get one more cheque. It is a medical cheque. I have cancer in the stomach. So I get medical welfare. I've got cancer. It's a bit of a melody, but... I am supposed to get a place. But I have been living on the street for too long. I cannot put myself in a room, I cannot. I am thirty years old. I have been on the street since I was fourteen years old. If I put myself in a room, I won't know what to do with myself. I will be lost.

This reluctance means that administrators who have been trained to deal with such problems will not have a chance to rule on the case unless they themselves take an active role in contacting the person, which is unlikely, or unless there is outside intervention from a mediator. This occurs in

Gérard Etienne's novel *Une Femme Muette* (1983), which describes Marie-Anne, a Haitian woman who is married to Gros Zo, a powerful, rich psychiatrist who works in an established Montreal hospital. In addition to his Western medicine, Gros Zo also practices voodoo and, in an attempt to eliminate his wife in order to marry a rich white Montrealer with whom he is having an affair, he plants a number of Haitian voodoo objects in the house and locks her up in a small room, expecting that she will commit suicide. His spells are doubly powerful given his privileged place in Montreal society, but just when she seems ready to succumb, Marie-Anne miraculously flees her captivity, and receives the assistance of a young *Québécoise* woman whom she meets in a park and who, out of compassion, guides her through a claim in court against her husband. Without this unexpected saviour, Marie-Anne would have either resigned herself to her fate, or killed herself, as her husband so desired.

Other examples of cultural residual obstacles concern, for example, marriage rituals and accepted pre-marital relations, as in Naim Kattan's short story *Les Rêves de la Mère* (1985). In this case, the residual values are embodied by the parents through their reference to tradition. Joyce, the female child of immigrant parents, must overcome their prejudices in order to achieve personal autonomy and a sense of self-worth. In Naim Kattan's short story *La Conquête* (1985), the main character, Habiba, is forced to overcome the cultural obstacle that prevented her (as a woman) from working in a significant job and actively participating (as a wife) in the commercial affairs of her husband. When her husband dies, she must decide whether to keep the business, which means that she must face up to and renounce his old inefficient methods. That she chooses to meet the challenge constitutes a liberation and an emancipation, effected through necessity. What is interesting here, though, is that she tries to change present circumstances by staying put, rather than looking for new adventures and possibilities (Maya), or by seeking out territory uncharted by her ancestors (Keiko). In this case the effect of the forced emancipation is clear: Habiba begins to *live* in ways she never thought possible.

Another kind of cultural adaptation that occurs is in the very fact that some of the characters write fiction, and then in certain cases publish their stories in Quebec. In the case of Dany Laferrière, for example, the process of writing becomes a means of entering more fully into society, which transforms him from a person observed to an observer. In the case of Fajardo, writing becomes a way of expressing that which cannot be expressed to persons around him, for although the narrator has become integrated in the society, he does not feel close enough to persons from the host country to recount his story: "I don't have anyone to whom I can tell the story of your death. For them, it would remain something abstract. It's always so terrible to lose one's mother. I don't want to talk about it with anyone from here. I don't think that they'd commiserate. I don't believe in their compassion" (30, my translation). And in the case of Maya, the main character in *Le Printemps Peut Attendre*, her writing (of letters) becomes a necessary link to the country of origin and to the past that led her into the (failed) adventure of integration into Quebc society. More recently, Eddy Garnier, a refugee from Haiti, has written a novel in which the main character describes his arrival in Montreal and the refugee hearing he has to undergo to attain status. One of the chapters contains the actual transcription from his refugee determination hearing, which was held in Montreal in 1973, thus once again blurring the line between autobiographical narrative in fact and in fiction.

Outsider Law versus Formal Legal Procedure

As we have seen in these fictional and non-fictional narratives, the kinds of norms that persons in need have to learn in order to resolve their problems are complex. They include such diverse skills as learning the acceptable method of representation, the criteria for establishing grounds and proof, the appropriate narrative techniques, the body of acceptable evidence, the levels of leniency and fairness, the nature of the adjudicator or judge, and, of course, finding out how to gain access to the appeals mechanisms and the administrative procedures pertinent to their case. Unfortunately, the very fact of being a welfare recipient, a refugee, or a homeless person makes people 'outsiders' to the whole array of procedures for legal redress, and the fact of living in limbo (on the street, in great poverty, awaiting a refugee hearing) exacerbates this problem dramatically. In certain cases, the degree of outsiderness is so severe that the victim cannot hope for a fair 'hearing' no matter how successful his or her narrative construction because, in Pierre Bourdieu's (1991) terms, the legal discourse marketplace doesn't recognize his or her discourse 'product'. For this reason, helping institutions, such as the Appeal Court for social welfare cases in Quebec or the Immigration and Refugee Board in Canada, have tried to set up hearing situations that will allow the claimants to feel comfortable and confident about telling their own stories in their own way. Is this type of flexibility likely to resolve the problems we have described? The answer to that question, and to most questions in administrative tribunals so heavily indebted to ideas of discretion and fairness, is that it depends not only on the goodwill of the adjudicators, but also on the context within which the hearing takes place. This latter point is increasingly worrisome, because with recent and on-going cutbacks of all sorts to social welfare, and with the newfound emphasis on 'security' over 'assistance', many claimants fear that if they so much as file a claim, they will be 'cut-off', in the case of welfare recipients, or sent back, in the case of refugee claimants; without more formal mechanisms this process unfolds with complete impunity from scrutiny. For this reason, it may be irresponsible or counter-productive to move towards a highly-discretionary adjudication and appeals system, despite the obvious benefits that are evident from the examples provided in this chapter.

The most glaring problem in allowing people to tell their own stories in their own ways, and in resisting a more professionalized and formal system, is whether it is possible in administrative hearings to treat 'like' cases in 'unlike ways', and to justify doing so with reference to vague ideas about custom, indwelling right, morality, fairness, or discretion. This leads us into a larger discussion about the virtues of a norms versus exception based legal system to address problems such as social welfare or refugee determination. The treatment of needy individuals in the so-called 'welfare state' is regulated according to standards specific to the State within which the claimants reside, which are in themselves underwritten by philosophical notions concerning the function and workings of law in society. Increasingly, according to William E. Scheuerman (1994), the tendency in Western states is to move away from a classical liberal notion of 'rule of law', with its insistence on consistent and universal legal standards, towards a form of law that "takes an increasingly amorphous and indeterminate structure as vague legal standards like 'in good faith' or 'in the public interest', proliferate" (ibid.:1). In the case of an appeal court, as we have seen, this can be quite advantageous because a quasi-judicial space, like its literary counterpart, is more flexible to claimants' narrative. But Scheuerman argues that basing a legal system on such tribunals has its dangers, evidence for which can be seen historically, notably in the approach taken by Carl Schmitt and Friedrich Hayek that was used to establish the legal basis for Nazism in the 1930s, and in the opposing efforts of Neumann and Kirchheimer, who supported the 'rule of law' and opposed Schmitt affirming that "state action must be based on cogent general rules". In their view, which is supported by Scheuerman, "only clear general norms restrain and bind the activities of the state apparatus, provide a minimum of legal security, and counteract the dangers of a 'creeping authoritarianism'" (ibid.:2). Rather than relying upon legislators, judges or bureaucrats to redress the wrongs of modern society, those who favoured a norm-based law found therein "a high degree of legal regularity and predictability to achieve autonomous and un-coerced political deliberation and action" (ibid.:3). This predictability is for Neumann strongly linked to the idea of a legal norm that overrides all other decisions. He defines this norm as "a rule which does not mention particular cases or individual persons but which is issued in advance to apply to all cases and all persons in the abstract; and ... as specific as possible in its general formulation" (Neumann cited in Scheuerman (ibid.:165)). Scheuerman is very sympathetic to this approach but is unsure about whether it could work in our society, because the complex areas of state activity "require equally complex (non-formal) modes of law" (ibid.:207). Furthermore, the rule of law according to Scheuerman "can never be rendered perfect, and legal gaps, exceptions, and irregularities are unavoidable side-effects of a social setting having particularistic power concentrations necessarily regulated by clandestine individual measure and administrative commands" (ibid.:207-8). What Scheuerman does consider a realizable goal is that irregular law be exercised in a regular and rational fashion, to overcome the dangers inherent in excessively vague laws that can "constitute little more than a blank check, which bureaucrats and judges are left to fill in; judges and administrators may end up regulating *like cases in unlike ways*" (ibid.:208). This is indeed the very problem that we are facing in the administration of social welfare or refugee determination, and it is indeed one of the *raisons d'être* of appeal boards. But two problems remain: first, as good as they sound on paper, it's difficult to find norms and consistent legal methods that are applicable to cases as intrinsically diverse and complex as refugee determination hearings. And second, appeal boards, when they do exist, often lead to uneven treatment of those whose claims have been mishandled in the first instance; some people will make appeals and some won't, and it is most likely that those in the know will do the right thing, and those who most need help will suffer.

Conclusion
Negotiating a Middle Ground

Fictional and non-fictional texts describing narratives of appeal contain a high degree of judicial 'messiness', for lack of a better term, and even if it is tempting to have formal procedures ruling over the rampant arbitrariness of adjudicators, the fact is that trying to impose a supposed scientificity, predictability, and formalism to narratives that, by their nature, resist simple categorization and rationalization, is not possible or desirable . The appeal to formal mechanisms for narrative analysis and for hearing procedures is also based on the assumption that language is more or less transparent, and that there's an intimate link between intention and utterance, which is not at all what we've seen in either the fiction or the interviews. If there is a hope of improving the plight of the people involved, such attempt must be grounded in a method of representation that can answer the needs of reticent claimants, while ensuring a degree of legal fairness and procedural predictability. Furthermore, administrators and lawmakers need to recognize the need to find strategies which will help educate both the adjudicators and the general public, about the plight of the marginal people described who are too often considered parasites of an otherwise homogenous legal system set up to meet the needs of the domestic population.

A promising avenue is described by Anne Coughlin (1995), who advocates adjudication systems set up to hear 'outsider narratives', stories told by people who are unfamiliar with the norms of our legal or administrative system but who are nevertheless welcomed into it for restitution and also to help us better understand the plight of those who are strangers to our system. The narratives these 'outsiders' produce are valuable because they are, in Coughlin's opinion, "politically interventionist and theoretically disruptive, and yet at the same time flexible, sensitive, and immediately accessible" (1995:1231). To allow people to tell their own stories in their own way in a legal setting can "disturb and then persuade insiders that law should reflect the reality of outsider experience" and reinforce "commitment to a resistant scholarship", of which this very chapter is an example. Such work may even "inspire other outsiders to offer their own autobiographies in support of the cause" (ibid.:1231). For Coughlin, hearing narratives which challenge conceptions of what typical narratives can or should sound like might allow for the development of "alternative methods and languages that will include their distinctive perspectives" in the hope of repairing "the partial accounts of 'outsiders' lives embedded in conventional scholarship and, ultimately, to supersede the type of self-effacing 'objectivity' exemplified in current legal theory and practice" (ibid.:1230). The suggestion here is that if outsiders are given the chance to speak openly they will challenge traditional narrative boundaries that exist in the legal domain, something that has evidently occurred already in these quasi-judicial settings, such as in the Appeal Court for social welfare claimants. As we've seen, this is indeed the case because these narrative spaces, fictional and non-fictional, allow us a view from the inside into marginalized people's experiences.

It is not enough to support efforts at re-casting judicial norms and expectations, however, because there is the danger that outsider narratives will simply create an authorized sub-genre of discourse that, ironically, would become the legitimate language for a successful claim. In other words, even if administrative tribunals are opened up to the recounting of 'outsider' narratives, it is possible that some narratives will become standard, eliminating the advantage of non-official discourse. The reasons for this are described in Pierre Bourdieu's *Language and Symbolic Power*, which reminds us that:

> ... the assertion of linguistic counter-legitimacy, and, by the same token, the production of discourse based on a more or less deliberate disregard of the conventions and proprieties of dominant markets, are only possible within the limits of *free markets*, governed by their dominated classes, haunts or refuges for excluded individuals from which dominant individuals are in fact excluded, at least symbolically, and for the accredited holders of the social and linguistic competence which is recognized on these markets. (1991:98)

To imagine that any 'outsider narrative' will be judged on its own merits is to assume that these 'free markets' exist, that the adjudicators will be open to whole new ways of telling stories, which, in the real world of time constraints, translation, security and so forth isn't likely to be sustainable in the long term.

Another assumption of outsider law is that once outsiders' autobiographies are uttered, others with similar outsider experience will both recognize themselves and, as a consequence, gain empowerment, if only through the precedents their cases set in the appeal courts. Unfortunately, the system as presently construed can't help those who are not making the appeal, because the precedents set in the appeal process don't bear upon the cases heard day-after-day by Commissioners or Immigration and Refugee Board members. So the same mistakes can be repeated *ad infinitum*, in which case only literature of the type we examined in this chapter can offer space for some kind of redress through the spreading of (potentially) useful information to the adjudicators and the general public. As long as the present administrative system remains in place, the telling of their stories by outsiders is but a band-aid solution, or even an outgrowth of present legal (and literary) norms. In light of these drawbacks, support for outsider narratives would have to be coupled with political efforts aimed at challenging the continued existence of those structures that thrive on, or cannot account for, displacement. Corporations, for example, *necessarily* combat efforts aimed at inclusion when they act to maximize profits, because this quest is incompatible with the type of compassion or fairness that emerges from the belief that the playing field is not a level one. It may be that in the long term certain efforts made to accommodate difference can be abandoned in favour of equal treatment of all people, as we're now seeing in Canada where multicultural policies are slowly receding because the society itself is increasingly set up to accommodate outsiders without special government intervention. This is a positive evolution, consistent with the idea that the eventual goal to which those interested in resolving the crises of displacement and relocation must tend is to dismantle power structures that dictate decisions over people's lives. From this standpoint, the eventual goal would be to eliminate categories of 'outsiderness', 'marginality', and 'interest groups', the code words for maintaining the business-as-usual approach to first-level administrative assistance, and the resistance to adequate forms of appeal for manifestly unjust decisions at lower levels. Only then will claimants be able to tell their stories with the effect that they seek, both in terms of the openness offered by fiction, and the concrete assistance provided by helping organizations. Along the way, we need to encourage efforts aimed at heightening public sensitivity to the challenges of displacement and dislocation by making people more immediately aware that the problems exist, and that they themselves could easily have been on the receiving end of similar troubles. The research I have described here allows the researcher, as interviewer, direct and privileged access to the kinds of difficulties people face, which leads to a sense of proximity and empathy; but if fiction offers an equally privileged glimpse into these tortured worlds, perhaps Multiculturalism Canada does well to fund such publications, and we'd do well to read them, and to teach them to our children and our students. Behind the words of these narratives are the people with whom we share sidewalks, institutions and lives, not beggars who undeservedly tap into our enormous sources of wealth and charity.

References

Literary texts [with country of origin]

Arnau, Y. (1988) *La Mémoire Meurtrie* [The Murderous Memory], Montréal: Cercle du livre de France/Pierre Tisseyre [Algeria].

Bakhtin, M. (1984) *Problems of Dostoevsky's Poetics*. Ed. and trans. by Caryl Emerson. Introduction by Wayne C. Booth. Minneapolis: University of Minnesota Press. Theory and History of Literature, (8):6.

Dahan, A. (1985) *Le Printemps Peut Attendre* [Spring Can Wait], Montréal: Quinze [Egypt].

Dorfman, A. (1994) *Death and the Maiden,* London: Penguin.

Étienne, G. (1983) *Une Femme Muette* [A Dumb Woman], Montréal: Nouvelle Optique [Haïti].

Fajardo, J. (1990) *Votre Manteau Mouillé/ Su Abrigo Mojado* [Your Wet Overcoat], Montréal: Humanitas/Nouvelle Optique, Récit, Translated by Chantal Chevrier, [Chile].

Garnier, E. (1999) *Vivre au Noir en Pays Blanc* [To Live Black in White Country] Montréal: Vents d'ouest [Haïti].

Ghalem, N. (1981) 'Le Recommencement' *in L'Oiseau de Fer* [Iron Bird] Sherbrooke: Naaman [Algeria].

Kattan, N. (1983), *La Fiancée Promise* [The Promised Fiancé] Montréal: Hurtubise HMH [Iraq].

------ (1985) 'Les Rêves de la Mère' [The Dreams of the Mother] pp. 159-180, 'La Conquête' [The Conquest] (pp.107-122), and 'Les Deux Fils' [The Two Sons] (pp.181-198), in *La Reprise* [Take Two] Montréal: Hurtubise HMH [Iraq].

Laferrière, D. (1985) *Comment Faire l'Amour avec un Nègre sans se Fatiguer* [How to Make Love with a Negro without Getting Tired], Montréal: VLB [Haïti].

------ (1987) *Éroshima,* Montréal: VLB.

Latif-Ghattas, M. (1990) *Le Double Conte de l'Exil* [The Double Story of Exile] Montréal: Boréal [Egypt].

Mallet, M. (1981) 'How Are You ?' *Les Compagnons de l'horloge pointeuse* (pp.110), Montréal : Québec/Amérique [Chile].

------ (1986) 'How are You ?', 'La Mutation' [The Mutation], 'Affaire Classée' [Classified Affair] in *Miami Trip* (pp.47-54), Montréal: Québec/Amérique, Translated from Spanish.

Orwell, G. (1972) *Down and Out in Paris and London,* London: Harvest.

Critical Works

Bakhtin, M. (1981) *The Dialogic Imagination,* Austin: University of Texas Press.

Barsky, R.F (2001) *Arguing and Justifying: Assessing the Convention Refugee Choice of Moment, Motive and Host Country*, Aldershot UK, Burlington VT: Ashgate.

------ (1994) *Constructing a Productive Other: Discourse Theory and the Convention Refugee Hearing*, Amsterdam, Philadelphia: John Benjamins.

Bissoondath, N. (1994) Selling Illusions: The Cult of Multiculturalism in Canada, Toronto: Penguin.

Bourdieu, P. (1991) *Language and Symbolic Power*, John Thompson (ed.), trans. Gino Raymond and Matthew Adamson, Cambridge: Harvard University Press.

Bruner, J. (1990) *Acts of Meaning: Four Lectures on Mind and Culture*, Cambridge: Harvard University Press.

------ (1991) 'The Narrative Construction of Reality', *Critical Inquiry*, 18:1-21.

Corradi, C. (1991) 'Text, Context and Individual Meaning: Rethinking Life Stories in a Hermeneutic Framework', *Discourse and Society* 2 (1):105-118.

Coughlin, A.M. (1995) 'Regulating the Self: Autobiographical Performances in Outsider Scholarship', *Virginia Law Review* 81 (August):1229-1340.

Hutcheon, L. (ed.) (1990) *Other Solitudes: Canadian Multicultural Fictions*, Oxford: Oxford University Press.

Kymlicka, W. (1996) *Multicultural Citizenship: A Liberal Theory of Minority Groups*, Oxford: Clarendon Press.

------ (2001) *Politics in the Vernacular: Nationalism, Multiculturalism and Citizenship*, Oxford: Oxford University Press.

Linde, C. (1993) *Life Stories: The Creation of Coherence*, New York: Oxford University Press.

Norrick, N. (1998) 'Retelling Stories in Spontaneous Conversations', *Discourse Processes* 25, Vol. 1:75-97.

Polanyi, L. (1985a) 'Telling the Same Story Twice', *Text* 1:315-36.

------ (1985b) 'Literary Complexity in Everyday Storytelling', in D. Tannen (ed.), *Spoken and Written Language: Exploring Orality and Literacy* (pp. 155-170), Norwood, NJ: Ablex.

Scheuerman, W. (1994) *Between the Norm and the Exception: The Frankfurt School and the Rule of Law*, Cambridge, MA: MIT Press.

Taylor, C. and A. Gutmann (eds.) (1996) *Multiculturalism: Examining the Politics of Recognition*, Princeton: Princeton University Press.

Afterword: 'Story, Place and Encounter'

JAMES COLLINS, *University at Albany/SUNY, USA*

In the introduction to this collection, the editors lay out with admirable clarity the recent debates about narrative theory, identity-as-discourse, and the role of narrative in social orientation and institutional procedure. Rather than review these topics, I will take up other issues raised by the contributions to this volume, discussing salient themes and some remaining questions. But let me begin with a story about a story.

An Opening

While reading the chapters that make up this volume, I happened to be visiting my sister, who lives in South Texas in the Rio Grande Valley on *La Frontera*. This southernmost part of Texas is an area overwhelmingly populated by people who have emigrated from Mexico in their lifetime or are 'Tejanos', Texas citizens of Mexican descent. My sister's husband, Chavelo, is a Mexican from a village near the city of Guadalajara, who has lived and worked in the US. – Los Angeles, Chicago, South Texas – at various times throughout the last thirty years. Often he has been *sin papeles*, 'without papers' that is, official documents approving his residence and work in the US.[1] One evening as we sat outside smoking cigarettes and passing time, he told me (he with his partial English, me with my partial Spanish) about his first visit to the States, of a man who had appeared in his town and asked the fateful question *¿Quieres trabajar?* 'You want to work?' A short time later, at age 15, he was on a construction site in Los Angeles, where he and his fellow workers were warned about a power line that ran near the two-story building they were framing. One day a young co-worker raised up, his back touched the line, and he immediately fell to the ground dead. *Pobrecito* 'poor little one' Chavelo said, and later repeated, as he described with his hands how the body hit the ground.

Chavelo's story and life illustrate some common themes of migration (Sassen, 1999). People leave their homes in one country to work in another and after dislocating themselves, they may permanently relocate but it is also common that many move back and forth. Often the work that

---

[1] This is estimated to be the condition of five million immigrants in the United States (Rosenblum, 2000).

they find is harder, dirtier, and more dangerous, than the settled residents of the host country want to do – that is, they dislocate and relocate in order to meet systemic, crossnational needs for labour. Despite the necessary work that they perform, they are often stigmatized as threatening strangers and in a variety of ways treated as cultural-and-legal aliens. These are processes of several centuries' duration in both Europe and North America, but there have been significant developments in the 20th century. For one, the increased capacity of the state to regulate movements and otherwise register people has sharpened the contrast between citizen and non-citizen. For another, labour migrations have become intertwined with refugee flows, following declared and undeclared wars, which has resulted in heightened fears of immigrants and a familiar, distorting rhetoric of 'floods' of 'aliens'.

The chapters in this volume address the stories told by immigrants and refugees as well as by people displaced by internal migrations. The stories provide accounts of places left and settled into, incidents illustrating the complex experience of being displaced and coming to relocate. In these accounts, the form of language matters a great deal. It is the old sociolinguistic insight, given a narrative turn: how the story is told, says a great deal about the teller as well as the tale. Who it is addressed to also matters – for instance, whether an interlocutor is incidental or holds some official position. In grappling with the interplay of story, performance, and context, the studies in *Dislocations/Relocations* explore significant themes regarding the relation of story to identity and place, to power, to occasions for talk and for silence, and at most general to language itself. The contributions also suggest important questions, some of which are perhaps unanswerable, regarding the relation of story to truth and the reflexive dimensions of the use and analysis of narrative.

Themes in this Volume

Narrative expresses identity and relationship to place

It is a commonplace of psychology and now of the social sciences more generally, that individuals and groups provide accounts in order to express who they are (Ochs and Capps, 2001; Wortham, 2001). In his probing analysis of self-identity in conditions of globalized technical, economic, and cultural change, Giddens (1991) argues that the fundamental task of the self, whatever tribulations it may face, is to find a 'coherent story'. It may be that in the trauma that follows upon extreme experience and sharp dislocation, the ability to provide an account of oneself is crucial to feel oneself as a self – this is an explicit theme running through Barsky's discussion of the homeless and addicted and of socially displaced immigrants in Canada; Jacquemet's account of refugees, both real and apparent, from the Kosovo War; and Maryns' analysis of the fraught efforts by African refugees to render accounts of their lives and travels in languages they only partially control. As a subsidiary current in a more general concern with space in social analysis (De Certeau, 1984; Harvey, 1996), it is now widely recognized in disciplines such as history, anthropology, and cultural studies that the stories people tell often concern places. Ethnic and national groups fashion claims to places through myths of origin and descent (Anderson, 1991; Hobsbawm and Ranger, 1983), and stories about place can also inculcate a sense of morality, often quite subtle in its discursive indirection, as shown in Basso's (1990) work on Western Apache place-stories, Hensel's (1996) analysis of Alaskan Yupik subsistence discourse, and my own research (Collins, 1998) on the contested claims of Native Americans and settlers in Northwest California. Because most of the studies in this volume focus on political and economic migrants, place is often problematic for the narrator. The 'facts' of dislocating and relocating can be evocative of worlds lost and perhaps regained, as in McCormick's account of South African Blacks from the neighbourhood of Protea; they can be expressive of the migrant's often profound ambivalence about where he or she belongs, as in Haviland's analysis of Mamal's many conversations and letters with those 'back home'; and they can be important stakes in refugees' claims to status, as in both Maryns' and Jacquemet's studies.

Stories are told in contexts of power

As with language more generally, narratives are unavoidably implicated in relations of power. As Bakhtin (1981), Bernstein (1996), Hymes (1981) and Blommaert (2004) argue from differing theoretical positions, finding 'voice' often involves a struggle to be heard. Analysts as diverse as Barthes (1972), Gee (1996) and Levi-Strauss (1963) have argued that narratives are built upon mythical logics that articulate social positions and social contradictions, transforming the specific and contingent into the apparently universal and timeless. Put in simplest terms, stories are ideological. Some forms of story are dominant, and we easily find 'our' voice if it fits into those forms, but we must struggle to articulate accounts that go against received accounts or expected templates. Put in a Gramscian idiom, some stories are hegemonic while others are counter-hegemonic. This is a central thesis of both Baynham and Relaño Pastor and De Fina's chapters.

Baynham argues that there is a commonly told and expected narrative about migrants, an account of a young man who goes abroad looking for work and subsequently brings his family to join him. This story has currency, it gets circulated: told and retold by migrants, community workers representing migrants and news media depicting the immigrant situation. Baynham's point, well taken, is that in addition to the stereotypical account, there are other counter-hegemonic stories; in particular, there are Moroccan women's narratives of leaving fraught domestic situations and dealing resourcefully with the move to the UK. In these stories access to multilingual language resources, including literacy resources, together with the ability to activate social networks for referral and support, are key elements in the immigrant's struggle to survive in the new country. The emphasis on multilingual resources calls into question the dominant official assumption that the immigrant 'language problem' is solely a matter of immigrants learning the official language of the host country. The question of 'whose language is legitimate' is central to Relaño Pastor and De Fina's discussion of Mexican immigrant women's stories in contemporary California, where anti-bilingual/anti-Spanish language sentiment is politically mobilized and dominant. In the stories Relaño and De Fina analyze, the encounter with and struggle against taken-for-granted Anglophone supremacy is an expression of agency and moral vision. As the authors nicely bring out, emotion (affect) is a motivating force in such everyday struggles against linguistic-and-social domination as well as a structuring principle in the narratives themselves.

In addition to interactional domination and ideological constraint, state policy and institutional practice is often at issue in the interplay of narrative and power. When Moroccan immigrants in the UK or Mexican immigrants in the US encounter employment, social welfare, and education policies that presume monolingualism, then these newcomers are at a significant disadvantage in regard to the recognition and use of their often considerable linguistic resources. There are, however, more pointed exercises of state power, as shown in the chapters dealing with refugees. In Maryns' study of the narratives told by African asylum seekers in Belgium, immigration officials' expectations about linguistic competencies in world languages and about temporal and spatial consistency in refugee accounts impose powerful interpretive conditions on believability. In addition, the officials are agents of bureaucratic procedures through which stories are decontextualized and recontextualized in case files, a chain of texts to which asylum seekers will have little or no access, although the files become the basis for official decision making about asylum status. In Jacquemet's investigation of refugee resettlement after the Kosovo war,

the 'power of narrative' receives an ironic twist. Because of distrust between case officers from the United Nations High Commission on Refugees
(UNHCR) and applicants for political asylum, narration is blocked, that
is, applicants are not allowed to tell their story. Instead, they are interro-
gated about places in Kosovo in order to identify Albanians who might be
posing as Kosovars. As Jacquemet notes, silencing someone by forbid-
ding their story is a pointed, offensive, interactional move, and it is seen
and remarked upon as such by refugees. In the encounter between asylum
seekers and UNHCR case officers, interpreters play an important role and
wield considerable influence in compiling 'the file'. This reminds us that
official power, based on whatever abstract principles or implicit criteria,
must nonetheless be interactionally displayed and secured. As with Relaño
Pastor and De Fina's discussion of affect, Jacquemet shows that trust is an
important resource, and a frequent casualty, in encounters between displaced persons and official representatives.

Stories are occasioned and may be refused.

A third theme found in this set of studies is that the situation of telling
matters (Ochs and Capps, 2001; Hymes, 1981; Wortham, 2001). Otherwise put, stories emerge as part of other endeavours: presenting one's
case to officials, expressing outrage at how a fellow Latina is treated,
giving an account of what it is like to live homeless on the streets of Montreal, providing excuses for why you cannot return home, telling an
interviewer how you came to leave home. Those present at the telling may
strongly shape the account, what is remembered, and the grounds for judgements and assumptions. This is described in close interactional detail in
Liebscher and Dailey-O'Cain's analyses of the stories of Germans who
have moved from the former West to the former East Germany. In these
accounts, and Liebscher and Dailey-O'Cain's analysis, allusions to prior
political categories ('East' and 'West') commingle with assumptions about
the standard of living as narrators, their partners, and the interviewers
themselves make subtle judgements and equally subtle conversational interventions to support or call into question a claim or presumption. In
Haviland's account of Zinacantecans in Oregon we have an intriguing
interweaving of analyst and analyzed, perhaps reflecting the author's un-
usually close and long-term relationships with the people he has studied. It
is not so much that Haviland is the addressee of stories or conversations,
as that he is a communicative resource. *Xun* [John], the anthropologist,
travels back and forth a great deal carrying letters and cassette tapes, and it
appears that his telephone is frequently used for calls home. This allows

the far-from-home Mamal to communicate while not returning, and it gives the analyst and us an overhearer's insight into how Mamal's ambivalence about place of origin and migration, over a long period of time, is reflected in subtle manipulations of reference to 'here' and 'there' as he provides excuses and makes illusory plans regarding return. Both the occasion of the interview and the sharing of language, gender, and political viewpoint were important in Relaño Pastor and De Fina's elicitation of narratives of language conflict. As they say: "Since the research focus was on language experiences, *the interview became a locus of ideological exchange* in which the *women and the interviewer shared views and perspectives* on issues having to do with language rights, language tolerance, respect, prejudice and discrimination" (emphasis added). Jacquemet's study of refugee interviews depicts an opposite extreme, a situation in which interviewer and interviewee definitely do not "share... views and perspectives". Instead, the interviewer/translator is conducting an interrogation. In this situation, we reach a limiting case of addressee influence on narrative: the story is not allowed.

Finally, Barsky's, McCormick's, and Maryns' studies remind us that there are diverse forms of official sponsorship of narrative. The Multicultural Program of the Department of Canadian Heritage supports immigrants writing fictional accounts of the migrant experience. In post-Apartheid South Africa, the Department of Land Affairs and a local museum solicit accounts from displaced former residents of the neighbourhood of Protea, and the sponsorship matters to the production of accounts. As McCormick says: "I think it is likely that a sense of public purpose and audience influenced many of the narrators who weighted the communal more heavily than the individual in what they selected to describe about Protea".

As with language more generally, any aspect of linguistic form may be used to position the narrator and organize the tale

Reading across the range of studies presented in this volume, I am struck by how diverse are the symbolic processes and elements of language that may structure an account (Levi-Strauss, 1963; Hymes, 1981). In McCormick's study of the dislocated and subsequently returned inhabitants of Protea, we find the binary of nostalgia, an incessant symbolic contrast between the good old days of settled community, when neighbours knew one another, respect was shown, children played freely, and people spoke, and the bad new days of disorientating resettlement in townships, large and

filled with strangers, places where journeying outside the house, especially at night, is a dangerous endeavour, where one might have the
modern conveniences of electricity and running water but there is no safe
familiarity of person or routine. The backward-looking yearning, what
McCormick refers to as a contrast of 'mythical time' in Protea and 'historical time' in the townships, is similar to centuries old process that
Williams (1973) analyzes in *The Country and the City*: an ongoing contrast, rendered in diverse literary forms, such as the pastoral and the
detective mystery, between settled place and new development, between
knowable communities and an ever-changing scale of settlement brought
about by national and international capitalism.

In Relaño Pastor and De Fina's analysis of Latina women's resistance
to subordinate social placement, affect (feeling and emotion) is a central
expressive means. As they note, however, affect is signalled through diverse linguistic and paralinguistic conventions "such as facial expressions,
body postures, prosodic features, lexical and syntactic forms". Relaño
Pastor and De Fina argue, as do Liebscher and Dailey-O'Cain, that social
categories are intertwined with discursive processes. In their case, the representation of angry response to linguistic subordination – an anger
represented through finger pointing, swear words, raising the voice, extended paraphrases of one's emotional state – is a means for reporting,
reflecting upon and resisting a linguistic inequality that is also a social
subordination. In Blommaert's discussion of 'class and code' we are shown
that rapid shifts between varieties of language, which attain their interpretability as part of local, national, and international repertoires, are ways
in which interlocutors negotiate their position – locate themselves – socially and geographically. The chain of indexical inferences is familiar: if
you speak a certain way, you must be a certain kind of person, who comes
from a certain kind of place. But the linguistic forms which can be used in
such a play of presupposed and creative identity-in-position are diverse:
features of pronunciation, lexical items, and extended routines.

Blommaert makes an important point: that locating oneself is always
done in relation to other potential spaces, in his case globalized cultural
flows. This point is reinforced in Haviland's meticulous analysis of how
the Zinecantecan émigré, Mamal, plays upon deixis, the signalling of 'here'
versus 'there', as these contrasts are encoded in lexical items and grammatical categories in the Tzotzil language. In Mamal's letters and
conversations, an ongoing discursive process in which he locates himself
vis á vis his home village of Nabenchauk, the lexical-grammatical resources
are subtle, systematic, and essential means whereby the work of placing

oneself is achieved, both in direct reference, and in the 'transposed' forms necessary when, as in much narrative, the perspectives and voices of others are incorporated into one's own account.

Remaining questions

In reviewing the contributions to *Dislocations/Relocations* I am struck by how they raise, without necessarily directly addressing, questions about narrative truth and the strategic uses of story.

It is a commonplace that all narration is selective, and hence incomplete to the events it would represent. Indeed, as Shuman (1986) argues at length in her analyses of adolescent fight stories and the moral economy from which they emerge, an event is itself a categorization, a selective representation of experience, well before any ordering of events into the diachrony of narrative sequence. We also know, and have been reminded in this collection, that stories are sensitive to the occasions of telling. There is a widespread sentiment in contemporary popular (US.?) culture that narrative somehow gives a necessary and maybe more adequate account than other forms of representation. This may explain the popularity of *History* and *Biography* channels on US. television, if it does not explain the declining popularity of history as an academic subject. It also partly explains why the Department of Canadian Heritage supports the writing of fictional accounts, an 'as if' of the immigrant experience. It is presumably also at play in the oral history project that partly underwrote the collection of stories about the Eden of Protea and being cast of out Eden. I use this ironic phrasing to emphasize what McCormick brings out without dwelling upon: that the stories of Protea are 'mythic' in their evocation of time and reported practice of place.

But what is the relation of the fictional and mythic to other ways of knowing? The question of 'other ways' is patently at issue in the studies of refugee asylum procedures by Maryns and Jacquemet. Here, amidst fractured and fragmentary accounts, it would seem that a distinction of 'truth' versus 'lie' is operating – but in Foucauldian fashion, what-is-truth is revealed as that which is *sayable* in official encounters, whether a story of a certain kind or a non-narrative response to questions. On my reading of the studies that make up this volume, it seems that in providing accounts people wish to be as truthful as possible, to adhere to the Gricean maxim of Quality "try to make your contribution one that is true" (Grice, 1999:78). There are many influences, however, that work against 'the plain and unadorned facts': the pressure of advice when dealing with officials, resulting in the formulaic, exaggerated accounts Maryns and Jacquemet refer to; the influence of tacit social logics that organize much of social life, whether the contrast of 'good old' and 'bad new' in McCormick's analysis or the hegemonic masculine and counter-hegemonic feminine Baynham discusses; or, most interestingly, the invitation to fictionalize that Barsky reports.

Stories are elicited and told for a purpose, perhaps merely to entertain or pass the time, but often for more consequential ends. In both Barsky and McCormick's cases, it would seem that stories are elicited as part of an official ameliorative effort, to gain further insight into the place of the displaced in multicultural Canada or to record and presumably reconcile the breaches of Apartheid. In the Canadian case, the narratives enter into what Barsky calls a 'messy' judicial process which cannot be rectified by better procedure but must somehow grapple with "a method of representation that answers to the needs of *reticent* claimants" [emphasis added]. In both Maryns' and Jacquemet's accounts, there is some evidence that claimants may intend – for understandable reasons – to mislead. Maryns notes that the refugee narratives that she analyzes "are vague and share a particular pattern", which immigration officials take as evidence of 're-hearsed narratives' and a strategic linguistic incompetence, "[an] instruction to stick to vague notions of English in order to hide one's real linguistic identity". Jacquemet begins his account of UNHCR procedures with a frank discussion of the situation in Tirana. In addition to the many Kosovars displaced by the war, "[b]y the winter 2000, a growing number of Albanians, locked out of rich countries by immigration restrictions, increasingly resorted to scoring an asylum card as the only legal means of achieving the right to migrate". Faced with the power of narrative – in particular, that stories "appeal… to a human need for …coherence", that once told they are texts with rhetorical potential, and that the act of storytelling "force[s] [participants] to take sides" – UNHCR officers forbade stories and sought, in Barsky's words, other "methods of representation".

In such circumstances there are no clear grounds for arguing the truthfulness of accounts, although Barsky, Maryns, and Jacquemet all suggest that something like the fullest and most empathetic interpretation of stories is important for achieving a common humanity in a much divided and deeply unjust world. Barsky takes this issue up most sharply in his self-critical reflections on fieldwork among the socially dispossessed. Perhaps it is sufficient that all three argue that narrative can serve important purposes: allowing a perspective on that which people do not want to discuss

(Barsky), enabling people to locate themselves by articulating their transition from old to new place (Maryns) or achieving catharsis by telling about horrific experiences (Jacquemet). And perhaps this is a larger lesson from the entire collection: whatever the relation of narrative to experience, it provides occasions to articulate a sense of self by recounting what happened on the route from there to here; whatever the relation to official purposes or researchers' agendas, it is an occasion for assuaging the 'need for coherence', for giving voice to emotion and playing with the ambivalence of place.

References

Anderson, B. (1991) *Imagined Communities* (2nd edn.), London: Verso.

Bakhtin, M. (1981) *The Dialogic Imagination*, Austin, TX: University of Texas Press.

Barthes, R. (1972) *Mythologies*, New York: Hill and Wang.

Basso, K. (1990) *Western Apache Language and Culture*, Tucson: University of Arizona Press.

Bernstein, B. (1996) *Pedagogy, Symbolic Control and Identity*, London: Taylor & Francis.

Blommaert, J. (2004) *Discourse*, Cambridge: Cambridge University Press.

Collins, J. (1998) *Understanding Tolowa Histories*, New York: Routledge.

De Certeau, M. (1984) *The Practice of Everyday Life,* Berkeley: University of California Press.

Gee, J. (1996) *Social Linguistics and Literacy* (2nd edn.), London: Taylor & Maxwell.

Giddens, A. (1991) *Modernity and Self-identity*, Cambridge: Polity Press.

Grice, H. (1999) 'Logic and Conversation', reprinted in A. Jaworski and N. Coupland (eds.) *The Discourse Reader* (pp. 76-88), New York: Routledge.

Harvey, D. (1996) *Justice, Nature, and the Geography of Difference*, Cambridge, MA: Blackwell.

Hensel, C. (1996) *Telling Our Selves,* New York: Oxford University Press.

Hobsbawm, E. and T. Ranger (eds.) (1983) *The Invention of Tradition*, Cambridge: Cambridge University Press.

Hymes, D. (1981) *In Vain I Tried to Tell You,* Philadelphia: University of Pennsylvania Press.

Levi-Strauss, C. (1963) *Structural Anthropology*, New York: Basic Books.

Ochs, E. and L. Capps (2001) *Living Narrative,* Cambridge, MA: Harvard University Press.

Rosenblum, M. (2000) 'U.S. Immigration Policy: Unilateral and Cooperative Responses to Undocumented Immigration', Paper presented at the *International Studies Association*, 41st Annual Convention. Los Angeles, CA, March 14-18, 2000.

Sassen, S. (1999) *Guests and Aliens,* New York: The New Press.

Shuman, A. (1986) *Storytelling Rights*, New York: Cambridge University Press.

Williams, R. (1973) *The Country and the City*, New York: Oxford University Press.

Wortham, S. (2001) *Narratives in Action,* New York: Teachers College Press.

List of Contributors

Robert F. Barsky is the author or editor of numerous books on narrative and refugee law (*Constructing a Productive Other: Discourse Theory and the Convention Refugee Hearing* and *Arguing and Justifying: Assessing the Convention Refugees' Choice of Moment, Motive and Host Country*), on radical theory and practice (*Noam Chomsky: A Life of Dissent* and an edition of Anton Pannekoek's Workers Councils) on discourse and literary theory (Introduction à la théorie littéraire, an edited volume with Michael Holquist entitled *Bakhtin and Otherness*, an edited collection with Eric Méchoulan entitled *The Production of French Criticism*, and, most recently, an edited collection entitled *Marc Angenot and the Scandal of History*) and on translation – in both theory and practice (including the translation of Michel Meyer's *Philosophy and the Passions*). He has been involved with a range of journals, including SubStance, for which he served as an editor, and he is the founder of 415 South Street, a literary magazine, Discours Social/Social Discourse and most recently AmeriQuests. He is Professor of Comparative Literature, French and Italian, Vanderbilt University.

A sociolinguist by training and applied linguist by affiliation, **Mike Baynham's** research interests lie in the application of insights from sociolinguistics to a range of educational and social issues, particularly literacy and English for Speakers of Other Languages (ESOL). Mike has been active in the field of applied linguistics since the mid 1980s and his interest in narrative and migration originated in his doctoral research. He is currently Professor of TESOL at the University of Leeds.

Jan Blommaert is professor of African Linguistics and Sociolinguistics at Ghent University, Belgium. His research interests include linguistic ideologies especially in multilingual environments, linguistic inequality, discourse theory and narrative. Major publications include Language Ideological Debates (edited, 1999), *State Ideology and Language in Tanzania* (1999) and *Debating Diversity* (with Jef Verschueren, 1998).

James Collins is Professor in the Departments of Anthropology and Reading at the University at Albany/SUNY. He has published on social theory and linguistics, critical studies of language and education, and Native American languages, cultures and societies. He is the author of Understanding *Tolowa Histories: Western Hegemonies and Native American Responses* (Routledge, 1998) and the co-author, with Richard Blot, of

Literacy and Literacies: Texts, Power, and Identity (Cambridge University Press, 2003). He has recently completed six months fieldwork on immigrants and language contact in Belgium, collaborating with Stef Slembrouck and Jan Blommaert of Ghent University, and he is beginning a related investigation of social class and language learning among Spanish-speaking immigrants in Upstate New York.

After doing her Ph.D. at the University of Michigan, **Jennifer Dailey-O'Cain** came to the University of Alberta, where she is currently Associate Professor of German Applied Linguistics. In addition to her research interests in language and migration in post-unification Germany and in language practices in the bilingual classroom (both together with Grit Liebscher), she also works in sociolinguistic variation.

Anna De Fina is Assistant Professor of Italian Language and Linguistics and Coordinator of the Italian Language Program at Georgetown University, Washington D.C. Her research interests focus on narrative, the relationship between language practices and the construction of identity, the discourse of immigrants, and language contact phenomena. Her major publications include *Identity in Narrative, A Study of Immigrant Discourse* (John Benjamins, 2003), and the forthcoming *Discourse and Identity* co-edited with Deborah Schiffrin and Michael Bamberg, to be published by Cambridge University Press.

John B. Haviland is an anthropological linguist, with principal interests in the social life of language. His major research has been on Tzotzil (Mayan) in highland Chiapas, Mexico, and its neighbours, as well as on languages from the area north of Cooktown, in far north Queensland, Australia. He is Professor of Anthropology and Linguistics at Reed College, Portland, Oregon, USA, and concurrently Investigador Titular C at the Centro de Investigaciones y Estudios Superiores en Antropología Social, Mexico. His most recent book is *Old Man Fog and the Last Aborigines of Barrow Point* (1998, Smithsonian Institution Press) about the last speaker of the Barrow Point language.

Marco Jacquemet is assistant professor in communication studies at the University of San Francisco. His research focuses on the complex interplay of language and identity in globalization processes. He is the author of *Credibility in Court* (Cambridge University Press, 1996) and of a large number of other publications.

Grit Liebscher did her Ph.D. at the University of Texas at Austin and is currently Assistant Professor of German at the University of Waterloo. In addition to the interests she shares with Dr. Dailey-O'Cain, she also investigates communication among East and West Germans and learners' online communication.

Katrijn Maryns is a Research Fellow of the National Fund for Scientific Research-Flanders, affiliated to the Department of African Languages and Cultures of Ghent University. Her doctoral research, completed in 2004, focused on language in the Belgian asylum application procedure. She has published in several journals on this topic, and a book-length study is in completion.

Kay McCormick is a professor in the English Department at the University of Cape Town. Her research interests in sociolinguistics include language policy and planning, language and identity in bilingual communities, language contact, code-switching, and local dialects of English. In the area of discourse and narrative analysis, her work focuses mainly on narratives told in the public hearings of South Africa's Truth and Reconciliation Commission. Her study of language use in a bilingual, inner city community, 'Language in Cape Town's District Six', was published by OUP in 2002.

May Relaño Pastor is a Postdoctoral Fellow from Spain in the Department of Ethnic Studies at the University of California, San Diego. She received her Ph.D. in English Philology from the University of Granada (Spain), and holds a Master in Applied Linguistics and TESL from the University of California, Los Angeles. Her primary academic interests include language and Mexican female migration, Latino language socialization, intercultural communication, bilingualism, and language and identity. As a pre-doctoral fellow at the Center for Comparative Immigration Studies (CCIS) at the University of California, San Diego, she carried out fieldwork with a group of Mexican immigrant women in San Diego County and studied intercultural communication experiences and discursive constructions of identity in narratives of language conflicts. Her recent publications include The Language Socialization Experiences of Latina Mothers in Southern California in Zentella (ed.) (2005), Language and Literacy in Latino Families and Communities (Teachers College Press), and Latino Diaspora in Chula Vista, San Diego, and Ciutat Vella, Barcelona: Comparative Approaches, with Guillermo Alonso in Henke (ed.) (2005). Crossing Over: Comparing Recent Migration in Europe and the United States (Lexington Books).

Index